Other
Voices

Edmund:

I don't have a "brown paper wrapper" in which to present this to you; but you can certainly provide the dark glasses necessary to read it!

I hope it may entertain; and it is a *very* small Recognition of your own work.

Seattle, 1980

Nick Read

CHANDLER & SHARP PUBLICATIONS IN ANTHROPOLOGY
AND RELATED FIELDS

GENERAL EDITORS: L. L. Langness and Robert B. Edgerton

Other Voices

The Style of a Male Homosexual Tavern

by

KENNETH E. READ

University of Washington

CHANDLER & SHARP PUBLISHERS, INC.
NOVATO, CALIFORNIA

For

*Ernest A. T. Barth, Michael A. Read,
and Nick Layne*

Library of Congress Cataloging in Publication Data

Read, Kenneth E
  Other voices.

  (Chandler & Sharp publications in anthropology and related fields)
  Bibliography: p.
  Includes index.
    1. Homosexuality, Male—Social aspects—United States
—Case studies. 2. Hotels, taverns, etc.—United
States—Case studies. 3. Etiquette—United States—
Case studies. I. Title. II. Series: Chandler & Sharp
Sharp Publishers. Chandler & Sharp publications in
anthropology and related fields.
HQ76.2.U5R42   301.41'57   79-26194
ISBN 0-88316-534-1

International Standard Book Number: 0-88316-534-1
Library of Congress Catalog Card Number: 79-26194
Printed in the United States of America.

Book designed by Joe Roter
Composition by Publications Services of Marin

Contents

Foreword

Those who write forewords are rarely perfectly objective bystanders. Let me make my biases clear. I was Kenneth Read's first graduate student after he arrived in the United States. With his assistance (far beyond the ordinary, I must confess) I was able to survive graduate school and, following in his footsteps, conduct ethnographic research in the New Guinea Highlands. Throughout the more than twenty years of our acquaintance he has remained both mentor and friend. I believe his moving personal account of fieldwork among the Gahuku-Gama, *The High Valley* (1965), to be the best example of its genre yet published. Now, in *Other Voices*, he again takes the lead by describing and examining, with rare personal insight, a segment of our social world which remains no less remote and exotic to most of us: daily life in a male homosexual bar in the inner city of an American metropolis.

This is the first book on contemporary American homosexuality by an anthropologist. The only thing close to it, as far as I know, is Esther Newton's book on female impersonators, *Mother Camp: Female Impersonators in America* (1972). For most of us this introduction to life at The Columbia Tavern will be as strange and challenging an experience as was our initiation into the world of the Gahuku-Gama. Although many recent books deal with the subject of homosexuality, very few deal with its social milieu (rather than the psychology of homosexuals as individuals). Few offer much insight into the ways homosexuals themselves experience their lives on on everyday basis. It is fair to say that we have no anthropological *theory* of homosexuality, and that analyses—both anthropological and popular—are only beginning to emerge. *Other Voices* sets up guideposts for the work ahead: first, by clearly indicating diversity of life styles embraced by the umbrella term "homosexuality"; and, then, by applying the insights of the existentialist writer Jean Genet to show us the ways in which, symbolically, homosexual and heterosexual life styles mirror each other, and, in reality, are often intermeshed.

The fundamental task of the anthropologist is of course to describe and examine other cultures. Practitioners of anthropology range the globe, locate themselves in remote and exotic places, and attempt to comprehend that fantastic behavioral variation which uniquely characterizes the human species. In more recent years, for a variety of reasons, anthropologists have found themselves increasingly involved in researches which focus upon American culture itself. This type of research, as in the present case, often proves more demanding both physically and psychologically than the more traditional variety. Maintaining an open perspective becomes more difficult the closer our personal lives are touched. It becomes harder to maintain the role of researcher as one is increasingly drawn into the lives of others. But wherever they work, and whatever the circumstances, the most essential requirement for a successful anthropologist is that he or she be a sensitive observer. Kenneth Read has proven himself to be an exceptionally keen and sensitive observer. He is also an unusually gifted writer. This is an exceedingly rare combination in a social scientist and helps to explain the enduring success of his earlier work, *The High Valley*. He brings these same skills to *Other Voices*, which should, I think, enjoy the same success. Read was the first anthropologist to publish extensively on the New Guinea Highlands. His work there stimulated all those who followed. I am certain this work will do likewise.

L. L. Langness

University of California, Los Angeles

Author's Foreword

This book attempts to delineate the style of a male homosexual tavern in a contemporary United States city. It may be called an essay in urban anthropology or urban ethnography. Both labels indicate the locale—a metropolis—and the discipline orientation of the research that underlies the writing. Of the two, I prefer to call it an ethnography, despite the rather formidable implications the word may summon to the general reader. There is no need, however, to be intimidated by it. Ethnographies are generally descriptions of the customs, institutions, and beliefs associated with a group of human beings. They attempt to portray a way of life—the skeletal framework of a culture—and of course the economics of description, of arranging and relating a vast assemblage of raw data, entail even at the minimal level some organizational framework: some theory.

The work reflects and possibly may add to theories of human interaction and communication, but it also possesses another dimension that is usually minimized in ethnographies—a subjective dimension that includes some of the feelings, the motives and reactions of the observer as part of the situation. In this respect, it repeats a former "experiment in ethnography" that grew out of my research in New Guinea. *The High Valley* (1965) was an attempt to depict the style or culture of an exotic people (the Gahuku-Gama) through descriptions of their natural environment, their customs and beliefs, their personalities, and my reactions to immersion in a strange, sometimes cruel, sometimes repulsive, but often tender and always human way of life.

This work has the same general thrust, but the locales are vastly different and there are some necessary elements in reporting and describing that some readers may find offensive. Possibly the new permissiveness in motion pictures, books and magazines, and the everyday speech of many young people absolves me of justifying the sexual explicitness of many passages. Indeed, the pantomimed acts in *The Last Tango in Paris* (not to mention *Deep Throat* and the unredeemed vulgarity of *La Grande Bouffe*) are more "obscene" than almost anything observed in The Columbia Tavern in Port City. The language and the tactile pantomimes are integral to the style, ritualized expressions of a lore of inclusion and exclusion. Language and tactile customs among the Gahuku were often quite as explicit as anything seen in the tavern, but the screen of culture tends to diminish their shock: the words are not English and the people are so different that conventional expectations of propriety are suspended.

However it may affront some sensitivities, the sexuality of The Columbia is absolutely essential to an understanding of its style, and I will try to demonstrate that it is mostly innocuous, that the language and accompanying gestures are principally symbolic. They are ritualized expressions (often greatly exaggerated) of particular experiences of stigmatism; and they are equivalent to the highly creative, richly descriptive, and humorously "detached" folk-idioms associated with many other stigmatized groups. They include a large component of "ethnic" humor.

Because the overwhelming majority of my research population are stigmatized by the larger society, all personal and most place names are fictitious. The necessary subterfuge probably will not conceal the urban locale, and the tavern itself will soon be relegated to a forgettable past as the block on which it stands is razed in the cause of urban renewal. It is quite possible (indeed, there is no doubt) that many of the tavern's patrons will recognize themselves and their acquaintances if they read the book. Pseudonyms do not conceal appearances and personal idiosyncrasies. I trust, however, that no one who sees himself in the following pages will feel he has been personally diminished. There are many reasons why I will not miss The Columbia when it is demolished to accommodate an extension to an inner-urban mall, but I will miss the "regulars" who have become more than mere acquaintances in the course of two years. They are not faceless members of some representative sample who are polled for their opinions from time to time in the cause of determining the direction of public thought on a variety of gross issues. Rather, they are people whom I know better, in many cases, than my next-door neighbors. They are fleshed and living human beings, variously flawed and coping in one way or another with existential problems. I hope that I have portrayed them with both understanding and affection.

The research for *Other Voices* had a completely accidental beginning.

One night after sharing dinner and drink with a friend, we were walking through the virtually deserted streets of the historically oldest section of Port City. We were feeling high and younger than our years, inquisitive and adventurous and not yet ready to separate to our respective homes. We came to The Columbia, whose interior light spilled across the sidewalk through uncurtained windows, and on mutual impulse, on the order of "let's have one for the road," we entered it.

The tavern was swinging, and the sudden irruption of light, in contrast to the dark street, provoked the feeling of having been projected onto a stage where some ongoing play was·in progress. The jukebox was blaring "La Paloma" and a man in his sixties—with dyed hair and pancake makeup—was twirling and pirouetting in the aisle between the bar and tables. His feet twinkled and his arms etched sweeping balletic gestures. He was completely self-absorbed. No other person in the crowded space seemed to notice him.

The level of noise made it difficult to attract the bartender and order a beer. My impression, standing somewhat euphorically at the bar, was disjointed, a curious combination of sharp images and detachment from an apparently disorganized scene. After a while, the sexual ambience was obvious. It did not offend me, but I felt as though I was a tourist having a night out in some unfamiliar town. It was interesting, yes, but completely forgettable, even less than tangential to my proper life—an escapade, an episode I might recall and laugh about at some later date; but no more than that.

The steps by which I became more deeply involved with The Columbia cannot be ranged one above the other in a precise progression. Many students, undergraduate and graduate, were pressing my department to develop through research and teaching the "field" of urban anthropology, not necessarily as opposed to but as complementary to more traditional areal studies. Political developments in many foreign countries had already made it difficult to pursue research wherever one chose; and national reductions in funds for research were hurting both students and, through them, the discipline. Lastly, it had been a long time since I had done systematic and intensive research on any human population.

Port City's rich variety of ethnic groups and socioeconomic "subcultures" had not been overlooked entirely as research resources. Over the years, a handful of students, some of whom I had helped to direct, had collected material and written theses on gypsies, prostitutes, Native American (Indian) drinking patterns, psychiatric institutions, and some others. Undergraduates in my regularly scheduled course on religion were required to visit and report upon varieties of organized religion ranging from the occult through fundamentalist and ethnic churches to middle-class and upper-middle-class religious institutions. I participated personally in some of these limited studies, not merely advising and directing from my office but visiting a few of the groups over a longer period of time than any undergraduate could afford in one academic quarter; but I did not contemplate becoming more intensively involved.

Virtually on impulse, though actually responding to the influence of all the factors mentioned above, I decided to demonstrate that it was not necessary to have vast logistical and financial support in order to do traditional anthropological research in situations that are closer to home than Nepal, Tanzania, or New Guinea. No foundation has supported or has been asked to support research for *Other Voices*. The costs have been born entirely by myself, and in purely monetary terms they have been minimal: gas to drive the few miles from my home to the location, a number of—sometimes too many—beers, and an inexpensive birthday gift here and there. There have been other costs on which I cannot place a monetary value; and it is also true that I did not intend to use any expensive and sophisticated ancillary services or equipment. It has been research conducted on a shoestring budget according to the classical method of "participant observation."

There have been relatively few attempts by sociologists or cultural anthropologists (who sometimes seem to annex the method by divine right) to explain what is meant by and entailed in participant observation. Mostly, students are expected to acquire the method by osmosis. And perhaps this is understandable, for it is impossible to reduce to rules or simple maxims everything that is required to live with and to understand other people. I recall that at age twenty-six when, in wartime 1944, I was being sent to New Guinea on my first anthropological research, I asked my distinguished mentor: "What should I do? How should I respond to the people?" "Oh," he said, as though it was the least important question, "treat them like gentlemen. *You* know how to do that." This was the extent of my training in the method of participant observation. Of course there is more to it than that; but my friend's remark summarized one absolutely essential dimension of the method: a willingness to interact personally with your subjects and to immerse yourself in their lives.

The "participation" is always qualified by the fact that you are also an "observer" and, particularly in exotic situations, an "outsider." The investigator plays a divided role, trying to identify with those whom he is studying but also attempting to preserve a clinical distance from them. It is possibly the most ambiguous and least precisely structured method in the entire arsenal of sociological enquiry; but without any doubt at all it has produced the richest qualitative data in all the social sciences.

The involvement required by participant observation often, perhaps characteristically, generates strain and stress, so much strain, in fact, that it is not a method suited to all temperaments. The possibility of experiencing personal trauma is probably more obvious in traditional anthropological fieldwork situations where the observer is often alone in a culture that is entirely alien, where initially he may have only minimal verbal communication—or none at all—with his subjects, where the only links with his own background are his few possessions and his scholarly purpose, a purpose he cannot explain to those on whom he is depending. His intellectual training does not, cannot prepare him for the palpable experience of difference, of personal isolation and disorientation. The trauma that may result—and may abort the enterprise—is referred to as "culture shock."

It is not necessary, however, to journey halfway round the world to experience a degree of culture shock. In the early nineteen-sixties I used to take my undergraduate students to a storefront black church where I had established a relationship with the pastor. The students were all young whites from mainly middle-class homes, and their experience of organized religion was also middle-class—Roman Catholic or one or other of the more widely acceptable Protestant denominations. Their prior church experience—and their other social contacts—had not prepared them for some of the highly expressive variations on rituals that many of them regarded as formalistic and boring. The orchestrated emotional intensity, the different idioms, and the in-group understandings and implications created shockwaves that I could see on their faces as they sat side by side in their pews, stiffly and properly erect, restrained by their own conventions from stamping, clapping, and interjecting verbal appreciations. At the end of the service, many of them were shaken and subdued. Some were so close to tears that they wanted to leave immediately, refusing a standing invitation to share a meal in the basement of the church. There were also some who did not seem particularly moved at all, whose preformed cultural shell could not be shattered and who probably regarded everything as a confirmation of the superiority of their own values.

I have touched upon my own experiences of culture shock in *The High Valley*. The illness that terminated my research in New Guinea cannot be attributed solely to the stress of the field situation, but without that stress it probably would not have occurred at that precise time. Research in The Columbia has generated similar personal tensions and some comparable physical consequences, and it may be of more than passing interest to ask why this has been so. After all, the first language of a majority of the tavern's patrons is English. Their ethnic origins are diverse, but one passes thousands like them on any downtown street, and physically the tavern is like a multitude of others whose presence is announced by a neon sign in the urban streets and along the dark highways of America. The backgrounds of almost everyone, even allowing for my foreign origin, are different from mine, but not as different as those of New Guinea villagers. Possibly because they are so superficially familiar, there is a greater inclination to place them in a preconceived frame of cultural reference, attributing to both verbal and tactile behavior meanings that are based unconsciously upon folk-stereotypes. It is known—and it is not the paradox it may seem at first glance—that the possibilities of observer-distortion increase as gross cultural differences diminish, and exposure to personal affront becomes greater precisely because many things that occur are considered either improper or demeaning in more conventional and familiar contexts. Moreover, it is more difficult to maintain the role of the "outsider." In the New Guinea village some very obvious differences separated me from my subjects, and at times the inherent separation became a welcome form of insulation. The insulation was far less easily achieved in the tavern. It is a public place, and, unless you employ certain strategies that are learned only slowly, it is assumed that you may be approached and are familiar with the elements of the style. Your very presence means that you can't be ignorant.

The polar experiences of "inside" and "outside" sometimes generated devastating tensions in New Guinea, and they have been no less devastating in the tavern. But there was one overwhelming, redeeming, and solacing dimension to the former setting: the vast landscape of grasslands and mountains that was as near to me as my next breath. When my fellow creatures became too demanding and their cues too difficult to understand, it was always possible to withdraw into a more congenial world and to indulge myself in the purely personal exercise of trying to find words to describe the heroic volume of clouds, the calligraphy of bamboo leaves, and the bright candy-jewels of wild raspberries hiding in russet grasses.

There have been scores of occasions on which I have felt so confined, so constricted by the atmosphere of The Columbia that I have left suddenly, seeking to place some personal distance between myself and the noisy, crowded, and apparently chaotic scene—even if the distance is no more than a banal, macadamized parking lot or a bench in a newly cobblestoned minipark where old men are like a shadowy Greek chorus as they pass their bottles of wine to one another in the darkness of very chic, plastic-canopied shelters. And there was always the ultimate retreat not available in New Guinea: to return to my own home with its pictures, books, and furniture that represent some kind of personal statement. But even this statement was frequently open to question as I placed it against the lives of those persons I observed.

The experience of conjunction and disjunction is surely felt less acutely and managed more easily by those who are strongly convinced of their purpose, their role, and the values of the life they have made. Opposite temperaments—and I suppose I must count myself among them—the less sure and more doubting, are more inclined to find themselves facing existential questions with a degree of "fear and trembling." But probably the method of participant observation leaves no one completely unchanged.

Apart from the emotional components, there were also physical strains I had not anticipated. Though The Columbia is open during the day, it is mainly a nighttime place. My hours of work were principally between 5:30 pm and 2:00 am, when the tavern closes. There have been many occasions on which I have been there for this entire period; but whether I arrived and left early or arrived late and left in the early morning, the schedule added hours to my working day; and since I am not young nor particularly robust, my other work suffered. Moreover, for two years I was probably more of a fixture at The Columbia than the patrons whom I came to recognize as "regulars," whom I saw possibly four out of seven nights a week. The purpose of the research might have been accomplished by a less intensive immersion, but I do not think so; for it was necessary to observe the tavern and its patrons through all the hours of its day-to-day, week-to-week and month-to-month cycle. The personal moral—if there is one—that might be drawn from the experience is that the unconventional hours of research are more suited to the young and resilient who can bounce back to classes, exams, and papers with a morning-after Alka-Seltzer.

To speak again to the "outside-inside" polarities, I should say that I never concealed the academic purpose behind my ubiquitous presence in the tavern. The owners, the bartenders, and virtually all the regulars know my full name, my profession and institutional affiliation, and, in itself, this is somewhat unusual in a situation where conventions place a premium on anonymity. Over the entire period of the study there have, of course, been innumerable people with whom I have interacted who were unfamiliar with my personal background and who sometimes responded with suspicion when they discovered it. On two occasions, for example, I introduced a professional photographer to the tavern, having received prior permission from the owners and bartenders. The photographic essay was conducted as unobtrusively as possible, since we wanted cinéma-vérité records rather than composed shots. It is difficult, however, to conceal even a small camera in a situation where cameras are suspect. The regulars did not object even when they knew they were being photographed, but there were some casual visitors who confronted us with a warning to desist. Their suspicion, I think, is a reflection of the "passing" quality of their lives outside the tavern. It was not necessarily related to misdemeanors, felonies, or crimes that they may have committed—though not necessarily unrelated either—but rather the response of people for whom some degree of dissembling is necessary to maintain a foothold in a cultural system that continues to project them as figures of fun or as unreliable, not-to-be-trusted deviants.

Though I did not plan it deliberately, I also discovered that my customary style of dress contributed to an "outsider" image. "Why the hell do you always wear your fucking parka?" one man demanded belligerently, referring to my jacket and tie; and on another occasion two men stood in front of me as I sat at the bar and in succession slowly emptied their schooners of beer over my shoes and trousers. At the time, I was not sure what their demeaning gesture was meant to convey except, perhaps, a degree of hostility toward someone whom they perceived as an intruder.

The total experience, however, has been one of qualified acceptance and inclusion that seems to reflect the great tolerance The Columbia's patrons have for personal eccentricities of appearance and behavior. Unlike Laud Humphreys (*Tearoom Trade*, 1970) in his research on the far more clandestine, more ephemeral, and more immediate sexual activities in public urinals, the structure of relationships in the tavern did not include any formal role, equivalent to "watch queen" (lookout), that I could assume as observer-participant. Because of the highly stigmatized and criminally sanctioned tearoom activities, Humphreys was compelled to resort to an academic subterfuge in attempting to gather data on his subjects outside the anonymous setting of the urinals. Whether his tactics raise ethical questions is not an issue I wish to attend. The settings, apart from the fact that both are public places, are vastly different; and I mention the formal deception he found necessary only to add to what I have said already concerning my attempts to publicize my purpose within the tavern: namely, that every person who has been interviewed in depth has given his permission within the tavern, has known the focus of the enquiry before submitting to it, and, of course, has had the opportunity of refusing to participate. Tape recorders have been used in some private interviews, but it has been a quite open procedure conducted in the living quarters of the subjects, and all of them have listened to replays of the sessions.

At a different methodological level, it is necessary to state that I never made any notes inside the tavern; observations were recorded in writing at home at the conclusion of work. Perhaps this could be construed as a form of deception, but everyone with whom I have had more than passing contact has known I am writing about him or her. The method, however, may raise questions of veracity based upon the notorious fallibility of the human eye and memory. There are three responses to this. First, the reader must accept with a degree of faith that for more than thirty years—beginning long before I entered academia—I have trained myself to *see*. Visual properties have had a compelling fascination for me from my earliest remembered years. Second, the observations have been purposeful and sustained for a period of more than two years. They are not equivalent to recollections of an entirely unanticipated event. And last, some of The Columbia's patrons have read portions of the manuscript and have generally agreed with its descriptive dimensions. Indeed, their comments when confronted with the attempt to delineate the style and structure of the tavern have been positive contributions to it.

Since *Other Voices* departs occasionally from more conventional ethnographies, it may be useful to explain the book's structure. The Introduction defends my use of the term "style" to summarize the common understandings and particularities of behavior—the "lore"—associated with the tavern. I reject more commonly used concepts such as "subculture" and "subgroup" because I think they often carry pejorative implications and are not useful analytic tools in trying to depict the order of The Columbia. Similarly, I do not think the term "culture" is properly applicable to the lifeways of the total population of homosexuals, nor "community" to their relationships with one another and with the larger society. Of all anthropological concepts "culture" virtually alone has been accepted into popular lay usage and together with "community"—primarily a sociological construct—has been invoked as a charter of legitimacy for the activist causes of many (most) minority groups. Once one group joined it, the "cultural bandwagon" attracted—follow-the-leader fashion—others seeking acceptance of coexisting pluralism rather than the melting-pot theory that sat most comfortably with the privileged orders. This does not mean that the term "culture" is always misused; but the very popularity of the concept, its almost magic and charismatic quality as a rallying call, sometimes bends it out of reasonable recognition and utility.

C. A. Tripp in *The Homosexual Matrix* (1975) has made my point succinctly in remarking that "part of the difficulty in viewing homosexuality is that it is largely amorphous—a behavioral category of individuals who are about as diffusely allied with each other as the world's smokers or coffee drinkers, and who are defined more by social opinion than by any fundamental consistency among themselves." I have thought it necessary, however, to address the issue at greater length because of the opposition and hostility it has generated in many gay activists when I have expressed it in public. Gay activists, of course, represent only a minority of a minority, and I appreciate the social and political leverage of the terms "culture" and "community"; but they are misused if they are intended to subsume characteristics that bond the total homosexual population. "*The* gay community" and "gay culture" are patent misnomers when applied to the population at large. There are *some* gay "communities" and there is a minimal "lore" which is understood by a considerable number of homosexuals. There are, however, many more specialized "lores" that are not shared and that are often mutually exclusive. Paradoxically, too, the constant misuse of the terms "culture" and "community" may be a disservice in the long run to the achievement of laudable goals, fostering the perpetuation of the long-standing heterosexual myth that homosexuals generally are members of a "subversive conspiracy."

The Introduction concludes with a brief reference to the interpretive framework used to provide an understanding of certain ritualized behaviors that are conspicuous elements of the tavern's style. I have borrowed from Jean Genet the metaphor of "a hall of mirrors" in attempting to clarify the symbolic content of these behaviors. My thesis is that they are essentially ritual enactments of heterosexual myths of homosexuals, using deliberate distortions to disvalue the "truth" of the myths and, through a process of refractions, thereby communicating and intensifying the homosexual's existential experience of inclusion and exclusion. While the dominant metaphor is taken directly from Genet, the symbolic analysis relies heavily upon other writers associated with "the theater of the absurd" and on the work of that name by Martin Esslin (1969).

Chapters One and Two are almost entirely descriptive. They respond to a question I presented in the Preface to *The High Valley*. "Why," I asked, "is so much anthropological writing so antiseptic, so devoid of anything that brings a people to life? There they are, pinned like butterflies in a glass case, with the difference, however, that we often cannot tell what color these specimens are; and we are never shown them in flight, never see them soar or die except in generalities." These two chapters hope to provide the reader with some feeling for the life observed within the tavern, presenting it with a degree of vividness and immediacy that is possibly more novelistic than most ethnographies.

The first chapter describes The Columbia's urban "neighborhood" and touches briefly on its history and on the various homosexual styles that are found there or distributed more widely in the city. The styles are not regional. All of them, and many others not discoverable in Port City, can be found in reasonably large metropolitan centers across the country, and there are numerous references to them in the growing literature on homosexual "territoriality" (Leznoff and Westley, 1956; Cory, 1960; Hooker, 1967; Cavan, 1966; Rechy, 1967—to mention only a few). There are, however, several reasons for giving space to materials that won't be new to many readers. They will not be familiar to academicians who have no reason to read the scholarly journals and monographs in which they are enumerated, and the general public—including many homosexuals—is largely unaware of the diversity of specialized styles, for, despite the recent "surfacing" of homosexuality, the public settings remain essentially clandestine.

The last statement may seem to be disputed by the availability of national and international "travel guides"—as well as by advertisements in homosexual newsletters—that locate the places on city maps and list them, Baedeker-style, according to their different characteristics; but an unmotivated general public does not have access to much of this literature, which is often sold and distributed in the settings or in "adult" bookstores. Many heterosexuals in Port City know the location of its gay quarters but are generally completely ignorant of the different kinds of associations and "services" that are offered in them. Finally, the differentiation of styles allows me to position The Columbia relative to others in a typology.

Chapter Two is an impressionistic treatment of the tavern on a crowded night. It tries to convey the contrapuntal quality of encounters and to display a cross section of the population. The vignettes are not meant to be in-depth character studies, and although the treatment leads sometimes to excursions beyond the tavern, to the homes and into the private lives of a few customers, they are not case histories. Since I am not concerned with homosexual motivation—simply assuming its presence—there is no point in addressing all the possible cause-and-effect linkages built into traditional psychoanalytical studies. I am not asking the questions "how" or "why" The Columbia's patrons "chose" their sexual life-style; rather, I want to know what—having "chosen" it—they find at the tavern: how its style responds to their needs and expresses the shared experience of stigmatization. Their sexuality is the dominant component of that experience, but the majority of the customers are branded with the multiple stigmata of other social, economic, and ethnic disadvantages, and these are also reflected in the tavern's lore. Most of the additional disadvantages, however, are so well known and documented that it is redundant to recount their individual details.

Chapter Two also includes some subjective impressions and reactions. They are not merely self-indulgent. The personal approach I used throughout the research is often regarded with suspicion by "formalist" colleagues in anthropology and sociology. I do not wish to debate the relative merits of different methodologies or the value of their respective contributions to knowledge, but I think that a reader is entitled to know my personal tastes and prejudices, not all of them—for a complete accounting would transform the book into an autobiography—but enough to allow an independent assessment of the extent to which they may have affected my judgment of events. Moreover, these personal digressions and insertions may help to give laymen some feeling for the ambiguities inherent in the method, whether it is applied to people in geographically distant and exotic places or to "submerged" lives in our own society. If I say that I "did not like" much of what I observed and in which I participated in the tavern, this personal judgment also applies to many things observed among the Gahuku of New Guinea. "Liking" is not, however, a prerequisite of "understanding," and the transformations between these affective and cognitive poles are the essence of the anthropological experience. In the end, they merge, for I do not think it is possible not to "like" an individual once you have acquired some "understanding" of him. But it takes a long while to achieve the synthesis, far longer than most of us are prepared to spend.

The third chapter deals with the formal properties of interaction—with the social structure of the tavern. It begins by considering the extent to which Sherri Cavan's (Liquor License, 1966) delineations of the characteristics of a "home territory bar" are applicable to The Columbia. The differences noted are not intended to discredit her model; rather, the model is presented as highly valuable for pointing up the characteristics of The Columbia's order of activities, characteristics that do not locate it precisely on her continuum of "convenience, neighborhood, and home territory" bars. Following this discussion, the greater part of the chapter is concerned with the relationship between the physical subdivisions of the tavern's space—its "stages"—and the prosecution of different goals. An uninstructed visitor entering the setting on a crowded night will very likely receive an impression of merely undirected chaos—of incessantly fluctuating activity that lacks any order. It is basically a false impression, for what I refer to as The Columbia's "stages"—barside, table area, poolroom, and rest room—are associated with different "codes" and used or exploited for different purposes. Ignorance of these codes often produces misunderstandings and causes affront to newcomers who have unwittingly adopted a particular position in a particular space with no thought that it may signify motivational interests to other customers.

The following two chapters (The Hall of Mirrors 1 and 2) deal with the more ritualized behaviors that are elements of the style: the first with language and particularly with verbal dueling, the second with sexual pantomimes. Characteristics of many of the behaviors I describe are treated by C. A. Tripp in *The Homosexual Matrix* (1975). He approaches them, however, from an essentially social-psychological perspective whereas I am concerned primarily with their cultural symbolism. The symbolic analysis appears in the two chapters but is not fully developed until the Conclusion.*

I have found some difficulty in maintaining a consistent usage for the term "homosexual" and its related adjective "homoerotic." Homosexual, though also used adjectivally, is a class noun that encompasses both males and females who have sexual relationships with members of their own biological gender. The difficulty in consistency is not a major concern where there is an exclusive interest in members of the same sex; all one has to do is add the qualifying adjectives "male" and "female"—or to use the term lesbian—to identify the respective populations. But there is a more indeterminate population of both sexes who have had or who resort to "homoerotic" experiences but who do not consider themselves "homosexuals" nor, for that matter, "bisexuals." For example, many men who participate in the activities of "tearooms" (public urinals) regard themselves as "straight" and vehemently reject any implication that they are homosexuals or bisexuals. In some other homoerotic encounters between males, the pretence that it is not a "homosexual" encounter may be maintained by the "straight" partner's refusal to "kiss above the waist." Sexual acts between members of the same sex are clearly, by dictionary definition, homosexual acts; but in this very sizeable gray area of sexual conduct self-identification must be taken into account before generalizing labels are distributed indiscriminately.

I have used the term "bisexual" only for those who consciously accept the label and manage their sexual life-style accordingly. Similarly, I have tried to confine the term "homosexual"—both as a noun and adjective— only to people, male and female, whose sexual activity focuses exclusively upon members of the same biological gender. It is roughly equivalent to the term "gay." "Homoerotic" is applied principally to the more ambiguous sexuality associated with such public male meeting places as

---

*It will not escape anthropologists that some of the ideas of Clifford Geertz (1973), Edmund Leach (1976), Nancy Munn (1973), and Victor Turner (1967; 1969) could have provided alternative or supplementary theoretical frameworks in which to deal with the ritualized behaviors of the tavern. Erving Goffman's *Frame Analysis* (1974) also uses the "theater of the absurd" to illustrate his approach to "the manufacture of negative experience." I did not read this book until the manuscript of *Other Voices* was in press, but it is clear that my approach is similar to his (see especially Chapter 11 of *Frame Analysis*).

urinals, parks, certain movie houses, and "peep shows." Of course there are homosexuals who frequent these places—and the acts they engage in are homosexual acts—but they are also patronized by men whose self-identification is unequivocally "straight."

A note is also needed on my use of the terms "transsexual" and "transvestite." As I use it, "transsexual" is synonymous with the older and more esoteric term *berdache,* and following Angelino and Shedd (1955) and Lurie (1953), *berdache* designates an individual of a defined biological gender who has assumed the role and status of the opposite sex and is viewed in this manner alone. Euro-American culture, as distinct from many Native American cultures (Jacobs, 1968) does not provide any status recognition for the *berdache,* though there are individuals who have assumed a transsexual identity with or without the assistance of cosmetic surgery. There is only one regular customer of The Columbia who is a transsexual. His ethnic identity is Native American. He has not had any surgery to effect a sex transformation, but he presents himself *only* as a woman, whether it is in the tavern, on the streets, or in the quarters he shares with his "husband." "Transvestism" means cross-dressing, that is, dressing in the clothing that is culturally assigned to the opposite sex. While all transsexuals are transvestites not all transvestites are transsexuals. Moreover, Tripp (1975) asserts that the majority of male transvestites are not homosexual. With one possible exception, however, The Columbia's transvestites—men who appear there occasionally in "drag"—are homosexual. One of them has begun the preliminary medical and psychiatric screening that may lead eventually to transsexual surgery. If this takes place, he will probably leave the scene of the tavern; for while the transvestite role is generally accepted and understood—if not universally approved—the transsexual has removed himself from the essentially man-to-man bonding of the style.*

Since *Other Voices* is directed to a general public as well as to academicians, I have with a few exceptions, avoided the scholarly convention

---

*My confusion on the use of all these terms is warranted. The psychological and sociological literature on homosexuality is shot through and through with inconsistencies in definition and usage. A recent attempt by Masters and Johnson (1979) to distinguish between "bisexuals" and "ambisexuals" provoked Martin Baulm Duberman to comment in a review of their book in *The New Republic* that their "ambisexuals," a sample of twelve, possibly should not only be distinguished from their "bisexuals" but also from the entire human race!

Given the focus of *Other Voices*—the cultural patterning of male homosexual behavior and its symbolic implications in a particular setting—I think my possibly simplistic differentiations serve my purpose adequately.

of footnotes. Where it has been necessary to acknowledge the work of others, I have tried to do so in the body of the text. The works cited are listed in a select bibliography (Selected References) at the end of the book.

Finally, in a work of this kind it is customary to acknowledge all those who have contributed to it. Foremost among them, I would like to thank the people of The Columbia, for, obviously, without their willingness to cooperate the research could not have been done. But I also want to thank them for accepting me and for the protection they often offered me—for an "instruction" that on occasion prevented me from making a complete fool of myself and helped to avert consequences I had no way of anticipating. Like all anthropologists studying unfamiliar ways of life, I was virtually a child when I began my work in The Columbia. There were numerous occasions on which some people took, or tried to take, advantage of my abysmal ignorance—Gahuku, of course, did the same thing when I lived with them—but the majority of the tavern's customers were supportive and protective in the ways in which adults are supposed to act toward the socially immature.

Many colleagues in anthropology, many students, and many other friends have read all or portions of the manuscript and have encouraged me or have provided valuable commentaries. Among them, I would like to thank particularly the late Margaret Mead who (and it won't be a surprise to those who knew her) gave more time to reading my material than anyone might reasonably expect; my friends Professor Melford E. Spiro and his wife Audrey; Professor Morris D. Morris and Ruby Morris; Professor Simon Ottenberg and his wife the late Norah Ottenberg; Dr. Gil Herdt, Barbara Young, Charna Klein, Darleen Fitzpatrick, Dr. Robert Schroeder, Professor Jean-Paul Dumont; and Craig A. Hanson, founder of the Los Angeles Gay Community Alliance, has provided valuable information on public male homosexual styles, some of which are not found in Port City. He has not agreed with the position I have taken in the Introduction, but in correspondence (we have never met) it has been possible to arrive at some understanding.

I am also truly grateful for the Foreword Lewis L. Langness has contributed to *Other Voices*. He was the first graduate student in anthropology who studied with me after my arrival in the United States in 1957, and he went on to make important contributions to the anthropology of New Guinea, an area that was then my own principal interest. Our long relationship has been personally and professionally rewarding and is one that I continue to cherish.

Last, I owe a particular debt to three people: to my friend and

colleague in sociology, Ernest A. T. Barth, who has listened to me—
without expressing boredom—over innumerable luncheons, and who
has directed me to pertinent literature; to my son Michael, who has
shown extreme patience with my unconventional hours, frequent
distress, and irritability; and to Nick Layne, who has provided a humorous commentary on the entire enterprise. The book is dedicated to them
as a grateful expression of support and trust without which I might not
have persevered.

Other
Voices

We have lingered in the chambers of
    the sea,
By sea-girls wreathed with seaweed
    red and brown
Till Human voices wake us, and we
    drown.

T. S. Eliot: "The Love Song of J. Alfred
                Prufrock"

Darling and Divine will always baffle the "normal" reader, and the more they elude him, the more true we think them . . . .

Although [Darling's] other features are only dream images, they have, nevertheless, the gratuitousness, mystery, and the stubbornness of life. . . .

We can be sure our dreamer never leaves reality: he *arranges* it.

Jean-Paul Sartre: Introduction to *Our Lady of The
                Flowers,* by Jean Genet, Bantam,
                New York, 1964.

Archibald: The time has not yet come for presenting dramas about noble matters. But perhaps they suspect what lies behind this architecture of emptiness and words. We are what they want us to be. We shall ` therefore be it to the very end, absurdly.

Jean Genet: *The Blacks,* trans. Bernard Frechtman, Grove Press, New York, 1960.

Fantasy is revealing; it is a method of cognition; everything that is imagined is true; nothing is true if it is not imagined.

Eugène Ionesco: "La démystification par l'humeur noir," *L'Avant-Scène,* Paris, February 1959. Quoted by Martin Esslin in *The Theatre of The Absurd.* Doubleday/Anchor, New York, 1969.

But where the comic and the tragic (for want of a better word) are closely interwoven, certain members of an audience will always give emphasis to the comic as opposed to the other, for by so doing they rationalize the other out of existence.

Harold Pinter: Letter to the *Sunday Times,* London, 14 August, 1960.

Solange	*(she steps back to the wardrobe):*
	I'm ready. — I'm tired of being an object of disgust. I hate you, too. I despise you. I hate your scented bosom. Your . . . *ivory* bosom! Your . . . *golden* thighs! Your . . . *amber* feet! I hate you! *(She spits on the red dress).*
Claire	*(aghast):*
	Oh! . . . Oh! . . . But . . . .
Solange	*(walking up to her):*
	Yes, my proud beauty. You think you can always do just as you like. You think you can deprive me forever of the beauty of the sky, that you can choose your perfumes and powders, your nail-polish and silk and velvet and lace, and deprive *me* of them? That you can steal the milkman from me? Admit it! Admit about the milkman. . . .

Jean Genet: *The Maids* (translated by Bernard Frechtman), Grove Press, New York, 1954.

Introduction

The Columbia tavern in Port City is listed in many "Gay Travel Guides" as a meeting place for male homosexuals. Some lesbians visit it infrequently, and its regular patrons include a few people, male and female, who are straight or bisexual. The straights, apart from those who enter unwittingly and leave suddenly, are mostly older members of the lowest economic strata. Some of the asserted bisexuals are married and appear there occasionally with their wives. The ambience, however, is unequivocally male homosexual.

This delineation of the style of The Columbia is, therefore, a description of a male homosexual style; but it is not a study of homosexuality in the most inclusive sense.* To begin with, I have a minimal interest in the psychodynamics of homosexuality. While I have read many books on the subject, I have not found them particularly illuminating but, rather, variations on Freudian dogma—commentaries to a largely discredited gospel. In a brief but devastating critique of the classical Freudian position, C. A. Tripp (1975, pp. 77–80) quite correctly questions its emphasis on the negative motivations in a person's life, remarking that "it was a pointless effort at best, since all sexual attractions are based upon positive motives: the real or imagined benefits a person hopes to gain by a

---

*It is also clear that my material is a far cry from the philosophical idealization of homosexual relationships in classical Greek literature (particularly those between teacher and pupil) and in many English-language classics including some works of contemporary American authors. There is no doubt that there are homosexual couples whose relationship approximates in quality the ideal advanced in Plato's *Symposium*. That the majority of relationships do not do so is no more remarkable than the fact that the relationships of many heterosexual couples are a poor match for a romanticized ideal.

1

sexual conquest or by "possessing" the partner." Tripp, however, is interested in the motivational bases of homosexuality—and provides the most lucid and reasonable discussion I have read—whereas I am not. I have assumed that a sizeable minority, maybe as many as thirteen percent, of the population of the United States are either exclusively homosexual or have intermittent but recurring homoerotic experiences. I have chosen not to ask "why?"—the question of genesis—preferring to address the patterned (cultural) ways in which the sexual preference is expressed. The focus is very close to that presented by Maureen Mileski and Donald J. Black in their paper (1972) *The Social Organization of Homosexuality.* Like me, Mileski and Black simply assume the existence of homosexual motivation in the population at large and state their position in this way: "If the motivation to act in a given manner is assumed in a theory of human behavior, then the question becomes a matter of what else besides a particular psychological state must be present before the behavior can occur. In the case of homosexuality, what besides psychological homosexuals must be present before homosexual behavior can take place? Simply put, what *social mechanisms* [italics added] make homosexual behavior possible?"

In the United States, gay bars and taverns, public urinals, some parks, and steam baths are among the "social mechanisms" that facilitate the expression of psychological motivation, but clearly, too, they are not the only mechanisms; for large numbers of homosexual men and women do not have recourse to any of the available public settings. There is, then, a second sense in which my work is not a study of homosexuality in general; it is a study of *public* male behavior and, moreover, of a particular style of such behavior.

Addressing the first point in this statement, The Columbia is not a private club where it is necessary to present a membership card or to pay a cover charge to gain admission. Its large plate-glass windows flanking the sidewalk doors are uncurtained. A lattice-like design in gold covers the lower half of the glass surfaces but does little to reduce outside-inside visibility. The premises are licensed by the state to sell beer and wine but no hard liquor. Any passerby looking for a drink may enter it. On this score, the activities in the tavern are not as furtive as male homosexual and homoerotic encounters in public urinals, parks, or the peep-show booths in "adult amusement arcades." Though the Port City Police Department has The Columbia under surveillance, its patrons do not run much risk of arrest for sexual misconduct. At the beginning of my study—before police attitudes toward homosexuals became more tolerant—they were often harassed outside the tavern, but the continuing interest of the police is prompted by other "biographical blemishes" on the lives of many customers rather than their sexuality. Neither the owners, who are a straight married couple, nor the bartenders approve sex on the premises, though they tolerate the explicit pantomimes. Nevertheless, despite the fact that it is an open, public place, the atmosphere of the tavern is enclosed and clandestine in the sense that the sexuality communicated within it is normatively disapproved and negatively sanctioned outside. I shall attempt to show eventually that these poles of inclusion-exclusion not only constitute the basic common understanding of those who frequent it but also underlie the more ritualized elements of their behavior.

Turning to my second point—the particularity of the tavern's style—I do not think my data lend any support to popular notions of "a homosexual community" or an inclusive "homosexual culture." My contentions are that no such generalized entities can be identified and that the tavern exemplifies merely what I call a "style," one of many constrastive styles. I feel I should speak more fully to both positions.

There is no doubt that within the past decade the subject of homosexuality has moved from the cloistered domains of scholarships and elliptical literature into the arena of the popular media. It is entirely inappropriate to refer to the sexual preference as "the vice without a name" when syndicated columnists bring it to the breakfast table and plays and motion pictures dealing with it reach not only sophisticated audiences but also the patrons of suburban drive-ins. The admitted homosexuals appearing on late-night television shows produce a retrospective sympathy for E. M. Forster agonizing over the manuscript of *Maurice* and withholding it until after his death, and for Oscar Wilde whose hubris compelled him to ignore the sensible advice of Mrs. Patrick Campbell that "you may do anything in London—if you don't do it in the street and frighten the horses." Wilde's folly, in the eyes of those who belonged to his circle, lay in confronting the Marquess of Queensbury and exposing what was widely practiced but prudently concealed; and comparing the destructive notoriety of his case with what is publicly known of lesser contemporary figures, there is a strong temptation to sing the television commercial promoting cigarettes for the feminine market:

> "You've come a long way, baby,
> [But you still have a long way to go!"]

The catch lies, of course, in the second and unvoiced line of the jingle; for despite the increasing tolerance that might be assumed from current publicity, admission or discovery of homosexual preferences may mean the loss of employment, of friends, and of reputation. Indeed, the legalization of homosexual acts between consenting adults is not likely to eradicate majority prejudices or to promote "open" and unevaluated acceptance of the "alternative sexual life-style." At least, one must assume this probability from the prevailing situation in societies of "Western origin" that have "legitimized" the sexual preference, for even there the "official" acceptance is halfhearted and imposes codes of decorum upon homosexuals that, in a sense, are designed to "keep them in the closet." Statutory "legitimacy" doesn't—as anyone should know—legislate unequivocal acceptance, and Tripp (1975, pp. 2–3) suggests that the liberalization of laws concerned with homosexuality may have the inverse effect of "tightening" surveillance of homosexuals, a condition which he finds in England, Switzerland, and Illinois, citing them as examples of "just how thoroughly entrenched classical mores are." The upshot is that, indeed, homosexuals have "a long way to go" and, more importantly, I do not think they will, in the foreseeable future, get "all the way" to unevaluated acceptance of their sexuality. This is virtually impossible so long as there are no fundamental changes in the dominant heterosexual and Judeo-Christian values of the culture. Difficult as it may be for them to accept it, homosexuals, despite hard-won partial recognition, will remain a possible scapegoat in American culture, and the long-run prognostication for them isn't much different from what it is now—a position that hasn't changed greatly from the one enunciated by Mrs. Patrick Campbell.

The tangled complex of legal, economic, and cultural sanctions and prejudices that continues to discriminate against homosexuals is the target of gay activists whose current movements follow chronologically behind those of other civil rights groups. This is not intended as a criticism either of their indignation and sense of injustice or of their sometimes selective efforts to disabuse the general public of its stereotypical images of homosexuals. These images are clearly caricatures, though it is necessary to remember that where stereotypes exist some people may adopt them and thus tend to confirm them. The apologetics of the gay spokesmen draw upon studies of behavior in animal species other than man, on the historical record within the tradition of Western culture, and on the cross-cultural anthropological record. The case is easily made that homosexuality is a panhuman phenomenon, and it is equally easy to document the creative contributions of homosexuals to literature, art, science, and philosophy. This is not a revelation, and the apologists occasionally seem to belabor small issues with overlarge sticks. The legitimacy of their anti-defamation protests aside, however, a pertinent question is *what* do they represent—for whom do they speak; what is their constituency?

About one year ago spokesmen for gay liberation, protesting alleged police harassment, testified before the City Council that Port City's population (approximately 600,000) included 50,000 homosexuals. The city is one of five major urban centers on its coast that are known for a degree of permissiveness in tolerating public homosexual meeting places. It is regarded—in the phraseology of male homosexuals—as a relatively "good city," though it is not as "open" or as tolerant of some styles as three of its coastal neighbors. Moreover, the tolerance extends only to some off-the-street establishments. Street "cruising" and park and public-urinal sex are negatively sanctioned. It is also my impression that over the past sixteen years the number of specialized places has increased threefold. Twelve years ago, for example, a colleague expressed disbelief when a student in one of his undergraduate classes suggested there were 12,000 homosexuals in the city and named half-a-dozen bars and taverns as homosexually oriented. The number now—though I have not made a precise count—is in the twenties.

It is quite unlikely, however, that the male homosexual population has doubled in a little over a decade. The discrepancy in the figures (neither being more than educated guess) probably reflects some of the easing of attitudes toward the sexual preference; and if one wishes to accept the figure of the local gay liberationists, my own educated guess is that less than four percent of all homosexuals, male and female, are affiliated or care to be affiliated with the activists.

Patrons of The Columbia dismiss the liberationists as "freaks." When one activist organization announced the formation of a "Lavender Patrol" of male homosexuals wearing identifying armbands who would walk the nighttime streets to observe police harassment, reaction to the notion was contemptuous hilarity: "Shit! Them queers are out of their gourds!" And on a visit to the tavern the organizer (who had appeared on local television) of the movement—ordained pastor of a homosexual Christian church—was informed he was unwelcome.

Leaders of other minority movements have encountered similar opposition from members of the constituency whose rights they hope to protect. There are always individuals who have learned to live with discrimination, and groups subject to discrimination often develop ways to reduce or to avoid confrontation with those who vilify or demean them. The "Uncle Tom" figure may be any color and may belong to diverse social strata. But of all minorities in the United States, homosexuals seem the least likely to organize successfully on a national level. Significantly, during the annual "Gay Pride Week" in Port City—supposedly a public declaration of sexual identity sponsored by a few gay organizations—spokesmen expect no more than about 250 individuals—male and female—to participate in the "open" activities

held in confrontation with the general public.* Admittedly, some of
these activities smack of juvenility—a hand-in-hand daisy-chain dance
a landmark fountain—and probably appeal to an extremely small and
immature minority, but I think the figure is more or less typical of the
state of overall cooperation and inclusive identification. Quite prudently, the vast majority of homosexuals remain "in the closet" and are
unlikely to leave it.

If the focus is the *total* homosexual population, there is nothing
nationally or in any given city that may properly be called "*the* homosexual community," at least not by any usage that respects the term's
usual reference in sociology. There is a sexual preference common to
many men and women, but this preference is subordinate in day-to-day
life to other tastes, interests, and forms of association. On any criteria
other than the sexual direction, homosexuals are the most fragmented of
minorities. They are often as racist as straights, even when the shared
sexual preference is acknowledged. "Nigger lover" is often used pejora-
tively by white male homosexuals to describe a member of their ethnic
group who is sexually involved with blacks; and by the same token,
there are blacks who resent other homosexual blacks who are sexually
involved with whites. Interracial "marriages" not only encounter the
prejudices of the larger society where interracial living is involved but
also similar prejudices within the homosexual population. And since the
sexual preference encompasses every ethnic group in the United States, it
is not surprising that generalized ethnic prejudices also color relationships other than those between black and white. "Rice queen" is the
equivalent of "nigger lover" for male Caucasians who are sexually
attracted to orientals; and although it is often used humorously, it also
reflects ethnic-based attitudes and divisions.

Ethnicity aside, there is a multitude of other factors that divide homosexuals—quite as many as those that contribute to divisions among the
heterosexual population, whether they are education, economic status,
profession or occupation, religion, or politics. The heterosexual
belief—still produced from time to time—in an inclusive "homosexual
conspiracy" has absolutely no basis in reality, far less basis, for example,
than the belief in a "communist conspiracy." But as with any convenient

*In 1978, according to newspaper accounts, this event drew about 2,000 demonstrators
to a downtown march and rally. The number is still a small proportion of the total population of homosexuals and many of those who participated were heterosexuals demonstrating
against an impending local initiative to rescind an existing city ordinance protecting the
rights of homosexuals in housing and employment (see Appendix 1). As far as I know, there
was no mayoral proclamation of "Gay Pride Week" in 1979 and there was no heterosexual
media coverage, not even a one-line mention, of the rally held this year.

scapegoat, the heterosexual majority is disposed to ignore the great diversity within a minority that is only a minority by virtue of a single criterion: a sexual preference. As Tripp (1975) has said, the national population of homosexuals—male and female— is as diffusely inter-related as those who smoke or drink tea or coffee.

Heterosexual stereotypes of homosexuals are patently exaggerated and oversimplified. The limp-wristed, lisping, flitty, and "feminine" male—so dear to television comedians—is, at best, minimally descriptive. Certainly, there are some homosexual men whose behavior could be construed as "feminine," but it is equally true that not every male exhibiting "feminine" characteristics is homosexual. Indeed, there is probably nothing less reliable than voice, mannerisms, and physical appearance in reaching conclusions on sexuality. From the conventional cultural perspectives of "maleness," a majority of male homosexuals would score 100 percent for "maleness," and, by the same token, many of those placed at the lowest end of the stereotyped scale are being misjudged. There is nothing that unequivocally identifies the homo-sexual in visible ways. And if mannerisms are entirely unreliable, so is occupation. The most "masculine" of occupations, from construction workers, truck drivers, and cowhands to the armed services and profes-sional athletics, include homosexuals, and, by contrast, not all male ballet dancers, hairdressers, ribbon clerks, couturiers, and interior decorators are gay. It is possible, of course, to find a sufficient number of homosexuals in certain occupations to reinforce the assumption that these occupations are homosexually dominated and directed. Only a few known cases are needed in the self-justifying game of stereotyping—no more than are ignored or, hopefully, swept under the rug where the popular occupational image will not entertain them.

Preferment in employment for homosexuals in any occupation is absolutely minimal. Where it exists, it is confined mostly to service roles, to salesmen in some chic men's haberdasheries, attendants in steam baths, waiters and bartenders in homosexual restaurants and taverns; but even the specialized establishments may have heterosexual employ-ees in positions of authority, and homosexuals—if their sexual direction is known or suspected—are more often the subjects of employment discrimination than recipients of special favors. It is far more ludicrous to speak of "gay power" than any other brand of minority "power." The vast majority of homosexuals are "Middle Americans" in everything except normative sexuality, and the values of Middle America are more important to most of them than open identification by sexual preference.

I repeat that these remarks are not intended to denigrate the efforts of the relatively few public activists on behalf of a largely noninvolved and

sometimes antagonistic constituency. Homosexuals presently have bene-
fited immensely, if mostly indirectly, from the dedication of the relatively few activists who have been instrumental in bringing the "vice" out
of the "closets." All blacks and all women have derived similar benefits
from liberation movements, even though many of both groups have not
been active in the respective causes. Pride in being black—self-
identification with color—is a ripple effect of the civil rights movement
of the early sixties and the various power movements spawned by it; the
rewards of activism are spread throughout the group as, indeed, women
generally have been the beneficiaries of the antisexist crusade. Male
chauvinism has not been eradicated; but at the very least women's liberation has sensitized many men to cultural attitudes toward the opposite
sex and has generated changes in linguistic usages as well as promoting,
for those who want it, some acceptance of freedom to choose their
domestic role—all this in addition to efforts to secure constitutional
guarantees for equal rights.

The thrust of the gay liberation movement is directed precisely at
securing the right to choose a sexual life-style without encountering
social and legal penalties. The climate of receptivity was prepared by
others whose causes were sometimes cultish and sometimes, as with the
black movement, more firmly grounded on sweeping, idealistic social
principles; and for homosexuals, male and female, it remains a grudging,
skeptical, and often completely antagonistic climate, possibly because
the cause, like the women's movement, strikes so directly at the tender
heart of cultural definitions of sexual roles. Nevertheless, there has been
progress, witnessed not least by a recent pronouncement from the
American Psychiatric Association—reversing a long-standing position—
that the sexual preference is not necessarily "sick."

Quite certainly, none of this would have happened if there had not
been individuals who had the temerity to confront prejudices, to
proclaim their preference at considerable personal risk, and to work with
others to remove the stigma associated with homosexuality; but there are
significant differences between the gay and other minority movements.

The black population is not homogeneous with respect to wealth,
education, occupation, religion, or politics. A majority of blacks,
however, unlike homosexuals, are employed in the lower-paying and
unskilled jobs, and discrimination in employment, housing, and other
areas of civil liberties is clearly of more concern, past and present, to
them than to homosexuals. Obviously, too, blacks, like homosexuals,
are the subjects of grossly misleading folk-images. But the very visibility
of blacks—their color—adds a dimension to the group experience that
may transcend sexuality. Many blacks are as intolerant of homosexuals

as whites are; but whether heterosexual or homosexual the black *is* black, and being black in a white-dominated society is something shared by all of them—a focus for identity and common aspirations, for group-wide feelings of injustice and experiences of gratuitous indignity. There isn't such a basic, *visible and focused* common denominator for the *total* population of homosexuals.

Cultural values associated with biological gender also tend to override a sense of common cause and to inhibit cooperation between male and female homosexuals. At Port City University, for example, there are two "gay students' associations," one for men and one for women; their offices are separated, and there are few jointly sponsored programs of social activities.* The city has only two lesbian taverns, a ratio of male-to-female homosexual establishments that is characteristic of all metropolitan centers and may require an explanation that does not rest solely on relative numbers. In the United States, bars and taverns have been principally male preserves. Women have not been "socialized" to the bar scene, which has been presented to them negatively by the male attitude that they would not intrude without an escort unless they were seeking or open to a sexual encounter. Sexual encounters are acceptable in lesbian taverns; but the public bar or tavern, as a customary meeting place even for merely social purposes, has been off limits to women, their presence there being regarded as a breach of the domestic roles tradition-ally assigned to them. Thus, the lesbian bar is a relatively new—as well as specialized—element in the cultural experience of women. Moreover, the normative values of American culture give women a far greater lati-tude than men in displaying affection for and intimacy with one another, a difference, Mileski and Black (1972, pp. 195 ff.) suggest, that is respon-sible for the not surprising fact that "many females first engage in homo-sexuality with a friend in an ordinary social setting rather than in an organized homosexual territory." The "territories" are, at best, supple-mental rather than central mechanisms for female homosexuals (Mileski and Black, p. 197).

The point, however, is that even in organized territories, where the homosexual preference is "openly" acknowledged, the sexes tend to maintain a public segregation. The lesbians who come infrequently to The Columbia are always accompanied by a male, and homosexual males seldom go alone to lesbian establishments. This is understandable, commonsensical enough if you are either male or female and looking for a trick; but one might expect that the "common bond" of homosexuality

---

*At the present time these two organizations have been amalgamated, but I doubt that the gender dichotomy has been resolved.

would be more productive of cooperation outside the organized territories. It isn't so. On the contrary, male homosexuals seem to have more female friends and acquaintances who are straight rather than lesbian, and many of them tend to regard the latter as "odd"—subjects of a snide lore concerning their sexual practices. Similarly, a possible majority of activist lesbians—and some lesbian organizations—identify with the much more inclusive feminist movement. Some of the more radical of them see lesbianism as only one issue—and possibly a subordinate one—in the struggle to secure freedom from male domination for all women. The male is the "enemy" while women, heterosexual or homosexual, are "sisters" with whom one should identify in pursuit of goals sought by the entire sex. The institutionalized male-female dichotomy—like the black-white dichotomy—provides a framework for social and political activism that often transcends sexual preferences.

Contrastively, male homosexuals (particularly whites) are in a kind of activist limbo. As males, they inherit a legacy of vested social and economic privileges, and many of them are as sexist (chauvinistic) as heterosexual men. Unlike women, blacks, Latinos, or Native Americans, they have *only* the sexual preference—with its avoidable and unevenly distributed discriminatory consequences—as a possible focus for population-wide unity.

The emphasis placed upon "only" does not imply that the cause is unimportant, and men have borne the brunt of obloquy, ostracism, and prosecution for deviation from the ascribed biological norm. Single individuals in a culture that defines heterosexual marriage as the expected adult state encounter discrimination in tax laws and more diffuse areas of their lives; and characteristically both single males and females are subjected to sexual gossip and innuendo. It is a little easier, however, for female homosexuals to pass in a world that is dominated by male heterosexual values and in which males are largely ignorant of female sexuality. The intra-sexual norms of American culture discourage expressions of physical affection between males even in family situations—in the relationship, for example, between father and son, where "intimacies" are supplanted very early in the child's life by conventions that prescribe a "manly" physical separation: the firm handshake and the "discussion" conducted in face-to-face positions across an invisible boundary. Adult men are allowed few ways in which to express even Platonic affection for one another—a slap on the back or, more rarely, a jocular *abrazo*— whereas women are permitted to embrace both publicly and privately, to walk hand in hand or arm in arm and to kiss one another in greeting. Perhaps the differences in permissiveness contribute to and also reflect a generalized male anxiety about homosexuality that does not seem to be so characteristic of women, but they also help to account for the relative ease with which possible homosexual motivations can be expressed by women and probably, too, for some noticeable differences in the ways of expressing them. For example, it has been said (Tripp, 1975, p. 154; Mileski and Black, 1972, p. 197; Gagnon and Simon, 1967, pp. 214–215) that the promiscuity and anonymity of many male homosexual encounters is totally absent or at most completely minimal in homosexual relationships between females. Quite certainly, there is nothing equivalent to street cruising and tearoom activities among the "mechanisms" that facilitate the expression of homosexual motivations between women.

Putting such differences aside, however, it is clear that discrimination against homosexuality has been directed principally at men. The nineteenth-century British statute proscribing "obscene" (homosexual) acts specifically excluded women because, it is said, Queen Victoria believed it was impossible for them to have sexual relationships with one another. The attribution may be apocryphal, but it is generally descriptive of the direction and enforcement of legal statutes in the United States. Such laws have been framed by men primarily with men in mind. To most men, male homosexuality is tantamount to "letting down the team," to identifying with women and subverting the ideally asexual bonding and ethos that "justify" culturally entrenched sexual oppositions of superiority and subordination. Perhaps the same attitudes and values should also color male responses to female homosexuality, and there are certainly heterosexual men who perceive lesbianism as a threat to their sexuality; but as I have said—and as spokespersons for the feminist movement reiterate—men have not been required to concern themselves with the sexuality of those whose "natural" role has been construed as "servicing." The situation has been similar to "Upstairs, Downstairs" replicated on sexual lines: what occurred in the servants' hall impinged only indirectly on the noble members of the household.

The "bond" of male homosexuality, however, is not associated with a comprehensive complex of shared values, mores, and patterned ways of behaving that are subsumed, with other commonalities, by the concept of "culture." Not only is it bending the culture concept too far to apply it to the lifeways of male homosexuals generally but, similarly, these lifeways cannot be regarded—except with minimal implications—as characteristic of "a subculture."

Most heterosexuals—subscribing to the popular view that "it takes one to know one"—tend to believe that homosexuals have special, almost subliminal ways of communicating their sexual preference to one another—a "secret language" of identification. The belief that such a specialized system of communication exists obviously reflects the majority norms that negatively sanction the sexual preference and, except in specialized situations, impose "passing" as a mode of accommodation on most homosexuals. It has numerous parallels in the "languages" of other groups whose interests and activities are clandestine or illegal; but the popular assumption, as with almost everything concerned with homosexuality, is an exaggeration.

Specialized languages that include both verbal and nonverbal elements are part of the learned lore of many occupations, client relationships, and ethnic minorities. The linguistic patterns and usages subsumed by "black language" exemplify the ethnic instance; the argots of prostitution and the drug trade are the most obvious examples of those associated with illegal activities. Similarly, there is a homosexual argot. It is possible to produce a compendium of words having homosexual references. Many of them are in general usage. "Queer," "faggot," "dike," and "fairy" hardly require explication to anyone, and even "drag" and "drag queen" have been brought "out of the closet," becoming commonplace among heterosexuals as well as homosexuals. There are words and phrases, however, that are more arcane: for example, the euphemism "tearoom" for men's public urinals; "shrimper" for a male homosexual who has a foot fetish, and "S and M"—an abbreviation of sadomasochistic—to designate the "leather" scene or relationships involving sexual bondage. Such more specialized words not only require an explanation to the heterosexual public but also to many homosexuals, for the entire lexicon is not shared. Many of the words and phrases are familiar only to those who participate in the particular style with which they are associated.

Purported nonverbal forms of communication and identification are even less significant than the argot on a population-wide basis. I have already discounted the reliability of mannerisms and occupation as indicators of sexual preferences, and dress must also be included, for even cross-dressing may have no relationship to sexual roles. There are a few "costume signals" which have a changing currency among some segments of the population. For example, wearing one's keys on the left or the right side of one's belt has been a recent fad in some bar and tavern territories as a means of advertising a preference for either a "passive" or an "active" sexual role. Handkerchiefs positioned in hip pockets—right or left and also by color—have also been adopted for the same purposes. The "in" fads change so frequently that it is difficult to keep abreast of them; but the important point is that they *are* just fads associated with a very small minority. They do not have any generalized currency and no significance for homosexuals who do not participate in the trendy bar and tavern scene.

Heterosexuals also commonly believe that male homosexuals communicate their preference to one another by "eye contact"—by subtle, "knowing" glances exchanged in mixed public and private settings. They do; but such nonverbal signals are not peculiar to them: they are elements of interpersonal communication generally and are no more mysterious than those used by heterosexuals in their search for partners. For the most part they are "situationally specific"—part of the activity of cruising public streets, parks, and many ostensibly heterosexual bars and cocktail lounges that are known as places where it is possible to find men who will respond to homosexual overtures. As with heterosexual prostitution and other kinds of pickups, there are locations in all large cities that are worked by men who are interested in homosexual encounters, and the "signals" transmitted between possible partners are not appreciably different from those used by heterosexuals in the same kind of public search. Clearly, homosexuals also "find" one another in mixed and private settings where it is necessary to conceal their sexual preference. But once again, the process of discovery is basically no different from the maneuverings of heterosexuals—in the same settings—who are interested in initiating or pursuing a relationship which it may be improper or inexpedient to acknowledge openly. In both cases, the clues lie "between the lines" of what is said rather than in anything that transmits an unmistakable message. Homosexual men, questioning this point, have sometimes told me that they can "tell" by the way in which another man positions his feet during conversation or by other subtleties of body presentation. I do not wish to discount such clues entirely; but I suggest that they are not distinctive of homosexuals and that interpretation—if it isn't to result in egregious mistakes and possible rejection—depends upon their relationship to other elements in a behavioral complex that has virtually no uniquely homosexual characteristics.

My point is simply this: all the assumed population-wide interests and behaviors are overshadowed by a tremendous diversity in lifeways and lores. It is as minimally useful to speak of "homosexual culture" as it is to speak of "heterosexual culture"; indeed, there is less justification, less warranty, than in postulating and identifying a "black" or Latino "culture" or even a "street" or "ghetto" culture.

It is for these reasons that I wish to emphasize that my delineations of behaviors in The Columbia tavern are not "typical" of homosexual behavior generally or even typical of behaviors in all public territories. The territories—principally bars, taverns, and steam baths—differ greatly in salient characteristics—in what is offered or permitted on the premises; in the age and socioeconomic class of their clientele; in their "encouragement" of interethnic mixing. They are often "mutually exclusive," presenting a particular homosexual image that excludes those who do not "conform" to the valued mode of self-presentation, and the sexual lores associated with them also differ in many significant respects.

Because of the differences, I have chosen to use the term "style" to identify the sum of The Columbia's order of activities. "Style" has a perfectly acceptable intellectual lineage in literature, the graphic arts, and other humanities, where it is used not only to differentiate "schools," or genres, but also to distinguish the idiosyncratic characteristics of those who represent a "school." Transforming the analogy into the language of sociologues, "genre" represents the category of a population who are "associated" by the "constant" of an exclusive sexual interest in members of the same biological gender. As an inclusive category, "homosexual" —the genre—has only gross application, merely identifying a population whose sexual preference is the opposite of heterosexual. "Style" narrows the focus, recognizing that there are many independent variables within the gross population that are associated with different varieties of public expression.

This, as I said earlier, does not mean that the style of The Columbia is unique—a one-only example that is not replicated anywhere else in the United States. The male homosexual who uses the organized territories can find places almost anywhere in which to pursue his particular tastes, in which he can feel "at home" because the establishments reflect both sexual or nonsexual values and understandings with which he is comfortable. The sexual preference is minimally significant in determining the kinds of public associations that are sought.

The variables that contribute to the style of The Columbia include, first, the ethnic mixture of its population: blacks, whites, Filipinos, Latinos, Native Americans and Asian Americans, and Eskimos—representatives of all the ethnic groups in Port City but with blacks and whites, almost evenly divided, forming an expectable majority. Most of them are socially and economically disadvantaged, earning the minimum hourly wage when they are employed and otherwise living by their wits or on welfare and social security. Few of them have had any more than a high-school education, and the majority have not completed this level of schooling. Their ages range from the early twenties to seventies, with the average probably in their late thirties. Some are alcoholics for whom the tavern is virtually their only "home." A far larger number of both the regular and transient customers are familiar with the mores and participate in the associations of "street culture," of an "underground" and exploitive way of life that is not linked to any single kind of sexuality: trading in stolen goods, in "grass" and "smack," in food stamps, and in all the other forms of "hustling." The experiences and understandings of these more generalized lores are woven into the fabric of the tavern's style and are among the reasons why its patrons say it is "real," contrasting it with the "phoniness" of activities in more "establishment-oriented" places. Similarly, male homosexuals who frequent the more decorous public territories have often been appalled on learning of my involvement with The Columbia. "How *can* you go there?" they have said. "Aren't you uncomfortable; isn't it dangerous?" And I feel them looking at me disapprovingly, probably suspecting I must have a déclassé predilection for the "low-life" sexuality.

Clearly, it is not simply the sexuality that produces these negative and moralizing attitudes. It is true that the style of The Columbia allows more direct approaches and expressions of sexual interest than those that are considered "proper" in some other territories; but its order does not include anything as "open"—as normally expected—as the sex available in steam baths and some taverns that have special areas set aside not only for cruising the available studs but also to complete sexual acts on the premises. Moreover, some of those who moralize about The Columbia are regular patrons of the steam baths. Apparently, they make a distinction between the "socializing" characteristics of the bars and taverns they frequent and the immediate and mostly anonymous opportunities for sexual gratification associated with steam baths. Recourse to the sex available in these settings does not place a question mark against the values and associations they seek in far larger areas of their lives, and it is not the sexuality of The Columbia that provokes their distaste and rejection but, rather, the variables mentioned above, which give a distinctive and pervasive cast to most elements of the style, even to some ritualized behaviors whose recognizable counterparts are distributed more widely.

These ritualized behaviors are the focus of the second half of my study, and my admission that their counterparts can be found in a more inclusive range of both public and private settings may seem to contradict my denial of any entity deserving to be labeled "homosexual culture." But it isn't so. The behaviors concerned are not typical of the population at large: they are not generally approved and are often negatively sanctioned by many homosexual men, who perceive them as unwelcome confirmations of heterosexual stereotypes of homosexuals. The more general categories include drag costuming and public events associated with the "drag scene," "camp," "nellyisms," "fag talk" or "fag chitchat," formal and acerbic verbal dueling, and pantomimed sexual acts. Examples of all these ritualized modes of self-presentation and interaction are components of The Columbia's style, modified, however, by the variables of ethnicity, of socioeconomic class, and by other understandings of a "world view" whose experiential—existential— conditions include far more than the "commonality" of deviant sexuality.

Yet while The Columbia's examples have a distinctive coloration that distinguishes them from others in the general categories, I believe that all of them have basically the same symbolic implications. Despite the

emphasis I have placed on differences within the total homosexual population, *all* of its members share one fact of knowledge and experience,
namely, that their sexuality is not only disapproved but is also generally
construed as a betrayal or reversal of the roles and characterological
traits culturally assigned to them by gender. The entrance to the homosexual "hall of mirrors" is through cultural definitions of "the feminine"
and "the masculine" and the contradictions and antinomies between
these definitions and their own sexuality. By cultural norms and values,
the male homosexual is unsexed, and, since there are no "intermediate"
sexual roles and statuses in American culture, he must be "feminine." It is
precisely this assumption that some gay activist movements protest most
strongly, emphasizing for the purposes of public relations that a man is
not necessarily less "masculine" because he is homosexual. The most
valued and promoted spokesmen for these groups are men who before
"coming out of the closet" would have been identified as "manly" and
straight by the cultural criteria of appearance, occupation—the armed
forces, for example—and by other extra-sexual Middle American interests and identifications. For the same reasons, the conspicuous "faggots"
and "nellies" are seldom placed on public display and tend to be regarded
as an unwelcome but possibly unavoidable element at demonstrations
for the cause—as confirming examples of the heterosexual myth that a
male homosexual *must* be "womanly."

While is is not a matter I wish to attend at length, it is possible to argue
that the emphasis placed upon conventional "masculinity" serves, in the
long run, merely to entrench further the cultural dichotomy of male and
female. The desirable model is "manly" as opposed to "womanly," and
the larger intersexual bind is not resolved, for the objective of acceptance
is sought by reiterating that homosexual men are "men" and that their
sexual preference does not challenge other "manly" qualities and characteristics that are supposed to bond men in the more inclusive sexual
matrix.

Anticipating my final analysis of the categories of ritualized behaviors
and their variations in The Columbia, I shall try to show that they are
essentially symbolic enactments of cultural myths of sexual roles and
identifications. Jean Genet is said to have justified his life as a thief by
deciding to be what others—*les justes*—had branded him ("if that's what
they say I am, that's what I'll be"), a position which is a useful starting
point in trying to understand the implications of behaviors that are
widely disparaged by many male homosexuals and heterosexuals alike.
Obviously, I do not deny that there men who are psychologically motivated to be "women." The male transsexual is an example, and I assume
that the psychological disposition is present, though less pronounced, in

some male homosexual transvestites, but I discount its importance for most of them. Moreover, I do not think that "feminine motivation" is either a necessary or adequate explanation for many kinds of ritualized and "female-like" behaviors. My own interest in them focuses upon a different level of meaning, upon how they relate to and what they convey about heterosexual myths of homosexuality. In other words, the psychological disposition—"feminine motivation"—has a minimal import, for the behaviors are essentially symbolic expressions of what male homosexuals are *assumed* to be rather than what they *are*. From this point of view, they are a Genet-like riposte to the "absurdity" of conventional sexual assumptions and role stereotypes—a deliberately contrived and characteristically exaggerated commentary upon the cultural anomalies that are elements of a far more generalized homosexual experience and awareness. In metaphorical language, they are a distorting mirror whose images reflect already distorted heterosexual images of male homosexual interests, motivations, and traits of personality, and, by compounding the absurdity, they deny the "truth values" of the heterosexual myth that they enact. I think it is useful to view them not only as patterned responses to and rejections of cultural definitions of "the masculine" and "the feminine" but also as "rites of intensification" through which those who are stigmatized for their "betrayal" turn the stigmatization into a "virtue," into a statement that recognizes the absurdity of conventional ascriptions and emphasizes existential understandings of living in an "absurd" world.

At this point, one example will show the analytical direction I will take. There are many male homosexuals who occasionally cross-dress in both private and public situations and who refer to it as a "gender fuck." The cross-dressing, like many of the stylized elements of "camp," has more often than not an insignificant correlation with the roles assumed in sexual acts or with any other "feminine" identifications. What is being "fucked" is the heterosexual myth that homosexuality is necessarily a reversal of roles and motivations that are culturally assigned by gender. The behavior speaks most forcibly to the anomalous position of the male homosexual in a sharply "black-and-white" sexual dichotomy—a cultural dichotomy in which there are only two basic and opposed role models ascribed for gender identification, such that behavioral departure from almost any of the ideal components of one role complex provokes the kind of suspicious and stigmatizing reaction accorded to "subversives" in national politics. The "gender fuck" of cross-dressing is often, though not always, an in-group "put-down" of heterosexual values that divide the world into "male and female." The satirical commentary upon cultural ascriptions is conveyed most explicitly by gay performing troupes whose members affect a deliberately exaggerated androgynous appearance, complementing their masculine beards and other identifiable biological endowments with female dress and "feminine" body movements and vocal patterns. The "fuck" is a cartoon-like recognition of the absurdities of the cultural straitjacket of normative gender ascriptions concerning sexual preferences, social roles, and "natural" oppositions.

I shall apply this thesis not only to the "female-like" behaviors that are a part of The Columbia's style but also to other sexual and nonsexual elements of the ritualized categories of interaction. Though the behaviors, verbal and nonverbal, are seemingly highly personal in direction, they have at best only the most generalized biographical reference. Like the "gender fuck" of many instances of cross-dressing, they represent a deliberate play upon straight lores and stereotypes of those whose values and way of life position them outside the normative moral and social order. They are "rituals of stigmatization"—formally patterned responses to and expressions of "outcast status" that use and distort the shibboleths of *les justes* to intensify the experience of stigmatization and of opposition to those who are "responsible" for it. The rituals carry a message that is contained in Jean Genet's *The Maids* (1954) and other works in the genre of "the absurd" and is echoed, too, in a statement Charles Manson made to the court during his trial for the Tate-LaBianca murders (Bugliosi and Gentry, 1975, p. 256). While there is absolutely nothing comparable to those faceless, violently bloody assassinations in the biographies of The Columbia's patrons, Manson's rather eloquent defense—which I do not accept for a moment—touches the existential metaphor of the rituals. Addressing the judge and jury, he said:

> I can't judge any of you. I have no malice against
> you and no ribbons for you. But I think it is high
> time you all start looking at yourselves and judging
> the lie that you live in.
>
> I can't dislike you, but I will say this to you . . .
> you are all crazy. And you can project it back at me . . .
> (but) . . . I am only what you made. I am only a reflection
> of you. . . I have ate out of your garbage cans to stay
> out of jail. . . I have done my best to get along in your
> world and now you want to kill me . . . Ha! I'm already
> dead, have been all my life. I've spent twenty-three
> years in tombs that you built.

Most of those who go to The Columbia have also spent all or a large part of their lives in "cultural tombs"—tombs of ethnic and social disadvantage, of failure to achieve, and the "tomb" of being homosexual. It is the sum of these experiences and their cognitive and perceptual correlates that account for the style of the tavern—for the "recruitment" of its regular and transient customers; for its physical appearance; for the associations sought and provided, and for the content and quality of its ritualized encounters. To be sure, the last are related to more inclusive categories of rituals of stigmatism, sharing many basic elements and metaphors with more widely distributed male homosexual behaviors. Indeed, the basic metaphor can be applied, I believe, to all similar "ritualizations" of what *les justes* suppose to be the character, motivations, and "gender identifications" of male homosexuals generally. Thus, my thesis can be extended beyond The Columbia, providing, perhaps, a key to the symbolism of many other institutionalized ways of expressing the "bind" of those who are excluded from the normative sexual value system, even including behaviors that seem to be diametrically opposed to the "female-like" examples in emphasizing an exaggerated machismo.

... this

Millere

He nolde his wordes for no man forbere,
But tolde his cherles tale in his manere:
Methinketh that I shall reherce it here.
And ther-fore every gentil wight I preye,
For goddes love, demeth nat that I seye
Of evel entente, but that I moot reherce
Hir tales alle, be they bettre or worse,
Or elles falsen som of my matere.
And therfore, who-so list it nat y-here,
Turne over the leef, and chese another tale;
For he shal finde y-nowe, grete and smale,
Of storial thing that toucheth gentillesse,
And eek moralitee and holinesse;
Blameth nat me if that ye chese amis.
The Miller is a cherl, ye knowe wel this;
So was the Reve, and othere many mo,
And harlotrye they tolden bothe two.
Avyseth yow and putte me out of blame;
And eek man shal nat make ernest of game.

The Canterbury Tales, Skeat edition,
Oxford University Press; The Miller's Prologue, lines 59–78.

... this Miller

Would not control his tongue for anyone
But told his low-life story in his style;
   Now I'm of mind to tell it here again,
Entreating you, so be your taste polite,
For love of God, please don't believe that I
Have bawdy taste, but that I must recount
All of these tales, both good and bad alike,
Or else be false in some of what I say.
Therefore, whoever wishes not to hear
Can turn the page and choose some other tale.
For he can find enough, both short and long,
Of anecdotes about the genteel life,
Moral behavior, even holiness.
If you choose wrong, don't put the blame on me—
The Miller is a roughneck, well you know;
So is the Reve, and many others too.
And both their stories reeked of harlotry.
Keep this in mind and don't discredit me,
Nor take such trivial stuff too seriously.

(Modern version by W. L. Parker.)

ONE

Neighborhood and Public Territories

In summer when the evenings are prolonged into the nighttime hours, when the sky takes a slowly orchestrated farewell, withdrawing in shades of topaz, pale emerald, and imperial blue, the old buildings flanking Occidental Square glow and pulsate like echoes of the aerial splendor: fired in burnt reds and golds and pale yellows and creams before darkness extinguishes them. The falling hush is broken only by the voices of lingering tourists and the petulant, complaining cries of children who have tagged along with their parents for too many hours, pulled in and out of shops and eating places and standing on one foot then the other in front of displays of pottery, ethnically derived clothing, continental breads, and contrived gardens implanted in glass flasks and bottles. The hum of downtown traffic is like the sound of surf breaking against a distant reef and drawing the loiterers back to their hotels and motels to prepare for another tiresome seventy-mile-per-hour journey to notable places in other cities.

In the early summer evening—around seven o'clock—the air in Occidental Square is cool and stirs gently in response to a breeze from the harbor. It is a perfect time to enter the cobblestoned arena, to choose a bench near a lion's-head fountain and to enjoy the hiatus between the departure of one population and the arrival of another. The spurting water raises a crystal shower in the stone basin, rippling its surface with veins of green and silver, and for a magic moment I am transported to the piazza of a walled town in northern Italy. It could be the *Campo* in Siena where on similar summer evenings I used to sit with friends drinking bitter Campari and trying to fix in my memory the campanile of

21

the *Palazzo Publico* and the balconies of the surrounding houses that had blossomed recently with ancient banners and had been festooned with carpets for the medieval contest of the Palio. On the screen of my mind I can see the flags of the municipal quarters tossed high in the air beneath the windows of the bishop's palace, so high—thrown with such joyful, practiced, and consumate skill—that they fill the sky like a vast flock of birds escaped from an aviary; and I remember the excitement as I tried to identify the emblem and caparisoned procession of the quarter to which I belonged through temporary residence in an old, deteriorating, and ilex-shrouded villa poised on a hill outside the walls.

It is not merely a conceit to invoke Siena or other ancient places in attempting to depict a summer evening in Occidental Square. The flanking buildings are not very old. They are merely an infinitesmal dot on a time scale that includes Lascaux, Stonehenge, and the Siena *Campo;* but they stand like a signpost to the past against the soaring cubes of solar glass and travertine veneer that canyon the downtown streets in plagiarisms of Mies Van Der Rohe: buildings that lift into the air like inverted icebergs whose upper halves lie outside the normal trajectory of human sight.

The buildings in Occidental Square have a low and comfortable profile. The technological ingenuity of glass and curtain-wall construction hasn't imposed on them the blandness of efficiency. It is still possible to imagine the people who designed and built them, to enjoy their fancies and their craftsmanship. The results are eclectic: a mélange of Byzantine, Renaissance, and Neoclassical. Plain, good brick, mellowing beautifully, is the principal material, the almost infinite gradations in its shades offering far more to the eye that the black-and-white exclamation marks farther downtown. There are street-level arcades, gracefully arched, and pedimented entrances. Decorations range from the proclamation of civic virtues in the entablatured figures of Columbia and the American eagle to garlands of fruit; and here and there it is possible that some displaced stonemason from Italy has constructed his own memorial in a face that peers from the shadow of a richly decorated cornice.

Occidental Square is separated only by slightly more than one man's lifetime from the glass and marbleized cubes of downtown Port City. The Square was once the hub of the city. Its origins were a trading post on the edge of a spellbinding wilderness of forests of cedar, fir, and hemlock and snow-draped mountains, of lakes and vast silvery sheets of inland water. It is impossible to recapture it now, except vicariously in some remote and protected alpine region. In the late nineteenth century a catastrophic fire destroyed virtually everything that had been constructed around the original mud trails and tracks, and a new city literally rose

on the remains of the old. For a while thereafter Occidental Square and
its environs were the unchallenged standard of public elegance. Its Grand
Central Hotel had a palm-lined foyer, a tessellated floor, overstuffed
chairs and couches, and bright brass spittoons sitting plumply on oriental rugs. The long bars in the taverns and lunchrooms were solid cedar,
carefully crafted and polished and backed by mirrors whose reflections
of white tablecloths, wall sconces, and branching chandeliers produced
enchanting visions of present opulence and unlimited prospects. In its
heyday, the Square also received one of the most civic-minded of gifts
from a wealthy benefactor: a magnificently tiled and impeccably clean
below-the-sidewalk "comfort station" where uniformed attendants stood
outside the "Ladies" and "Gentlemen" sections, ready with a towel or
brush or some Florida Water to repair the appearance and esteem of
those who were hurrying from one important meeting to another.

But even at its apogee, Occidental Square coexisted with reminders of
a more sleazy past: of roistering waterfront beer joints and bordellos; of
dark alleys and Seamen's Missions and flophouses for the transient, the
unemployed, and the indigent. And as money and propriety moved the
center of the city farther north, the latter-day descendants of the roister-
ers, the drifters, and ethnically disadvantaged moved back. The Grand
Central Hotel closed its doors. The lunchrooms were stripped of everything except their massive bars and mirrors. Ladies did not walk there
any more to buy their ribbons and to look at swatches of material. The
magnificent urinal was boarded up. Who needed its sparkling tiles and
crisp attendants now that the inhabitants of the quarter were generally
designated undesirable, people whom civic-minded souls wished might
simply go away.

So for more than three decades the quarter continued to deteriorate as
the buildings rose higher and crowded more closely together in the newer
Metropolitan District. An unpleasant section of ribbon-development
connected it with its successful rival—a section of gaudy, flashing neon
announcing Loans, Bail Bonds, Fun Arcade, Eats, The Flamingo Lounge
or simply Tavern. Several all-night movie houses, playing reruns of
B-grade films, provided places to sleep for those who could afford admission; and a few of them were known as places where there were opportunities for homoerotic sex. As far as I know, there has been no study of
such movie houses, which can be found across the nation; but from a few
brief visits (I could not stand the furtive darkness, the odor of disinfectant, the surreptitious and suggestive movement of legs, and the eyes
boring into the back of my head), I suspect they are a style similar to and
a functional equivalent of urinal encounters. In a gesture to the Vice
Squad and conventional standards of morality, the dark recesses of the

balcony section are closed and ushers walk perfunctorily up and down the aisles, their flashlights directed at the threadbare carpeting. Not everyone is there to take advantage of the sexual opportunities, though few are there to see the movie; but the tapping of a shoe against the back of your seat and the stretching of legs beneath you can be interpreted as a signal by the cognoscenti—a signal to move around to the vacant chair beside the initiator or to visit the "Men's Room." Though the house is dark, the light from the screen, once your eyes have become accustomed to it, allows you to distinguish profiles and body movements that are situationally specific. It is quite formalized, though completely silent and anonymous. Men masturbate under the concealment of their overcoats while those who flank them play the role of "watch queen" as John Wayne storms ashore at Iwo Jima to the blaring sound of the Marine Hymn.

Respectable citizens seldom crossed this garish umbilicus to Occidental Square. The remaining hotels, advertising "Clean Beds" for a few dollars a month, were havens for the old and derelict who sat dejectedly in their dismal foyers waiting for the taverns and wine parlors to open. Panhandling and public drunkenness became the most visible elements of a submerged life whose relationship to the uptown area was similar to the underground remains of the original city below the buildings that not so long ago had been the hallmarks of civic pride. The unsavory reputation of the Square accounted for the ubiquitous presence of police cars patrolling it or lurking with lights extinguished in its alleys. Most of the taverns were lower-class and rough, many of them havens for dispossessed ethnic minorities. Ten years ago, for example, a graduate student and his wife asked me to accompany them to the Britannia, a tavern patronized by transient and "urbanized" Native Americans. The name and illuminated representation of the familiar mother figure touched me with a feeling of chauvinistic national pride similar to the comfortable recognition of the Union Jack in the quartering of the State flag of Hawaii, a surprise that nevertheless stirs some regret for the passing of grandeur and the loss of empire. Quite unwarrantedly—such is the power of symbols—I was prepared to find some common understandings with the Britannia's patrons; but obviously it wasn't anything like the hotels and bars with British homeland names that used to beckon colonial expatriates in a multitude of steamy settings, promising them a reasonable facsimile of Bournemouth and Brighton boardinghouses. We were clearly out of place and becoming more discomforted by the undercurrents of hostility when two armed policemen entered, marched directly to the booth where we sat, and stood demandingly above us. "What are you three doing here?" one of them asked. "You wanna get into trouble, get that nice girl inna trouble? Finish your beer and get out."

In the same period, I knew of and had visited briefly only two unequivocally male homosexual taverns in the quarter: one a beer and hard liquor lounge with an attached "greasy spoon" restaurant, the other a newer place converted from an abandoned and formerly fashionable lunchroom. I knew there was also a steam bath beneath the sidewalk of the Square itself, a place set aside like the entrance to a subway station— edged by an iron railing and a street-side sign over its stepped entrance that spelled the puzzling message: S * * * * B * T H R O O M S. The newer of the two taverns—The Maximum Man—had opened unpretentiously but with overtones responsive to the attitudes of the city police. Membership cards were supposed to be presented at the door and a uniformed but off-duty policeman, paid by the owners, stood inside, ostensibly checking the ID of younger patrons for possible violations of drinking laws. His presence, however, also reflected civic attitudes that homosexuality, if you could not stamp it out by statute, should be swept under the rug and watched by moral authorities. The sexual preference had not surfaced to its current level of public visibility; moreover, it was a time when payoffs for police protection were a common but unreliable form of insurance for those whose public activities were on the wrong side of legal and moral standards.

Before its recent demise, The Maximum Man aspired to greater ostentation, installing a dance floor, "black lighting," and offering twice-weekly drag shows. The uniformed guardians of respectability departed, their moonlighting jobs lost through a series of scandals connected with bingo parlors, punchboards, and other gaming devices where the rake-off was surely more lucrative than a tavern where drunkenness wasn't as common a sight as in the cocktail bars and restaurants of *grande luxe* hotels. It is said that the tavern was forced out of business because its building had been designated an "historical site" scheduled for refurbishing to attract more acceptable enterprises. This may be true; but there have been other homosexual taverns, lounges, and restaurants that have opened with greater ostentation and whose life span has been briefer, their sudden appearance and departure suggesting that someone who ought to know better has overestimated the potential market for the styles they hope to exploit.

Ten years ago, the three places were quite likely not the only homosexual public places in the quarter of Occidental Square, and certainly not the only ones in the city. But the quarter has tended to attract such establishments, possibly because rents for space in deteriorating buildings were low but also because the castaway qualities ascribed to the characters and modes of life of those who lived there fitted similar ascriptions for homosexuals. While the homosexual transients may not have been morally approved by the old and derelict, while their lives beyond the quarter were frequently a far cry from a sheltering viaduct or a pallet in a Salvation Army hostel, they, too, were members of a class of victims whose presence, therefore, could be tolerated and accepted in an area where most people were stigmatized by their failure to meet the soaring values represented by the downtown towers whose lights, even when everyone had departed them, were like a nightly celebration of achievement: skyward-probing banners inscribed *Excelsior.*

The quarter of Occidental Square gradually became a gay quarter, in the sense that it contained a concentration of taverns and other public establishments oriented to the sexual preference, and this element was recognized by the surveillant authorities. During the course of this study, when it was almost halfway through, a patrol officer who was a student in one of my classes invited me to accompany him on one of his regular assignments. I accepted, after having signed a release of culpability should anything happen to me, and sitting in the back seat of the police car I went the rounds from about 8:00 pm to 1:00 am. It wasn't a contrived "Adam 12" experience. We were called to a downtown hotel where a resident had lodged a complaint, and my uniformed mentors allowed me to accompany them, walking a pace or so behind them as we crossed the foyer to the elevator, rose, and entered the room of an obviously drunk and past-middle-aged woman who complained that her wallet, with all her credit cards, money, and other identification, had been stolen by a man who had sat beside her at the bar in the respectable cocktail lounge. The police questioned her dispassionately, but she clearly wondered who I was and why I was there as I sat silently in a corner. She kept her eyes on me rather than her interrogators, and I tried to reassure her that she need not be embarrassed as little by little it became apparent that she had run away from her husband and children in a brief but desperate gesture of defiance of conventional demands and that the man had been in her room when the theft took place. As we left, I hoped that her family would be understanding when she returned to them contritely the following day.

There were other calls that night, most of them connected with mugging and tavern fights, but I remember most vividly the experience of riding through dark alleys near Occidental Square, progressing slowly past garbage cans while a searchlight swept intermittently from side to side, peering into recesses at the rear of buildings. Enveloped in the mantle of legal and moral authority represented by the badge on the doors of the car, by the call signals on the chattering radio and the barrage of declaratory lights and sounds that could be activated at an instant, I felt as though I should apologize to those who were being watched—apologize to them because my position and the propriety of my life enabled me to work both sides.

We passed The Golden Slipper and my student announced across his shoulder: "That's a lesbian joint. They're all dikes there." Moments later we were approaching The Columbia. "Those faggots had a pretty rough night last week," one patrol officer said to the other.

"Yeah? What happened?"

"Someone drew a gun on another guy."

"Anyone hurt?"

"Hell, no. It wasn't even loaded." He laughed. "Just faggot stuff."

That night there were no calls to homosexual taverns, though the radio was directing other patrols to investigate domestic entanglements, reports of thefts, of stolen cars and suspected violations of drug laws in tidy suburban enclaves, downtown hotels, and heterosexual drinking places. I was mostly aware of a curious combination of detachment and involvement, a perspective similar to flying over one's hometown or neighborhood and finding it diminished and compressed in size as almost everything connected with our past is diminished when we return to it from the distance of maturity. I recognized people walking the streets and attached to them personal qualities and a multitude of remembered idiosyncrasies—gestures, inflexions of speech, and snatches of conversation—that the police could not know. Few of them had done or would do anything to enrich the material lives of those who lived on the surrounding hills in high-rise condominiums or in sprawling developments of overpriced ranch houses. Some of them were sexual hustlers out to make a score. Others could provide you with "grass," with "smack," or a discounted, stolen color television set. Many knew the inside of jails, and a larger number the demeaning experience— blunted, perhaps, by the frequency of its reccurrence—of trying to find someone, before the taverns and the bars closed, from whom they could obtain a dollar to retrieve from the custody of a desk clerk the key to a room from which they had been locked out for failure to pay their rent.

Certainly, the range of their experiences and problems was much greater than this suggests, and conventional criminality could not be attributed to the majority of those whom I could see through the open door to The Golden Slipper or who at that hour were lining the bar or dancing in The Roman Forum. On Monday, many of them would be returning to their offices in the downtown towers, to their classes at Port City University, to their medical and legal practices and a multitude of other professions in which they would pass as anonymously as millions of other people. But encapsuled in the squad car, I was faced with the inescapable evidence of changes that were once again affecting the quality of the quarter.

In a fairly recent and often divisive movement to recover and preserve the historical roots of Port City, Occidental Square had become a focus for civic action. Beginning with the vision, the taste, and the temerity of a relatively few members of the more art-oriented professions and occupations, the Square had graduated from virtual oblivion to a new chicness. The tone was set originally by an art gallery whose prices for a single painting were more than many patrons of The Columbia could hope to earn in several years. But the people who came to view and buy them—with some initial trepidation because of the quarter's reputation —were socially and financially influential, and the rejuvenation of the Square was not much farther away than the tiresome proceedings of trading for public funds in the City Council and the State Legislature, with the framing of ordinances for an Arts Commission and a statute for The Preservation of Historic Sites. Occidental Square had "arrived" again, as a belated and more architecturally varied and nostalgic contrast to the monstrous similarity of downtown monuments to the commercial conservation of space and profits. Little essays laudatory of the transformation appear regularly in the supplements enclosed with the Sunday editions of Port City's newspapers—essays that condescend to recognize the quaintness of the remaining "natives" and their colorful contrast with the suburbanites, the tourists, and the art lovers who have returned to browse the import houses filled with the industrialized crafts of Taiwan and Japan.

The changes occurring in Occidental Square are exemplified by an episode in which I participated in The Columbia on a Sunday afternoon in autumn. At 3:00 pm there are not many people in the tavern and its lights, at that season, are an antiseptic and depressing echo of the glow in the empty street beyond its windows. The house, like the patrons sitting at the bar, seems to be making an effort to pull itself together after Saturday excesses. It smells stale and looks dirty. Unemptied ashtrays litter the chrome and formica tables in one section of the room. The jukebox is silent. No one is in the mood for Roberta Flack singing "All the sad young men, sitting at the bar" or for Liza Minelli belting "Cabaret." They are turned inward, hands clasped around their schooners of beer and their "Logy Flips" (loganberry wine and 7-UP), and they talk in snatches, communicating little except a mutual understanding of their hangovers and a malaise of life.

As Chuck, the bartender on duty, mopped up spilled beer, some of those who were near me looked out to the lambent street, their attention focused speculatively upon a new establishment on the opposite sidewalk—a place identified in brass decorator-approved lettering as Primavera.

"What the shit is it?"

"Some fancy lunch joint."

"Faggots run it?"

"You ever heard of a cook who isn't a queer?"

Desultory laughter. And one man said:

"It ain't a soup kitchen, that's for sure."

"No sweat," Chuck said. "Anyone want a pepperoni sausage or a hard-boiled egg?"

"The fuck with you, fella! Those eggs oughta been banned by the FDA."

"Okay, buddy," Chuck replied without animosity. "Get off your ass and go to The Port City Plaza. Maybe you have the bread for some pheasant under glass."

But speculation returned again and again to Primavera, and, on an impulse to satisfy my own curiosity, I told them I would find out what it represented.

Crossing the street, I rapped on a glass door that carried a sign reading "Closed. Opening October 15." A woman came forward from the rear of the shop, initially suspicious but eventually sufficiently reassured to draw the bolts, unfasten the chains, and let me in. They were, as the sign implied, preparing for an imminent opening, and the place was not "some fancy lunch joint" but a craftsy art gallery. There were macrame key chains and pendants and batik wall hangings, examples of local pottery and superrealistic, emulsified, and varnished oil paintings of a sea captain, of a locally famous mountain, and of trees as brilliantly hued in fall colors as hothouse poinsettias produced for Christmastime supermarket trade.

When I returned to The Columbia and the people at the bar asked me what I had learned, I said:

"Nothing much. It's a gift shop—pictures and pottery. That sort of thing."

"Like Woolworth's?"

"Yes, but more expensive."

"Shit! I thought we might be getting a bit of class round here."

"Have an egg, fella," Chuck said. "I'll stick a feather on it and you can make as though you're eating with your academic friends."

On that fading autumn afternoon Primavera signified the demise of The Columbia and the displacement of a population who had made the quarter its own before its rediscovery. The rooming houses and the few remaining hotels advertising "Clean Beds" were closing down and the "natives" were being dispossessed, casualties to fashions and values that had made them expendable once and were doing so again. The new flowering of the Square—its trees and summer plantings of marigolds, its sculptures and cobblestones—was merely a reiteration of their past experiences of rejection and exclusion.

Sunk in my own Sunday mood, I thought of "Miss Rose," an old woman who comes regularly to the tavern and who could be described as grotesque. She has a heavily powdered face and brightly rouged everted lips divided by an extraordinarily pendulous nose. She sits customarily on a tattered, vinyl-upholstered bench near the street-side windows and is not averse to bumming a drink or a dollar to help with the rent of her room; but she holds on to vestiges of respectability in her little head-hugging turbans and a nosegay of plastic violets pinned to the lapel of her hand-me-down coat. I asked her why she came to The Columbia, and she gave the totally surprising rejoinder (in a Brooklyn accent I cannot reproduce): "It's so nice here. Everyone is so kind."

"Kind" in The Columbia! It seemed unbelievable considering the tavern's reputation for violence; but a young man came to her side and handed her a package which she placed in the contemporary equivalent of her reticule: a brown-paper shopping bag.

"They're sweet rolls," she said to me. "He's been to the Lighthouse and stole them. Have you been to the Lighthouse?"

She was referring to a charitable mission not far from the Square, and when I answered "no," she said: "Honey, you oughta try it. It's a real nice place. People serve you at tables. No one tries to put you down."

I have learned far more of Miss Rose since then. She has been as opportunistic as a New Guinea villager who exploits the assumption that you must have unlimited funds. I don't care for it particularly when she calls me "honey," suspecting that the conventional endearment is a preliminary to asking some favor, but she is a voluble conversationalist and likes to talk about herself. One of the few patrons of the tavern who lives nearby (in a room in one of the "Clean Bed" hotels), her visits to the Lighthouse and The Columbia (and an occasional walk-through, shoplifting excursion to Woolworth's) are the most important events of her week, for although she has the remnants of a family, a married sister, she does not get along with them.

"Honey," Miss Rose says, crooking her little finger as she maneuvers her "Logy Flip" under her overhanging nose, "she owes me money. I had a good job once, a saleslady at Kress's, and I loaned her the money for her furniture when she got married. Now she has this butch husband and clean kids, and I can't get a dollar out of her. She's a real bitch, honey."

Perhaps. One can't be sure how much of such confidences are fact or an effort to project a past gentility to someone she knows as "Doc." I suspect it is the latter; for one of the disadvantages of being known at The Columbia—of the "outside-inside" dimension of relationships with its regulars—is their attempt to play with one's sympathies and of being treated as an easy target for a hustle.

Miss Rose is a "hustler," but that doesn't disturb me any longer. Early in my acquaintance with The Columbia, "Miss Debbie" (a male), who had been sitting silently beside me at the bar, turned his modish dark glasses toward me and asked:

"What are you hustling, honey?"

"Nothing."

"Shit, baby! Every mother's hustling something." His left hand played distraughtly with his ponytail. "Jeez, I've got to get off them pills. Buy me a split of Cold Duck, baby. I'm going out of my gourd."

Thinking about it later, I realized that Miss Debbie was right. Of course I was "hustling," hustling my academic discipline. So the fact that Rose is a "hustler" has become quite immaterial to my relationship with her. Miss Rose's hotel, like The Columbia, is closing as the Primaveras take over, and I suppose there will be nowhere else for her to go than a welfare-supported senior citizens' complex of apartments stacked like boxes side by side and one on top of the other from which she can't get to the Lighthouse and where there won't be any young man to bring her stale and stolen sweet rolls.

Such a prospect is not peculiar to Rose. On summer evenings when the noise of the tavern has anesthetized my ability to sort and record impressions and I seek the open darkness of the Square and the comforting sound of water falling regularly into the basin of the fountain, it is apparent that the shadowy old men beneath the plastic shelters are fewer in number. At the edge of the mall, Das Gasthaus is a blaze of light, and red-jacketed waiters scurry in and out of tables arranged continental style on the sidewalk behind a trimmed hedge of box. No more than a score of yards separate the populations, but the distance seems immeasurable and points to a difference between reclaimed Occidental Square and the plazas of more ancient cities. It is becoming a kind of cultural plaything similar to reconstructed Williamsburg, allowing little room for styles that don't conform to the taste and the masterplan developed by its socially influential backers.

The Square, however, remains a gay quarter in the concentration of some public territories catering to homosexuals. Such places are dispersed far more widely within the city, but the Square retains its preeminence, and the styles it offers are representative of many though not all of those available.

Port City's public territories run the gamut from parks, urinals, "fun arcades," movie houses, and cruising streets to steam baths and various styles of bars and taverns. These places differ from one another to some extent in the anonymity and impersonality of their "contractual" relationships, in the opportunities provided for on-the-premises sex, and in the importance of "mere" socialization in their order of activities, but very few are as thoroughly anonymous and as completely impersonal as the popular heterosexual folklore suggests. This folklore, which is also presented as a fact by many sociologists and social psychologists, implies that male homosexuals are characteristically—by virtue, I suppose, of some "motivational" inadequacies—promiscuous and incapable of "deep" sexual attractions and attachments, but it is questionable if one compares the male *heterosexual* population with the male *homosexual* population.

Variety in sexual relationships has always been tacitly expected, "prior to marriage, at least," as a "natural" expression of masculinity for heterosexual males, and, legally speaking, there are no extramarital relationships among homosexuals. Obviously, too, there are heterosexual public territories and other mechanisms that respond to the motivation. Such gross similarities may not mean that there are no differences at all between the two populations, but the popular assumptions are almost certainly exaggerated. In the first place, the "statistical" base is unreliable because the activities of public homosexual territories have attracted most attention. Second, the sex in many of these places is homoerotic, but by no means all of the participants are homosexual. Many of the most promiscuous male homosexuals are also acting out the heterosexual model—not entirely disapproved—of the masculine stud. Indeed, the folklore concerning promiscuity reflects a double standard that winks at its occurrence among heterosexual men but places *all* male-to-male encounters in a stigmatized category. Variety is more or less accepted for the straight male because he is only "being a man," whereas male homosexuals do not qualify for such indulgence. And if there is a critical difference, which I doubt, it seems unnecessary to "explain" it by some "innate proclivity," for, surely, it is also reasonable to consider the extent to which cultural norms foster and contribute to it by denying to homosexuals the "institutional protection" given to most heterosexual relationships.

The anonymity and impersonality attributed to homosexual relationships is also frequently exaggerated, though there seems to be a difference between the male and female populations, "impersonal" sex—the pickup and sex with strangers—being far less common among lesbians than among male gays. "Impersonality," however, requires qualification for many—possibly most—male homosexual relationships, even those initiated and conducted in the public territories.

Some of these territories are highly impersonal in the sense that those who use them are looking for quick and immediate gratification and are not overly concerned with anything except its availability. The most impersonal settings include the movie houses, urinals, "fun arcades," some park encounters, and some transactions between client and male prostitute. I have deliberately qualified the character of relationships in a number of these places, for *all* relationships between client and male prostitute are not completely impersonal, not "never-to-be repeated" one-night stands, but may lead to an established connection that includes more than simply servicing, and it is questionable whether men who return to the same urinal again and again, using it as their preferred location, are indulging in completely impersonal sex; for many of the "regulars" can be said to "know" one another in the settings where they meet.

This does not deny the impersonality of many male homosexual relationships. It would be just as foolish to do so as to deny the existence of impersonal expressions of sexuality among heterosexuals. The activities of many public male homosexual territories, however, include far more in their interactional characteristics than a single-minded pursuit of sex. Steam baths, for example, are known for their encouragement of on-the-premises sex, and most of them affect a deliberately orgiastic style. Yet a good deal of socializing also occurs. Characteristically, patrons are on the premises far longer than those who go to urinals and movie houses; and while voyeurism or active participation in sex may be the main attraction for most of them, the settings also provide a meeting place—a place to talk and even, perhaps, to begin a relationship that moves out of the baths, transformed into the personal bond of "lovers." Numbers of men who use the baths for sex also use them occasionally as many heterosexual men use residential clubs, taking a room when they are in town at night and do not want to go home either because they are cautious about driving or simply because they want to spend the night in a familiar place where they can talk to others if they wish and sleep in a room that is half the price of the seedy hotels catering to derelicts and to prostitution.

Tavern relationships are seldom thoroughly impersonal. Almost all of them present opportunities to socialize that—on any given day or night—are just as important to most customers as the search for a trick. Taverns and bars are important territories for those who are looking for sexual partners, but they differ in the extent to which they encourage or permit it, some, for example, providing facilities that are as orgiastically impersonal as the urinals or specialized areas in the steam baths while others downplay sex, even prohibiting any kind of body contact except an innocuous touching of knees at barside or beneath a table. Male homosexuals are probably right in gently correcting Evelyn Hooker, whom they generally respect, for overemphasizing the sexual search in tavern activities. It is an ever-present element in most of them, but it is by no means the only attraction in all of them; and the same kind of search takes place, of course, in virtually all of their heterosexual counterparts and particularly in "singles bars." Sometimes, it seems that the stigma of "deviant" sexuality overshadows everything else in the eyes of the straight observer, predisposing him to see nothing except a "desperate" search for sexual gratification and to impute such motives to the behaviors of people who haven't the slightest sexual interest in one another.*

Anonymity is quite characteristic of most male homosexual territories. No names or any other personal information are exchanged in urinals or movie houses, and pseudonyms or first names only are generally used in steam baths and taverns. This isn't surprising, since, prudently, the vast majority of homosexuals remain "in the closet," compelled to "pass" in the areas where their lives touch the heterosexual order on which they largely depend for jobs and respect and for the achievement of nonsexual values. The generalized anonymity of the public territories does not, however, preclude "personalized" and nonsexual relationships of a satisfying kind, even though their scope is often limited to the premises. As I have said, I doubt that the "pursuit of sex for itself" is any more characteristic of the homosexual than the heterosexual population. The belief is that it is an element of a more inclusive folklore which holds, for example, that homosexual men are prone to violence and to prey upon and subvert the morals of youngsters. Neither of these is true. There is more sexual violence, including mass murder, in the heterosexual population (*vide* Robin Lloyd, *For Money or Love*, 1976), but any singular homosexual instance like the Houston murders (Lloyd, p. 47) tends to be presented to the general public as a confirmation of "outcast" characteristics and proclivities that are attached to an entire group, while no such blanket generalizations follow the discovery of comparable heterosexual atrocities.

Certainly, there is violence in the homosexual world at large, and, certainly, there is sexual exploitation, whether it is between consenting adults or between adults and minors; but the morals of most homosexual

---

*Most references to the activities of homosexual taverns emphasize the "frenzied" search for sexual partners. Since the authors (including well-known sociologists) are, presumably, heterosexual, it often seems that they have "seen" only behaviors confirming their heterosexual prejudices. While I do not deny that the search for sex is a motivation for some patrons (and more characteristic of some taverns than of others), it is also a motivation for some patrons of heterosexual taverns and bars and is not confined only to those that are known or advertized as "singles bars." Certainly, there is a good deal of heterosexual "ethnocentricity" (see Appendix 1) in many of these accounts of behaviors observed in homosexual taverns.

men are not appreciably different from those of heterosexuals when it is a matter of taking advantage of others. The "gay uncle" is probably less of a potential threat to his nephews than the "funny uncle" who likes to fondle his little nieces, and all in all, there isn't much difference in the range of "aberrations"; but the difference is assumed de facto by a folklore that casts the homosexual as mendacious, sexually unfulfilled, and questing incessantly for partners for a one-night stand.

Port City has its public parks that are similar to those described by John Rechy in his novel *Numbers* (1967). One of them is only a mile or so beyond the entrance to the campus of Port City University, on the very fringe of "Greek Row" with its colonial mansions flanking avenues of chestnut trees. The public urinal on the campus side of the park and the secluded glades at its center are widely known as "tearoom trading" places that attract mostly a young student or university-affiliated population.

A second park surrounds the Port City Art Museum, located on a hill that was once the most desirable residential area, a place where, in the nineteen-twenties, successful families built huge "Tudor" houses or incongruous "casas" in the Spanish-Californian idiom. No expense was spared on these dwellings. Tiles with acanthus and Della Robbia decorations were commissioned in Italy and artisans imported to install them. Pillared *portes cochères* were hung with massive lanterns and doorways were guarded by antique carriage lights. Now, however, the descendants of those who built them have mostly gone elsewhere. The great homes have been subdivided into apartments or have become halfway houses for the rehabilitation of unmarried mothers and drug addicts. And the austere, imperial name of the area is often facetiously transposed to "Lavender Hill" or "Fairy Fallout."

Art Museum Park is mainly a place for nighttime tricking. During the day, there are too many people traipsing in and out between the ancient Chinese lion figures at the entrance to the Museum, visiting the conservatories with their displays of tropical plants, or walking the *parterres* of seasonal flowers. Homosexual daytime activity is mostly confined to cruising in a location where a Noguchi sculpture frames, like an open lens, the graph of distant mountains. The daylight encounters—unlike those in the more secluded Campus Park—probably never result in "on-location" sex. Follow-up appointments may be made, and occasionally two men who have met for the first time may leave the scene together, and it is a reasonable assumption—given the "territorial knowledge"—that sex is involved. The park, however, isn't primarily a marketplace for prostitution, and many of the daytime encounters are merely socializing. But at night, sex is certainly an important motive to the men who sit alone in expensive sports cars in the parking lot in front of the Noguchi. Very few are there simply to admire the diminishing terraces of lights progressing to the dark void of inland sea. The sex that follows the acceptance of an invitation—which is really no more explicit than being there alone and, presumably, waiting—is mostly as anonymous as in the urinals; but it is subject to chance and seldom sought for commercial gain.

Parks, by their very nature, are among the most "public" of homosexual or homoerotic territories. Others that exist in Port City, as elsewhere, are cruising streets, urinals, movie houses, and amusement arcades. In this most public category, adult prostitution seems to be associated primarily with the streets and possibly some arcades rather than with the parks and movie houses. Many of the homosexual or homoerotic encounters in the peep-show booths of the arcades do not involve client and hustler, though these locales are worked by young male prostitutes whose legal nonage excludes them from some other territories. The "contracts" negotiated at the pinball machines, however, are generally honored in a movie house or a cheap hotel room (Lloyd, 1976, p. 13). Sex between adults that is *initiated in a movie house* has, generally, as little to do with prostitution as its counterpart activities in urinals and steam baths.

There are three homosexual steam baths in the downtown area of Port City. Like all other commercial establishments, they advertise their presence, though not their sexuality, in street-level neon signs, and, presumably, anyone who wants the proffered services—"jaccuzi pools," saunas, and so on—may enter them. The Vice Squad is well aware of their sexuality but does not bother them. Unlike the parks and amusement arcades, they are enclosed and off-the-street places where an unsuspecting public is not likely to be exposed to moral outrage, and they are not regarded as a front for prostitution as many heterosexual massage parlors are. Nevertheless, one of the baths attempts to screen its customers by refusing to admit strangers who have not been introduced by someone known as a regular patron. "Known" has to be qualified, for aliases are always used in signing for a room.

The police are quite correct in discounting prostitution or coercion on steam-bath premises. They are not "houses" in which the management has a permanently employed stable of sexual objects. Hustling isn't permitted. I suppose one could say that the sex "comes with the price of admission," but it is voluntary: money does not change hands between those who engage in it. Even the steam baths, however, differ from one another in style—in the range of sexual tastes recognized in their facilities. The most "closed" of those in Port City has an "S and M" room, restricted to patrons who have a special key, and a "glory hole"—a wallboard partition with genital-level cutout used for acts of fellatio in which the partners do not see each other.

Steam-bath opportunities for sex are so well known that it is puzzling why so many men who want the gratification use the criminally sanctioned situations of the parks and urinals. Of course, the steam baths are not free, and for this reason alone they are beyond the means of many who know what they offer. Most of them also have some minimum safeguards of decorum, refusing, for example, to admit customers who are obviously drunk. Age may also inhibit some people who might otherwise patronize them—the demeaning possibility of being cast as a lecherous and "dirty old man" if you are past forty-five. Nudity, too, is distasteful to many men, particularly to those who are sensitive about the "manliness" of their physiques and are embarrassed even in the approved asexual atmosphere of the locker room. Last, it is probably easier to maintain a straight self-identification in the urinals, parks, and peep shows. The baths are characterized as gay, and particularly in their private-room encounters the intimacy is more than may be desired by men whose self-image of straightness is not threatened by urinal activities. These are more easily viewed as an extension of adolescent experiences of group exhibitionism and masturbation, of a "buddy" activity carrying no implications of homosexual preferences, something "between guys" who, presumably, would marry and lead normal heterosexual lives. Contrastively, the steam baths are gay by definition, and having recourse to them represents to many men a crossing of boundaries between the homoerotic and the homosexual, between a peccadillo —an occasional aberration—and involvement in a life-style that was disparaged even in adolescent experimentation with members of the same sex.

A number of bars and lounges in *grande luxe* and first-class downtown hotels are known sexual trading places, though their public front is completely heterosexual. Some homosexuals refer to them as "cuff-link" bars, a term denoting the propriety of expected dress and gentility with which the trading is conducted. Patrons are relatively affluent and are mainly local or traveling business and professional men. Much of the trading involves prostitution and call-boy activities. In The Library of The Port City Plaza—a dimly lit lounge decorated with fake paneling and books and plastic trees—a man from out of state (he is probably in his early fifties) talks volubly to a barside companion. He is clearly a little high and is boastful, buying drinks for the bar and charging them to his hotel room. There is nothing particularly sexual in his conversation, though he emphasizes that he is alone and continually asks: "What does a guy do round here? Where's the action?" The man beside him leaves, excusing himself to make a phone call. Several minutes later he returns with a younger, handsome, and neatly dressed man whom he introduces by first name only to the spender at the bar. Refusing a drink, he leaves them together, and shortly after his second departure the out-of-state visitor picks up the room key and says to his new companion: "Let's go. I've got a bottle upstairs."

Though the trading in these expensive and ostensibly heterosexual places is not always commercialized, there is a certain irony in the fact that prostitution (if one has some moral objection to it) is more common there than in the parks and urinals. The arrangements are conducted as discreetly and elliptically as the commercialized heterosexual encounters that occur in the same places. Most of those occupying tables in the plastic environment or sitting at the bar would not notice what is transpiring under their noses. There is no physical contact in the public setting, nor any explicit verbal communication of sexual interests. It is necessary to listen for a long while to discursive conversations, identifying a cue here and there, before the purpose is identified and the arrangement cemented.

There are probably twenty male homosexual taverns, lounges, and restaurants that cater to different tastes and socioeconomic classes. Patrons of The Columbia refer contemptuously to some of them as "sissy." The term, when it is used in an in-group manner, is often interchangeable with "faggot"; but it implies much more than generalized sexuality when The Columbia's customers use it to distinguish different tavern styles. In their usage, "sissy" refers to middle-class and establishment decorum, to differences in social-class identification and accompanying tastes and privileges: it has social and economic connotations rather than any obvious correlation with "femininity." The category includes places that are widely recognized as "femme" as well as others that promote a conventional middle-class to upper-middle-class masculinity; but these differences aren't important criteria for discrimination to most of The Columbia's patrons. Almost anything from which they are excluded by their social position is "sissy" and "unreal" or "phony."

These bars and taverns generally emulate the taste and pretensions of places like The Library in The Port City Plaza. They are fully carpeted and dimly lit by colored glass lanterns; their barstools are upholstered in black vinyl and their tables topped with glass or wood veneers. Other ornaments frequently include one or more recirculating fountains splashing into basins hung with trails of plastic ivy or gardenias. Reproductions of Michelangelo's *David* are supplemented by blowups of the *Cosmopolitan* centerfold of Burt Reynolds and anonymous "Herbie," a naked young man in profile and holding an aggressively extended pneumatic drill. Color schemes are almost invariably in shades of red and black and gold with flocked wallpapers matching the rococo designs of the carpeting.

Some of the "sissy" taverns have dance floors (with dancing to jukebox music); a smaller and decreasing number provide drag shows as weekend entertainment. Port City is not on the principal drag circuit. The shows are merely second-rate by the standards of larger and better known cities, the talent of the gowned, wigged, and heavily painted impersonators running to exaggerated pantomiming to the amplified voices of Eydie Gormé, Barbra Streisand, Aretha Franklin, and an occasional interpretive dance that might have been resurrected from the decade of the thirties. Each performer has, however, his identifying style and surrogate professional voice; and backstage, in the dressing area, the atmosphere before the show is eminently theatrical, reminiscent of innumerable Hollywood movies that were part of the experience of my youth. Men stripped to their Jockey shorts sit on stools in front of mirrors, their elbows, positioned on a counter among jars of cosmetics, serving as a fulcrum to steady their hand in the application of eyeliners, eye shadow, and eyelashes. Behind them, their gowns wait on racks. The noise in the tavern is like the anticipatory sound of an audience filing to its seats behind a velvet curtain, and, momentarily, I expect to hear a summoning rap and a voice announcing: "Take your places! One minute to opening, Miss Starlet!"

Like the majority of Busby Berkeley's toe-tapping chorines, few of those in the dressing rooms will become the equivalent of an Alice Faye, a Betty Grable, or even graduate to Finocchio's in San Francisco; but their moment of glamour, posturing in a spotlight, and the applause from the crowded tables are deserved rewards. My own taste and critical judgment are suborned, and when "Miss Starlet," a tall, slim black man whose elegant deportment and classic features deserve a cover on *Vogue*, comes to my table in his white, sequin-banded dress, he has to be told that he looks quite fabulous and that his number was really great.

"Sissy" houses attract mainly a youngish crowd—early twenties to mid-thirties—who are neatly but casually dressed in jeans, open-necked shirts, and sweaters. They are similar to all the largely anonymous students walking to classes along the paths of the campus of Port City University, and, indeed, many professedly straight students can be found there on almost any night, exploring the style with an inquisitiveness and absence of embarrassment and censure that would have shocked the generation of the forties and early fifties. It is, I suppose, an expression of the permissiveness entailed in "doing one's own thing," a phrase that may be used as an excuse for doing nothing but which nevertheless expresses many of the virtues of the younger generation in their rejection of monolithic social, political, and moral orders and their determination to see for themselves the array of responses to the fundamental and unresolved problem of being human.

These taverns are worked by sexual hustlers, but the majority of encounters are not commercial. While those who frequent them tend to move from one to another during a night out, there are some differences of style that attract a regular clientele. The Chicken Coupe in the Occidental quarter caters, as its name implies, to "chicken queens," to men who prefer teenage trade. They are not necessarily "dirty old men" subverting the morals of youngsters. The upper age limit of the patrons is probably the early forties, and the legal minors are not innocent victims picked up in a street or park. From age fifteen upwards, they know what they are entering and employ various stratagems (false identification) to gain entry. The Coupe, however, has been closed more than once for violations of laws prohibiting minors on licensed premises. Outside the quarter, but only a block or so from its boundary, Spiffy's is a tavern that people in The Columbia refer to disparagingly as a "hangout for the intelligentsia," recognizing that it attracts students and members of the faculty of Port City University, airline stewards, travel agents, and members of other white-collar occupations.

The sexuality projected in "sissy" taverns is rarely as explicit as the tactile pantomimes of The Columbia but is far more open than anything observed in ostensibly heterosexual bars. Body contact proceeds from innocuous knee-to-knee touching to genital groping and occasional mouth-to-mouth kissing. There are variations, however, in permitted latitudes of sexual expression. In San Francisco, for example, some popular establishments allow no contact at all except while dancing; but the same city also offers restaurants where patrons are served by bottom-less waiters and others where sexual acts occur in full view of their patrons—not as pantomimed water-bed floor shows like those provided for heterosexual tourists but as part of a style in which there are no restraints on public exhibitionism. Port City is often (and perhaps justly) described as provincial in comparison with the range of styles discoverable in larger metropolitan centers. There are no bottomless waiters and only one tavern where go-go boys perform in monokinis.

From some points of view, the most "kinky" of Port City's taverns are those associated with the "leather" and "S and M" fraternity, where costuming is the exaggerated, semimilitary machismo of motorcycle gangs, of The Wild Ones and Easy Rider: grommet-studded jackets, tight jeans, boots, and menacingly peaked caps. On weekends when the members of a fraternal club visit Port City from a neighboring metropolis, the parking lot outside The Angels is filled with monstrous raked machines whose handlebars are shoulder height, machines that look as though they are ready to take off to the air at the kick of a booted foot to a starter pedal. Within the tavern, the costumes of the swashbuckling patrons are augmented by festoons of chains and padlocks. The peaked caps are positioned theatrically at eyebrow level and the faces below them are as expressionless as Marlon Brando at the height of his method period. Some of those who posture at the bar—legs extended as they lean against the counter—are chained to each other, an older and a younger man joined by their belts or flys. One is "master" (or "patrician") and the other "slave" (or "pleb"). "Virgil Youngblood" is a "slave" whose unzipped leather jacket displays most of his naked torso and the incredible revelation that his nipples have been pierced and are linked by a thin gold chain. Virgil's sexual role is to serve his "master" by fellatio and to allow himself to be chained to the coatrack in the closet of their apartment. He boasts of the number, most certainly exaggerated, of orgasms his master can achieve in one of their sessions; and since he does not mention it, I wonder how he obtains his sexual release. He has a frank and open young face, is respectably employed, and passes easily out-of-costume on downtown streets. "Well," he says, with no sign of embarrassment, "I jack off in the john."

There are similarities and differences between The Columbia and other places in this spectrum of public territories. From most perspectives it is an anonymous setting. Even the regular customers know little about the past and present circumstances of those whom they see perhaps four out of seven nights a week, far less, for example, than most regular patrons of heterosexual "neighborhood" taverns. Pieces of information are picked up here and there and sometimes put together in a garbled history; but there is a certain risk of offense in administering commonplace biographical questionnaires—"where do you come from," "what do you do," and so on—a risk that is related not only to the closet safeguards sought by most male homosexuals but also to other blemishes in the records of the majority of the tavern's population. Yet is is not an impersonal place.

Homosexual or homoerotic interests can be ascribed to most of its casual and regular customers, but the pursuit of sex isn't as obvious a motivation for going there as it is in street cruising, tearooms, parks and steam baths. This does not mean that the patrons are uninterested in the available sexual opportunities. They will take advantage of what is offered, and on any given night there are some whose principal objective is to find a partner; but it is a serious misunderstanding of the entire order of activities to assume that this is the all-consuming drive of those who go there. Some hustlers (male prostitutes) are members of the tavern's regular clientele, but few of them are working while they are on the premises. With some minor qualifications, which I shall come to later, it is not a lucrative place for prostitutes, and the more generalized bonds of disadvantage and the understandings of other "outside" or "street" experiences—all the additional elements of the style that are summarized by calling it "real"—are often as important to the hustler, and to other customers, as the sexual search.

This "reality" is the sum of the variables I mentioned earlier, and it confronts the stranger immediately in the physical appearance of the setting and the players who are onstage on a typical crowded night.

TWO

Players

Approaching The Columbia is always a theatrical experience. From the crosswalk half-a-block away, the tavern's sign spells out its name above an advertisement for a popular soft drink. There is nothing fancy about it, no jiggling neon, merely a plain announcement; but it is the only illuminated sign in the street, and it beckons like the lights of a marquee. The light spilling from its uncurtained windows casts bright rectangles on the dark pavement. Figures materialize suddenly within them, singly or in couples—a few staggering uncertainly—and disappear again to a blast of sound as they push open the battered doors. Hesitating on the curb, waiting for traffic signals to change, I wonder if I will be late for the performance.

Once inside, the physical appearance of the setting provides an immediate clue to some of the qualities of the play in progress. A sign opposite the street-side doors proudly draws attention to the absence of any decorative frills:

> *We have no wall-to-wall carpets here*
> *Only wall-to-wall good people*

The *David* of many "sissy" taverns is replaced at the entrance to the pool room by a common farm implement inscribed *The Columbia B.S. Shovel*. During the Presidential Elections of 1972, the mirrors behind the bar were plastered with bumper-stickers advising patrons to "Jerk Dick in 72." At Christmastime some bits of tinsel and a few plastic bells are draped and looped from lights to walls across the space; but in other seasons the decorations do not aspire to anything except revolving advertisements for brands of beer.

43

The lights are unshaded electric bulbs suspended from the ceiling by a
Rube Goldberg arrangement of exposed wires. They glare uncompromis-
ingly in counterpoint to the popular music of the overly loud jukebox
tucked into a corner near Miss Rose's "living room," and sometimes,
while sitting at the bar, the combined bombardment of sound and light
produces a kinetic effect—a hallucinatory experience as disturbing as
Nude Descending a Staircase must have been to the gallery-goers in 1913.
The visual properties share something with the heroic celebrations of
dispossession and exploitation associated with Orozco and Rivera; but
The Columbia isn't a place that is likely to spawn political manifestos or
revolutionary charters. Its atmosphere—to continue with the painterly
analogy—is closer to the works of the "Ash Can School" and many
minor public decorations inspired by the depression-days recovery
programs of the NRA and WPA. The few sagging wall-side benches are
upholstered in tattered yellow vinyl; the white formica tops of the tables
in the center of the room are scratched and pocked with the burn marks
of carelessly forgotten cigarettes; ash trays are the brown molded-plastic
kind that distributors of commercial products give to their customers.

Even at first glance, it is understandable why the patrons of
Spiffy's—who are among those who have disapproved of my connection
with The Columbia—regard it with distaste and generally accept its
reputation for violence. Only three months into my study of the tavern, I
remember a Saturday night when I was sitting at the bar and the owner's
wife appeared suddenly beside me, grabbed my arm, and pulled me from
my stool with an imperative command to follow her. Completely
confused, I allowed her to lead me to a bench beneath the street-side
windows. She gave no explanation, merely engaging me in small talk
while she looked beyond me to the far end of the crowded room. After
several minutes, she relaxed and excused herself, leaving me to wonder
irritably why she had ejected me from my barside vantage point. I taxed
her with it later and she said: "Baby, no one wants you to get hurt. Those
fellas at the end of the bar were coming on too strong." She smiled and
pressed my arm like someone reassuring a child in an unfamiliar situation. "You've got a *whole* lot to learn," she said.

It was only a minor episode; but had I recounted it, it probably would
have confirmed The Columbia's reputation to Spiffy's customers and
would have increased their skepticism of my publicized motives.
Certainly, they would not have believed me if I had told them that I was
really more comfortable in The Columbia than in their territory or in
The Library of The Port City Plaza. The difference between their stereotyped perceptions and my own eventual ease with a disparaged life-style
is, ultimately, the end product of a sustained period of learning—the

kind of learning that tends to distinguish the anthropological experience and judgment from those of "colonial masters" in far more exotic situations. Indeed, there is an unmistakable "colonial" ingredient in the distant relationships between the populations of The Columbia and Spiffy's; for most of Spiffy's patrons are predisposed to agree with folk-assumptions that the poor and ethnically disadvantaged are more prone to crude physical interaction than those who are educated and privileged.

There is occasional violence in The Columbia, but it is mostly fisticuffs, overturned chairs, and brief wrestling on the floor. I was there on the night referred to by the patrol officers when I accompanied them on their rounds, and the situation had been handled with aplomb. Two men were arguing at the bar, one sitting and the other standing. It was fairly common knowledge among the regulars that the men had a relationship with each other and that it was ending. At a high point in their altercation, the man who was standing broke away, banging the sidewalk doors behind him but returning soon in a comparably dramatic entrance. Running down the length of the bar, his face drawn in white lines of determination, he pulled a pistol from his Windbreaker, pointed it at the face of his opponent, pressed the trigger and tossed the weapon aside, sending it skidding over the counter in the direction of Chuck, the bartender, who picked it up, opened the chamber and, with a shrug of his shoulders, placed it among the glasses on his serving table. Only those nearby knew that anything untoward had happened. A police car, blue lights flashing, materialized like an authoritarian miracle as the man who had brandished the gun reached the sidewalk. A few heads turned with curiosity to the scene on the pavement, but there was no exodus nor even a momentary interruption to the scene within the tavern.

Perhaps the consequences could have been more serious; and the danger attributed to The Columbia seems to foster a degree of theatricality in some of those who frequent it less than regularly—young men who make a point that they are carrying a knife. But most outbursts are similar to what may happen on almost any licensed premises when too much alcohol has been consumed, relationships have become frayed, and egos wounded. Apart from the single incident when the two strangers poured their beer over my shoes and trousers, I have not been threatened; and on reviewing that occasion now I believe it had racial overtones, for the men were black and during most of the evening I had been talking closely with another black man on the stool beside me. It reminds me of an episode involving the older man who had been dancing, twirling, and pirouetting alone on my first visit to the tavern. I know him quite well now as "Yukon Amy." He always greets me affectionately and has given me a name that some of the regulars use instead of "Doc." Amy is a grandfather and is a fixture at The Columbia, where everyone knows that he is interested only in black trade. "Duchess," he says, using his name for me, "niggers are the best lovers." And on this particular night, Amy was standing at the end of the bar between two sharply dressed blacks. They left the tavern together, Amy, in passing me, rumpling my hair in a familiar fashion. Several minutes later, the sidewalk doors burst open and Amy, blood streaming from his nose, his face working distraughtly, rushed down the length of the bar. "Get them black motherfuckers off of me," he cried. "Look what them faggots done to me! They took me into the alley and beat the shit outa me!"

"Shit, Amy," Chuck said. "Go into the fucking john and wash your fucking face."

This matter-of-fact reaction to physical confrontation is typical of the tavern. People close to the antagonists may intervene, trying to cool things; but the majority remain aloof even when the police are called and come marching down the aisle with their weapons strapped to their thighs.

These are undercurrents of illegal activities, none of which, however, are peculiar to The Columbia. The subterranean lore of all such transactions is woven into the tavern's style, and sometimes it produces a conventional and self-righteous reaction. "Lucille" and his lover (now spending time in a state penitentiary) came to my house after closing time and offered me a "hot" color-television set. "Go down to Blumenfields," they said, naming Port City's most prestigious department store. "Look around. Pick out the one you like. It'll only take a month to get it." And I turned on them angrily, telling them to leave, showing them to the door and asking them never to come back.

Such underground activities are among the understandings shared by many of the tavern's patrons, and being jailed is often an element of the common experience. Most of the regulars have not been in prison; but those who have been arrested and convicted speak quite casually of their records, so casually, in fact, that it recalls the attitudes of the New Guinea Gahuku who, running afoul of the regulations of an imposed colonial order, were tried and imprisoned by white authorities. The supposedly corrective experience of punishment and shame simply did not bother either the convicted person or anyone connected with him. Why should it do so? The order prescribing the rules and the penalties for infringement of them was alien and "outside," having no moral authority; and although the analogy can be pressed too far, there are attitudinal similarities between the "excluded" Gahuku and the "excluded" population of The Columbia. "Chatty Kathy," a man in his late twenties who is prone to tears in the latter part of the night, holds his beer to his cheek and explains his recent absence from the tavern.

"Hell, man," he says, "I've been in the city jail. There I was, walking down First Street and there was this guy there, very big and butch (Jeez did he have a basket!), and he looks at me and I look at him. I'm feeling pretty horny, and he says to me: 'Want a ride, fella?' Then we get into this Impala. I'm not groping him, though his basket has given me a hard. And he says: 'What you like to do, buddy?' 'Fuck,' I say, 'fucking well fuck!' And the cop takes me to jail and books me for soliciting."

Experiences in The Columbia often produce an unnerving sliding of perspectives on what you have been taught and have assumed to be proper rules of conduct. Familiar boundaries are erased from your more or less comfortable cognitive map, and you know that somehow you will have to revise them to include, for example, the rumors concerning "Kenny."

Kenny is a sallow and rather emaciated man in his mid-thirties, his face, with its deep lines from nose to the corners of his mouth, looking much older than his years. He frequently presents himself in a knitted ski mask—an Andean-derived piece of headgear with embroidered cutouts for eyes and mouth. It is said that Kenny pushes "smack," and the rumor running round the tavern's regulars is that he has burned his suppliers by foolishly withholding from them the commission they expected. "Jeez," one man says, "these two guys come in here the other night and they marched Kenny out. They took the poor shit into the alley and killed him. It was in the papers. He got it in the face. You won't see that faggot here again."

But two weeks later Kenny came through the sidewalk doors, his ski mask gathered into a jaunty cap on the top of his head; and his old-young face crinkled with amusement when I exclaimed: "Kenny! Everyone said you were dead."

"Fucking faggots," he replied. "Sure, I had some trouble. No sweat."

The Columbia's "no frills" proclamation complements a costuming that runs to scuffed boots, tattered jeans, and "Marlboro Man" hats. "Clint" is a hustler and drifter, ranging up and down two thousand miles of coast like a latter-day member of the almost forgotten Beat Generation. Tall and slim, he leans against the bar, headpiece tilted forward and long legs extended, his pointed and high-heeled cowboy boots posing an unexpected hazard to those who pass him on their way to the john. The left leg of his faded denims has been torn deliberately to reveal the tattoo of a penis on his knee, a design that extends and contracts as he moves his weight from one foot to the other. It is an exaggeration of the most common costume, but there are other styles, particularly on Friday and Saturday nights, that are comparably flamboyant forms of self-presentation. Many have an ethnic flavor: fringed suede jackets with Native American beaded pendants and turquoise-studded belts, or the wide, cuffed trousers, platform shoes and nylon-fur hats favored by some sharp blacks.

The weekend atmosphere of carnival is also heightened by an increase in the number of patrons who appear in drag. "Pocahontas" ("the Indian broad") is the most conspicuous of them. He is huge, wears a mail-order wig and satin-finished miniskirts that display a quarterback's expanse of thigh and calves. One knows instinctively that it would not be wise to tangle with him: a single swipe of his arm would eliminate most men.

Pocahontas lives with "Charlie," a white wisp of an alcoholic whose head almost disappears in his spouse's armpit as they sit at a table in the tavern, pitcher of beer in front of them and Pocahontas glaring protectively at barside customers who may show an interest in Charlie. Late one night he threw open the tavern's doors and stalked down the bar on his stilt heels with a determination that seemed to rattle the glasses on Chuck's service table.

"Have you seen that fucking little shit?" he said to me, apparently referring to Charlie.

"No."

"Well if you see the faggot, tell him he's gonna get his ass beat. I'll break the fucker's jaw."

Several nights later they were there together, but Charlie, weaving submissively in the wake of Pocahontas, had his right arm in a sling.

"Did you do that to him?" I asked Pocahontas as he hesitated beside my stool.

"Shit, baby! The fucker only hurts hisself. He fell down some steps. I wouldn't hurt him. He's an asshole, but so's everyone in this motherfucking joint. That's my asshole guy, and no shitty faggot better badmouth him."

Full drag costuming (dress, wig, makeup, and heels) is relatively rare. Most of the identifiable "street fairies" among the regulars wear male clothing with face makeup and accessories that are merely cheap variations of styles that have become fashionable in the masculine haut monde. "Susie Wong" is a young (twenty-five) Japanese-American. Passing him on a downtown street during the day, he merges with the sidewalk population and you exchange no more than a distant nod of recognition. But when he comes to The Columbia at night, his costume includes a rhinestone choker, many Woolworth's rings, and a purse in which he carries compact, eye shadow, a vial of Evening in Paris cologne, and Magic Lash mascara. Holding the compact to the overhead lights as he repairs his lips and eyes, he sighs heavily and says:

"Man, it's *such* a drag to be in love."

"Are you in love?"

"Oh sure. I'm always fucking in love, but I guess it's gotta be real this time. He's a real neat guy—going to school at the 'U'."

"Do you live together?"

"Hell, no! I live with my straight brother and his wife." He turns his head to the side to study his handiwork, closes the compact, and returns it to his purse. "You see," he says, "that's the problem. I gotta be careful there or he'll throw me out."

"But how about your makeup? Doesn't he notice?"

"This crap? I take it off before I go home. But this guy and me want to be lovers. He's got a scholarship or something—lives in a dorm—and we can't afford a place of our own."

"Where do you meet him?"

"Both of us have gay friends. But, hell, it's not the same—not like being together all the time."

"Miss Debbie" is older than Susie Wong, probably in his mid-forties. His usual costume is trousers, sneakers, a T-shirt, and cardigan. His face, however, is a startling reproduction of the early Marlene Dietrich: penciled, arching eyebrows and the remote hauteur of hollow cheeks and a controlled, expressionless mouth from which words slide in a low-key baritone voice. He was the first of The Columbia's regulars to befriend me. Sitting side by side at the bar on a Saturday night, we had not spoken to each other. Indeed, I was scarcely aware of his presence, being fully absorbed by the inner exercise of trying to record the apparently chaotic scene—snatching a word here and there from the hubbub of conversation and the forefront blare of the jukebox; trying to fix a gesture, a facial expression so vividly that I could reproduce it later on sterile paper. Debbie may have mistaken my silent detachment for an echo of his current situation, feeling a bending recognition for a troubled brother. Suddenly he said, "I'll bet you're a Capricorn."

"Yes. But how did you know?"

"You look like one. Here," he took my hand, placed a small object in my palm, and curled my fingers round it.

It was a ring inscribed with my zodiac sign.

"Oh, shit," he said. "It's nothing much. I got it out of a Cracker Jack box."

"You look pretty lonely," Debbie said, as I tried to adjust to the possible implications of the unexpected gift.

"I'm okay."

"If you say so," he responded skeptically. "Jesus, I've got a problem. My old man is getting married to a real broad. That girl's got a lot to learn. I fucked him as much as he fucked me, and baby she hasn't got my equipment. What's she gonna do when he wants it in the ass? Use a finger or get a dildo! Well man, it's no big shit. I'm okay too."

Debbie's situation reminds me of "Larry" and "Clara," a couple who are not regulars and who appeared in the tavern toward the end of the study. I was sitting at a table with Debbie and some of his friends, observing the barside action from a different perspective and not paying much attention to the chatter near me. Because I had not seen them previously, Larry and Clara were projected from the line of more familiar faces. Clara, who was sitting on a stool, was obviously a biological woman (one learns to identify males in drag, partly because of cues supplied by those who know them and because of their tendency to overdress the role). I placed Clara at about forty years old. Her round face, beneath blond hair, suggested a doll-like and not too intelligent quality she may have possessed in the postwar era of the nineteen-forties—the era of bobby-soxers and the big-band sound, of Harry James and the young Frank Sinatra. Her softly formed and open mouth contributed to an impression of vacuity and troubled uncertainty. Larry, standing beside her at the bar, looked like her junior by more than a decade. He was darkly handsome and neatly dressed in white pants and casual black shirt ornamented with a silver necklace and medallion. Men approached Larry, standing beside him in a way that seemed to exclude Clara, whose doll-eyes wandered past their shoulders and their conversation as though she would rather be comfortably ensconced in more familiar domestic surroundings.

It was this last quality that held my attention; for it echoed the way in which I frequently composed my own face into a fixed smile as I sat at the bar, presenting one image to the tavern while reserving a different dimension inside me. Clara seemed lost, as lost as I had been when I began visiting the tavern, and I speculated that she may have been Larry's mother or an older sister trying to adjust to a sexuality that would not have been mentioned in the days of Harry James.

Clara and Larry were merely figures in a nighttime composition; but several weeks later a little more was added to my perception of them.

I had arrived late and all the stools at the bar were occupied, so I went to Debbie's table and asked if I could join him. Having ordered a pitcher of beer, I looked toward the bar and recognized Clara sitting there in her customary gray tweed coat with a fur collar. Larry, sitting beside her, was in drag. He wore an elaborate wig with shoulder-falls and a rhinestone ornament positioned behind the poufs of hair on his forehead. His dress was gossamer-thin, a hostess gown in beige and white. He tossed his curls when people spoke to him, patted his hair with a beringed hand, and frequently turned to admire his reflection in the mirror behind the bar.

It was such an unexpected embroidery to my prior speculation that I exclaimed with involuntary astonishment: "He's in drag!"

"Who?" the lesbian to my left asked, interrupting her conversation with Debbie.

"Larry. Over at the bar."

"Oh, that's no new shit. Where you been, fella?"

Chastened by her bantering tone, I said: "Well, he looks much better as a man. That's a tacky outfit."

She laughed. "He's wearing his old lady's clothes," she said. "She hasn't got much class."

"His old lady? You mean they're married?"

"Sure."

"Legally married?"

"Yes, legally married—confirmed by a judge. All the fucking shit. His old lady has the money. That's where he gets his bread."

"Well," I said, trying to fall into the same casual acceptance of a relationship I could not understand (and also using the language of the tavern), "well I suppose he has the necessary equipment."

"If he can get it up when she's around. She's got a faggot—a no-good asshole fairy—but I guess it's what she wanted. She was pretty depressed when her husband died two years ago. So that faggot hustler gets a hold of her. You know he was wanted by the cops?"

"No."

"Well, it wasn't much more than a crock of shit. Before he met the broad he passed some phony checks. He was taking an older guy at the time. The creep brought charges when Larry split."

"Did the police find him?"

"Sure, they found him," she said, "but the old guy was in the closet— some kind of banker. He got cold feet and dropped the charges."

I did not want to continue the gossip, for I felt a sudden bending sympathy for Clara, knowing, however, that it may have been misplaced. It is quite possible that she knew about Larry's occasional transvestism when she married him, and certainly she was quite familiar with it now, though I did not think her public acquiescence had been easily achieved, particularly in the trading setting of The Columbia. She has two small children by her former husband. Sometimes Larry brings them to the tavern on Saturday afternoons, leaving them in the family station wagon parked at curbside while he has a few beers. His appearance on these occasions is thoroughly "Saturday-suburban"—turtleneck sweater, jeans, white sox, and loafers, the weekend uniform of comfortably well-off fathers running domestic errands or dropping in to the country club. The blond children climb from seat to seat inside the glass box, their petulance increasing as time passes. Larry ignores their impatient and demanding faces pressed against the windows of the automobile, and I try to preserve a sophisticated detachment from a situation that is none of my business; but the after-image of Clara's vacuous moonface appears in the bleak space between the tavern and the children, reminding me of second-rate Tennessee Williams—of *The Roman Spring of Mrs. Stone* with its themes of middle-age bereavement, loneliness, and defiance of conventions.

Larry's participation in the drag scene is in fact greater than suggested by his occasional tranvestite appearances at The Columbia, or at least one must assume so if any credence can be given to his public statement on New Year's Eve in the Sixty-Niner tavern, whose owners belong to "The Queen City Guild."

The Sixty-Niner, like other taverns in the Guild, makes some effort to provide its patrons with additional entertainment on special holidays and Halloween. Drag queens, taking full advantage of the masquerading license, dress in their very best finery. "Live" music often supplements the jukebox; amateur talent contests, with token prizes, climax the evening.

Larry was there around eleven o'clock at the beginning of the talent competition. He was in drag and alone, though earlier Clara had been with him in The Columbia, totally ignored by everyone as usual—a drab housewifely contrast to her husband's empire gown of peach-colored chiffon, his silver shoes and a glittering coronet positioned on top of a wig whose falls cascaded over his shoulders. Clara had left in a taxi (going home to the children?), Larry barely noticing her self-effacing departure through the crowd of posturing, Western-costumed men. He was convivially engaged with everyone who passed him as he faced the room, back to the bar and feet delicately pointed, laughing and tossing his head, extending his neck—adorned with a yellow ribbon and cameo pendant—in a stagy manner that threw his hair behind him, allowing him to fondle it coquettishly as he gossiped. He seemed a little drunk, an impression later confirmed by an unsteady edge to his eye-catching entrance to the Sixty-Niner and his stately progress down the bar to the stage where Miss Debbie, acting as mistress of ceremonies, prepared to introduce a dozen contestants. Last in the line, Larry, who was announced as "Miss Cornelia," rather than making a simple acknowledging bow as the others had done, took the hand microphone from Debbie and launched into a self-promoting speech informing the audience that recently he had been chosen "Empress" of the capital city of a central state and hoped to receive the same distinction at a forthcoming competition in Port City. His pushiness wasn't well received. Miss Debbie was startled by the unexpected interruption; the other drag queens smiled like ladies trying to ignore a social gaffe; a few loud and derogatory remarks from the audience upset Larry's composure, sending him unsteadily back to the line with a petulant toss of his head.

Unlike The Columbia's patrons, who dismiss it as "no big deal," I am fascinated by the incongruous coupling of Larry and Clara. Once again, firmly drawn conventional boundaries slide like ink on moistened paper, leaving no more than a blur—no more than a puzzling, unidentifiable echo bounced back and forth from the walls of a Marabar cave. The same echo comes from "Tama" and "Lou," though their relationship is not cross-sexual; both are men.

Tama is of mixed Hawaiian ancestry, with a brown complexion, a broad face, and a large, generous, and smiling mouth. He wears his hair in a full, waved, and shoulder-length style that passes easily among today's fashions for men. A Columbia regular, he is employed as a cook in a "Polynesian" restaurant and after his shift he often appears in the tavern in his working clothes of white smock, trousers, and shoes. More frequently, however, his costume is jeans topped with an off-the-shoulder see-through blouse exposing a firm, masculine barrel chest.

Tama and Lou live in a modest frame house in an unpretentious, lower-income neighborhood some forty minutes drive from The Columbia, a street of little dwellings on narrow lots, not exactly run-down but depressing to someone accustomed to more space, to trees, a view, and the other privileges of a higher standard of living. The house sits cheek to cheek with others that are almost identical and looks at its reflection—its mirror image—across a ribbon of asphalt flanked by untended sidewalk strips of grass. There is nothing remotely nostalgic about it, nothing similar to the rediscovered qualities of brownstone terraces in some other cities. It is part of a low-income development probably dating to the late nineteen-fifties, a development that took advantage of the economic growth of Port City and a sidelong glance at the suburban conventions of more expensive neighborhoods. Behind the house, there is a narrow yard that Tama and Lou have planted with some flanking beds of summer-flowering dahlias and some grape vines trained to climb a corridor of trellises. Everything opens to the rear; for the front is merely an untended rockery (with a few persevering plants of

Aubrietia and *Alyssum saxatile)*, and a score of concrete steps zigzagging to the front door from the treeless sidewalk.

The interior of the house is cluttered with couches and chairs upholstered in deep-pile materials in shades of garnet and puce and occasional tables supporting lamps whose pleated shades are protected by their original plastic wrapping. It is probably this last and more widespread convention that promotes an automatic degree of cultural snobbery that is of-a-kind with the private laughter occasioned by the plastic "raincoats" that on-leave, wartime officers of the United States Army used to protect their military caps and gold-laced decorations—a custom almost as déclassé as wearing galoshes on your head or even a bone through your nose. Similar judgments move from the plastic-wrapped lampshades to the Norman Rockwell prints on the walls of Tama's house and to his Sunday hospitality of canned beer and cubes of processed cheese offered in the narrow yard between the regimented dahlia borders (and again, for reasons I cannot explain, I dislike this particular flower, finding it as stiff and lifeless as the floral designs on ten-cent Valentine's cards in the revolving racks of chain-style drug stores).

Lou never comes to The Columbia. He is middle-aged and has a minor administrative position in a loan company. His personal friends are downtown businessmen with whom he lunches daily and frequently joins for an after-work drink at a heterosexual bar. These people are not invited to the house he shares with Tama. The guests at Tama's parties (even at the celebration of Lou's birthday) are mainly male homosexuals and a sprinkling of unmarried men who are said to be bisexual. Only a few of them are familiar faces in The Columbia. One is "King," who stayed the best part of a week in my house when he was unemployed and completely without money or lodgings. King has never given me any trouble either in the tavern or at home, though eventually I had to ask him to leave because his hour-to-hour addiction to television was a totally frustrating and infuriating interruption to the quietness and isolation I need when working. His predicament, when I took him in, was not unusual. He is more often jobless than employed, and it seems to me that brief sojourns in the homes of other people are routine elements of his experience.

King is so "ordinarily" masculine that no one would single him out from thousands of other men on a twelve-block downtown walk. Thirty-five or -six, his face is a little ravaged, beginning to show his age, though his hair has no gray and his figure is tall and lean. He has a loose but manly way of walking and posturing at the pool tables in the tavern, and has often given me an unexpected and jocular prod with his cue, provoking me to turn to him and receive a laughing embrace of recognition. His

favorite joke is recalling the occasion when I accidentally locked myself
from my house, and, in bare feet and bathrobe, had to walk the suburban street looking for a housewife sufficiently trusting to unchain her
door and let me use her phone to call a locksmith.

King's humor runs to raunchy heterosexual jokes. When I met him,
I could not decide whether he was straight or gay. There is a tendency
to assume that the majority of those frequenting the tavern regularly
are gay (or they wouldn't be there), but King says he is straight.
His "straightness," however, does not exclude recurring homoerotic
encounters.

"Miss Julie," watching me observing King at the pool table, said:
"He's not much dice, dear. Sure, you can get him to bed, but it's not
worth the shitty effort. If you want to hold his dick, he'll fight and groan
like a virgin. Hell man, no fella has to go through that crap."

Tama always refers to Lou as his "husband." Their relationship seems
to be easy and affectionate, though Tama sometimes treats Lou in an
offhand and cavalier fashion. At his birthday party, Tama brought Lou's
cake from the kitchen to the living room, plunked it on the TV table in
front of his chair and thrust a single household candle into it, saying:

"Here it is. Light the fucker and see if you can blow it out."

On Tama's birthday, however, Lou kept his present until the guests
were about to leave and then assembled all of us around his car in the
driveway. Unlocking the trunk, he handed Tama a small package which
contained, when he opened it, a gold and jade ring. "Oh, baby!" Tama
said, passing the gift among his friends. "That's really great." And he
explained to me: "We saw it in a window on Fifth Avenue. It cost two
hundred dollars. Doesn't he look after me?"

Tama, however, often appears at The Columbia with other men he
also introduces as "my husband"; and one night, possibly responding to
some critical speculation in my rejoinder, he said, standing close to me
with his arm encircling my waist, "Honey, Lou's my *real* husband. We've
been married eight years. I don't sleep with him, though. But I don't take
these other fellas home. Lou doesn't mind what I do on the streets. He
loves me. He doesn't come to the bars, but he lets me do my thing."

Tama is gregarious and truly likeable: humorous and outgoing and
enjoying life, whether it is playing pool in the tavern or playing mistress
of the house he shares with Lou, three dogs, and a cat. I have only
Tama's word that he does not sleep with Lou, but Lou seems quite satis-
fied with the domesticity he provides, and I suppose their arrangement is
no more than a variation of some cultish heterosexual agreements that I
find as much difficulty in understanding. The sexual possessiveness
associated with marriage—and the wounds to self-esteem occasioned by

infringement of the rights of one partner to the other—tend to be transferred to homosexual couplings, and Tama's stated relationship to Lou, including its "extramarital" permissiveness, is almost as puzzling to me as heterosexual marriages of convenience and wife swapping.

Meeting Tama and Debbie in their homes always raises the question: "How do they pass in their neighborhoods?" No one has to pass in The Columbia, and in its enclosed space there is the greatest tolerance of eccentricities of appearances that are either contrived or physical. "Roger" is partially paralyzed and shuffles down the bar in a crab-like fashion, his stunted and withered arm waving like an uncontrollable claw. "Tina" and "Dick" are deaf-mutes, both young and attractive. When Tina joins a group in which there are people who do not know him, someone will say casually: "She can't hear you or talk to you, fella." Physical deformities, infirmities, and peculiarities do not provoke either private or public comment, and surely, this tolerant acceptance of personal handicaps or idiosyncrasies is an element of the kindness Miss Rose finds in the tavern. The young man who had brought her the sweet rolls from The Lighthouse saw me buying her a drink of muscatel (her favorite wine because, she says, "It's so good for my throat, honey") and remarked approvingly: "That's a good old broad. Shit, she hasn't got much, but don't you ever put her fucking down. Some of us faggots will look after her."

The acceptance Rose finds in The Columbia is incomprehensible to her sister, whom I met one night when she was sitting beside Rose on the tattered bench under the sidewalk windows. Rose is always "ladylike" when she talks to me, using little gestures of gentility to impress "the Professor," which was the way in which she introduced me to her sister, trying, I thought, to demonstrate that she had some respectable friends.

Her sister was very neat, a typical suburban housewife wearing a good coat and a stylish brocade hat. Her pale, composed, and regular features were the antithesis of Rose's struggling effort to project the same values. She was persevering, trying, like Clara, not to judge what she saw; but when Rose left us momentarily she said to me: "Look at her! She wasn't always like this. We were a good family. Now she has nowhere to go but *this* place," and her hand sketched a gesture that dismissed the entire tavern. "I can't do anything more for her," she said.

Rose may have come down in the world, but I think that even when she was a saleslady at Kress's (if her statement is true) she must have been an "outsider," looking for something beyond the store and her Brooklyn home. Rose writes. She showed me the first page of a short story titled "Viona and Her Great Love," asking me to give the correct spelling for words like caviar, champagne, debutante, and the meaning of au revoir. The story began:

"Viona Carstairs was beautiful. She lived in a big house near a lake where there were trees and flowers and servants. They had caviar for breakfast. Viona of the cornflower eyes trilled all through the day. She was like a fairy princess, loved by her family and flying in and out among them like a moth they could not catch. But Reggie caught her at the debutante's ball in the mansion and carried her off to Paris (France), Rome (Italy), and London (England)."

Rose's fantasies are not confined to her writing. A local newspaper runs a sweepstakes in which every copy is numbered and somewhere tucked away in the Sunday edition is a number readers try to match for a bounty of several hundred dollars. Rose cannot afford to subscribe to a paper, so she makes a daily collection from street-side trash cans. The two brown-paper shopping bags she totes to The Columbia are stuffed with old issues from which she clips the numbers to compare them with the Sunday edition. "Honey," she says confidently, "I'll make it. You'll see." And she brings the same optimism to her compulsive involvement with writing slogans and composing housewifely endorsements for commercial products, always anticipating that she will win.

I spend a great deal of time with Rose, correcting, but not altering, the manuscript of "Viona." Though she has never heard of Scott Fitzgerald, I think of him as the story unfolds on scraps of wrapping paper presented to me on the sticky surface of a table in the tavern. I am not a great admirer of Fitzgerald, and Rose, obviously, possesses nothing remotely similar to his educated style. "Viona" is best compared with the "penny dreadful" tales of romance that servants in late nineteenth-century England concealed under their pillows in their attic quarters. But Fitzgerald's themes appear in "Viona," distorted by distance from the high-life she attempts to describe; and I suspect her principal models are Hollywood movies of the thirties and early forties, of the star system and fan magazines.

Rose is clearly not alone in bringing her fantasies to The Columbia. All the men in their "Marlboro Man" costumes—their pointed boots, low-slung jeans, and wide-brimmed insouciant hats—are "coming on" in a style that is an exaggeration of conventional images of rugged masculinity; and on the "carnival" nights of Friday and Saturday, the visible elements of fantasy are underlined by contemporary replicas of "Sportin' Life": men costumed in cheap variations of the "outrageous" and assertive dress that television cameras seek—with patronizing implications—as the audience assembles at Madison Square Garden for a multimillion dollar match between Mohammed Ali and Joe Frazier.

It is cheap "Madison Square Garden," cheap Bette Davis, Joan Crawford, Donyale Luna, and Lee Remick, and, on the male side, Peter Fonda, Sammy Davis, Jr., James Coburn, and Rock Hudson.

The difficulties of passing in public outside the tavern are not a daily hazard to patrons who wear conventional "working-class" or sharp and funky male dress. There is not the slightest embarrassment in walking downtown with King, even though he is often unshaven, crumpled, and dishevelled and would certainly be out of place at a faculty dinner or cocktail party, and it wasn't only his addiction to television that prompted me to turn him from my house and back to the streets but also the suspicion that other friends who came to see me might treat him as a "native." Virtually all of them knew of my research in The Columbia and would have identified him as a "member of Read's population," and I did not want to present him as a specimen, exposing him to possible embarrassment and myself to subsequent questions concerning his origins, his job, where he lived, and how he managed to get by from day to day.

King could not pass in my house, and, if I have to admit it, there was no liberal-intellectual credit to be gained from having him there. Judgments on what he said and how he behaved would not be suspended because of some exotic origin. He was an affront, a statistic from welfare and unemployment rolls suddenly fleshed and sitting in my living room hour after hour in front of the television set; and most people do not want to see anonymity presented to them in palpable form.

King did not resent me asking him to leave. He left in the clothes he had been wearing when, one night in The Columbia, he had told me he was broke, had a cold, and had nowhere to go. Offering him lodging had seemed no different from buying Rose a muscatel to ease her throat or slipping her fifty cents when she said she was hungry; but I think I was as guilty of patronizing him as others would have been on meeting him in my home, perceiving him as a resource person rather than as *King* and making notes about him in my study while he sat downstairs. I could not lend myself to this deception. It seemed more honest to know him only in the tavern where he was completely at ease and not a possible object of intellectual charity, where no one would feel compelled to say in deference to me: "He *does* have an interesting face."

Curiously, Pocahontas and others like him also pass quite easily in the streets outside the tavern. Pocahontas has assumed all the visible attributes of a woman's role and never relinquishes them. He is bizarre. His calves bulge beneath his abbreviated skirts; his hair is fancily coiffed and his eyes disappear behind false lashes and layers of mascara as heavy as bruises. Passing him downtown during the day as he window-shops with Charlie (who clings to his arm like a satellite captured by his gravity), he stands out from the anonymity of the sidewalk. Heads turn for a second glance, fascinated by the grotesque; but very few would question his assumed biological role.

Curiosity about passing does not focus upon Pocahontas and all the "Kings" but, rather, upon the "Debbies" whose everyday appearance is thoroughly ambiguous. Debbie's male dress does not match his penciled, butterfly eyebrows, his pancake makeup and light, glossy lipstick, and these, in turn, are an absurd contrast with the manly tattoos on his forearms: patriotic American eagles and mottos (In God We Trust) that are indelible relics of his days as an enlisted man in the United States Navy.

Debbie, in his younger years, has been a member of a cheaper drag circuit. One night in The Columbia he took my arm and said: "Come with me, baby. There's two fellas I want you to meet."

I followed him to a neighboring tavern where once he had a job tending bar. He took me to a table and introduced me to two "impresarios" for whom he had worked in a variety of "middle" states, never getting to New York City, San Francisco, or New Orleans. I did not know their connection with him until, touching my hand, he said: "They have a poster of me when I appeared at the Pussy Cat in St. Louis. You really ought to see it, honey. The style is all coming back—the curly hair, the cupid's bow, that kind of class. I could tap dance as good as Ann Miller. I was a *star*, baby; and I've always been a lady of class."

Debbie does have "class" in presenting himself as he is to the agents of welfare and unemployment bureaucracies who must have serious misgivings when they confront him across a desk and he removes his dark glasses, revealing his Marlene Dietrich mask. Unlike Roger or the deaf-mutes or "Sky," whose face is a livid and contorted mass of scar tissue, Debbie is not physically deformed and eligible for conscience-saving charity. I do not have to steel myself as I receive his cheek-to-cheek greeting. There's no merit in it, as when Sky kisses me on the mouth or I engage in helpless and uninstructed sign conversation with Tina and Dick, flicking my fingers erratically and preserving that benign, fixed smile. Urban anonymity is, however, the principal protection of the Debbies, the Tamas, the "Miss Stars" (six-feet tall, black with bright red lipstick and eyelashes as spiky as the television image of Cher Bono), and "Cheryl" who is past forty, gap-toothed, with lank and thinning blond hair, a conspicuous five-o'clock shadow showing beneath his makeup, and who has a commission arrangement with five or six sexual hustlers.

Whether in drag or male dress with face makeup, there is something incongruous and exaggerated in the appearances of these queens, a quality that, as with Larry, produces the involuntary judgment that they're "tacky." I remarked as much again one night while watching an amateurish drag show at The Roman Forum, and the man sitting beside me said: "Hell man, that's what it's supposed to be. Don't you know anything?"

His matter-of-fact statement was so unexpected that I suddenly found myself watching everything from an entirely different perspective, realizing its connections with the theater of the absurd in which comfortable definitions of reality are deliberately distorted.

Examples of the distortion can be seen almost every night in The Columbia, but they are probably best observed at the Empress Ball at The Port City Plaza Hotel.

The Empress Ball is an annual event sponsored by about a dozen owners of homosexual lounges, taverns, steam baths, and a few attorneys, tax consultants, and other businessmen who are members of a loose organization called "The Queen City Guild." The ostensible purpose of the Ball is to select, crown, and install the "Empress" who will reign over Port City for the following year. The several contenders support their candidacy with posters and "benefits" in various taverns, with free "favors" such as a cellophane package of peanuts inscribed with the slogan "Bust a Nut for Frankie Doll," and more recently—possibly with the intent of improving their image with more "respectable" activists—by publishing their respective platforms in the local homosexual newsletter. As far as I know, the vote is not publicly reported. I assume it is small—a matter of hundreds only—and, in any case, it has to be an unreliable index of popular interest in the programs of the "Imperial Court," for many voters merely mark their ballots as urged by the bartenders in whichever or all of the sponsoring taverns they visit.*

---

*These voting practices have changed. Ballots are now cast at a central polling place (not a tavern) staffed by members of the "Imperial Court," a further indication, perhaps, of the organization's effort to improve its image. In the past, the "Imperial Court" and its principal sponsored event, the Ball, were not approved by some of the more influential and politically oriented gay organizations. The "recognition" it has achieved at present is still tempered by its déclassé image as an organization of "drag queens," but a former "Empress" is a member of the Board of the most conservative activist group in Port City. This is surely the result of an ecumenical movement within some of the organizations, but the quest for recognition and "respectability" has been accompanied by some changes in the public character of the Ball. In the early nineteen-seventies the event was held "openly" at a major hotel, guests were allowed to bring cameras, and even local television stations were not forbidden to videotape some of the proceedings. In the past few years, the Ball has been moved to other rented and less "conspicuous" auditoria, and in 1978 photographs were not permitted. The style of the Ball is a sensitive issue for public relations and is often decried by homosexual men and women. Indeed, the "surfacing" of homosexuality and the quest for respectability is often accompanied by a greater degree of caution in "exposing" some forms of behavior that seem to confirm heterosexual stereotypes of homosexuals and may result in ridicule.

Port City's newspapers report the Ball the day after the event. Their coverage, sometimes running to five or six half-columns and a photograph, could be cited as an example of "the new sexual liberalism." The tone of the writing, however, is snidely humorous, obviously composed by straights who do not understand the style they have observed and who link the event to the fictional "homosexual community." Most of those attending the Ball are men, though in glancing recognition of the distaff side there is a "court" and procession of an "Honorary Lesbian." The fact that this dignitary has such a qualified title may support my earlier characterization of relationships between male and female homosexuals; but the point I wish to make—and it is contrary to the implications of the newspaper reports—is that the Ball is merely an exaggerated example of a style, a carnival, a masque that has no more relevance to the total homosexual population of Port City than "cultural" benefits such as Symphoneve and Divas and Diamonds (inaugurating, respectively, the symphony and opera seasons) have for the entire heterosexual population. The so-called "Guild" sponsoring the event represents virtually nothing more than selective business interests. Its owner-members maintain a liaison with spokesmen for gay activism and do some lobbying—in their own financial interests—with state and municipal agencies; but neither their "organization" nor the Ball represent "the community."

The Ball is a spectacular, visually exciting, and sometimes outrageous charade, equivalent, in its own way, to opening night at the Metropolitan Opera, to the costume parties of the late Marquis de Cuevas and a multitude of similar events that are reported in the "Society" pages of newspapers. It is conducted with an astonishing panache and a magnificent theatricality that maintains, however, room for a smile that is not permitted at other "galas" that serve as its models—a smile announced in the "theme" of the 1973 Ball: Fairy Tales.

The "Grand Ballroom" of the Port City Plaza, where most of these events are held, is a cavernous and balconied room hung with row after row of plastic chandeliers and decorated in red, white, and gold, with plaster wall embellishments derived from Grinling Gibbons and a ceiling in the worst rococo taste. It is rather like the movie palaces of the thirties in which "clouds" moved across a midnight-blue sky, "stars" twinkled, and painted cypresses and balustrades flanked false-front temples on each side of the soaring proscenium arch; but it is perfectly suited to the pageantry of the Empress Ball and the fantastic procession of the members of various "Courts" as they enter from the far end of the room and proceed down a football field of carpeting to make obeisance to the outgoing Empress who is enthroned on the stage among banks of scarlet tulips, elaborate ice sculptures (including the *David)* and illuminated fountains. The multitude of wall sconces and the chandeliers are dimmed, and, watching from a balcony table, the arc lights focused on the runway are moving and cross-cutting celestial shafts dancing to the rhythm of the band that heralds each "Court" with an appropriate pop tune.

Suddenly, all the lights are extinguished, with the exception of the candles on the ranks of tables. Veils of smoke drift back and forth in the high darkness above the after-image of the arc lights, and an announcer's voice proclaims: "Mister George, Port City candidate for Empress honors our gracious Queen!" Trumpets sound. Everyone stands, craning toward the far end of the room as the band breaks into Elgar's *Pomp and Circumstance* and something like a Christmas tree materializes in the distance—a "burning bush" of twinkling fairy lights that approaches the stage at stately pace. On the streets, Mr. George is a comely, jeaned, and bearded young man; but now he is a magnificent apparition gowned elaborately in hoop-skirted, transparent gold tissue wired with a multitude of tiny lights and crowned with a headdress of gold-foil curls studded with reflecting ornaments. As he proceeds toward the throne of the outgoing Empress "Della," the lights slowly return and reveal his retinue of young men clad only in gold lamé codpieces and gilded Roman wigs.

Unfortunately (I thought at the time), Mr. George did not become the succeeding "Empress." But he was "first runner-up" and therefore on stage when everyone formed a line to "bend the knee" and "kiss the hand" of "Miss Zenobia" (the successful candidate) whose ample masculine arms enfolded triple bouquets of American Beauty roses as he looked at his subjects under sequin-studded eyelids.

Visually, this scene is as remote from The Columbia as an exclusive country club differs from a bowling alley or a downtown poolroom. Male dress, befitting the grandeur of the occasion, is the very latest in tuxedo styles and colorful ruffled dinner shirts—most of them rented. Drag costuming runs to extravagant, individual variations and adaptations of "show business" fashions. It isn't Dinah Shore but, rather, Cher Bono mixed with Phyllis Diller. Indeed, male homosexuals watching these ladies on the screen often laugh at their appearance more than their material. "Oh, there she goes, Mary!" they say. *"Will you look* at that broad in drag! Jesus, she's as tacky as a two-bit whore. They wouldn't let *her* out on the streets."

The exaggeration of assumed roles and fashions is thoroughly understood by everyone except the reporters who merely see grotesque impersonations of upper-class values. Their aesthetics are both confused and offended by the inverted implications and the high-camp commentary on serious occasions that range from The Miss America Pageant to the selection of a statewide Dairy Queen. They lack the necessary humor and detachment to see that it is not meant to reflect a "reality" equivalent to that of Symphoneve, that it is both fantasy and an "in" joke, a Mardi Gras in which, for those in drag, the boundaries of conventional taste are deliberately erased.

The Empress Ball is the highest of camp, and it is expensive. Tickets are $10.00 a person. There is no food. All drinks are "no-host," and the other extras include tuxedo rentals, expensive wigs, gowns, and makeup. It is far beyond the means of most patrons of The Columbia, and, anyway, the majority of them have as little interest in it as the majority of the city's heterosexuals show for Divas and Diamonds. It is relevant, however, to the style of drag observed in the tavern.

Larry in curls, hostess gown, rhinestone tiara, and heavily lashed and painted eyes is an incongruous contrast with the naked lights, the bare floors, and the western-booted men. It is like finding yourself in a scene from *Destry Rides Again* (the Dietrich version) or any saloon in western movies featuring overdressed ladies of questionable virtue. Even Susie Wong and "Maria" (who has both speech and hearing impediments) embroider outrageously upon the fads expensively photographed for the more glossy magazines. It would be quite wrong—missing the whole intent—to expect reproductions of Mary Tyler Moore or, from an earlier era, June Allyson. There is no profit in applying the aesthetics of Sunday brunch at the country club to the impersonations in The Columbia.

"Misty," who is a hair stylist, stands at the bar talking to "Gary," who has a part-time job behind the counter. Misty is in drag: short, chiffon shirtwaist dress, silver high-heeled shoes, a profusion of shoulder-length chestnut curls, Cover Girl makeup, and layers of green and blue eyeshadow. As he banters with Gary, his eyes con the tavern—the poolroom, the tables, and the barside patrons. He is on one of many stops he will make that night, and he says: "Jeez I want a man, and there isn't one in this whole motherfucking joint!"

Misty's remark, lifting out of the Saturday-night chorale, causes speculation on the sexual intent of drag-costuming. Presumably, there are men who are sexually attracted by the ambiguity and whose masculinity is supported by it; but assuredly there are also many whose possible sexual interest is diminished or totally erased.

For most of a Friday night "Arlene" had been trying to make it with "Derek." It was a drag night for Arlene, a Columbia regular who out of costume is a perfectly ordinary white male in his mid-twenties. Derek was new trade in The Columbia, only three weeks in the city. His casual clothes (flared blue double-knit trousers cinched by a massively buckled belt and an open-necked red jersey shirt clinging so tightly to his chest that it seemed to breathe with his skin) were more expensive than the customary tavern dress. His blond hair was fashionably styled and his healthy tan accentuated the extraordinary blueness of his eyes. Very much at ease, he sat on a stool with his back to the bar, confronting the room with parted legs and polished boots tucked under the lower rung of his seat. Arlene reached him in the course of a gossiping, posturing progress from one barside customer to another, halted beside him, placed a hand on his knee and said, with eyes suggestively widened:

"Why, hello! I'm Arlene. What's your name?"

"Derek."

"You didn't say *Dick* did you? No, Well, it *could* be," Arlene said, pressing his pelvis against Derek's knee and looking at his groin. "That's meant to be a joke. I'm a bit high tonight, but I could use a 'Logy Flip.' "

Derek ordered the drink.

"Thank you, dear," Arlene said, and slid his hand along Derek's thigh. "Do you mind me doing this?"

"Whatever turns you on."

"Fella, I know what turns *me* on. This for instance." He placed his hand squarely between Derek's legs and groped him. "Nothing phony about *that*," he said, "not like these tits," he added, looking down at his chest: "Jeez, I think they're slipping. I've gotta be drunk!" He made some casual adjustments and returned his hand to Derek's leg. "There, that's better. No need for Amy Vanderbilt to worry. So, as I was saying before that crisis—what closet have you been hiding in?"

"None."

"Well, wherever it was," Arlene replied, dismissing the denial with a wave of his "Logy Flip," "you're out of it now, and Arlene found you first."

The dialogue continued, with Arlene making most of the conversation and receiving little information in return. It seemed to me that Derek was becoming bored and edgy, not embarrassed but merely uninterested; and on one of Arlene's frequent visits to the Ladies' john (always prefaced by: "Don't you go away. I've got to pee"), he turned to me and made a wry face.

"Those drag faggots turn me off," he said. "There was this night I met a butch-looking guy and went home with him. He had a pretty fancy apartment, and while I sat on his couch he gave me a Scotch-on-the-rocks and said he'd be back in a minute. So I waited, thinking he had to piss. And he comes back in heels and a long dress with feathers. 'Don't you like me?' he said. 'Hell, no.' I put my Scotch on his coffee table and got ready to split. 'Fella, if I wanted a woman, I could get one,' I said. I didn't want to hurt his feelings, but that stuff's not my scene."

Placing his half-finished beer on the counter, he rose from his stool. "See you around," he said with a friendly nod. "I'll leave while he's in the can."

Derek's personal distaste for the drag scene is stronger than anything openly expressed by the majority of The Columbia's regulars. Most of them have a bantering attitude toward those who make intermittent tavern appearances in full costume, responding with such remarks as:

"That's a great outfit, dear."

"Where'd you find those tits?"

"Jeez, I bet you make a mint with that pussy."

"You hustling for a bit of dick, honey?"

"Fella, I didn't know you had those sexy legs!"

"You pregnant, baby, or just forgot your girdle?"

"Tuck in that butt before I bust it."

"Honey, you're losing a fucking eyelash."

"If I wasn't already married I'd go for you, baby."

"Turn it on, sister. Shake that keister."

"Act like a lady, now. Don't fall on your fucking ass."

"Honey, take your fucking shoe off my fucking foot. I don't mind your boots in my face, but that heel's *hurting.*"

Full drag costuming in The Columbia is taken no more seriously than the more extravagant examples of The Empress Ball. Covering the 1973 event, a reporter for *The Port City Examiner* quoted a candidate identified as "Mame": "We're not like this outside," Mame said. "We work for The Children's Orthopedic Hospital, The Cancer Society—all the charities."

The tone of *The Examiner's* story was skeptical, and, certainly, The Columbia's patrons are unlikely to give either time or money to charity; but Mame's remark applies to the tavern's drag scene in the sense that everyone knows that the visible reversal of roles is a game, a "play" to which they respond with a badinage that underscores an essentially comic and excluded understanding.

As I became more familiar with the tavern, more at home in it and more comfortable with its style, I began taking friends there when they wanted to see where I worked, selecting, however, only the younger of them, because I felt they could behave properly, that they would neither offend nor be offended by anyone. "Richard" and "Stephanie" are a young (early twenties), highly attractive heterosexual couple who are quite close. Their backgrounds are upper-middle-class suburban. Richard owns a fire-engine red expensive sports car; Stephanie's hair is ash-blonde, her face as clean and fresh as a Noxema model. After dinner in Richard's apartment, they wanted to go to The Columbia, so I took them there without misgiving and introduced them as friends to Chuck behind the bar.

"Stephanie?" Chuck said. "Better I call you Steve."

And Stephanie was "Steve" for the remainder of the night.

The nicknames, the sexual banter and complementary pantomimes are elements of a style that, paradoxically, is as "masculine" as a men's locker room. "Watch your mouths, fellas," the bartenders often say when women like Stephanie are present. "Keep it low. We've got some real girls here."

No two nights in The Columbia are precisely the same. Except for the steadfast regulars, the population is in constant flux. Even after two years of study I am left with the impression of a kaleidoscope of faces and people who are known mostly by first names only. Chuck tosses dice at the bar to see if the house will pay for the next selection on the jukebox. The pool players in their high-heeled boots posture at the tables and the conversational banter hurtles back and forth—point and counterpoint. Superficially, it seems as chaotic as first impressions of any of the unfamiliar ways of life that have provided most of the source material for anthropology; but in these distant and exotic situations, the investigator expects to discover an order eventually: a "system" within which people move in relationship to one another, in which there are certain standing rules, shared affects and cognitions, symbols and ritualized expressions of common understandings. However remote and unconventional the situation may be, this is the basic hypothesis; and, with perseverance, the initial impression of chaos yields to it, as it does in The Columbia tavern.

THREE

Stage Directions

Fridays and Saturdays are the most crowded nights at The Columbia. Pushing open the sidewalk doors, the first impression is a painful explosion of light and sound—of the jukebox, the naked electric bulbs, a hubbub of voices, and the click of pool balls one against another. It is a mass of people lining the bar, sitting at the formica-topped tables, or posturing around the two emerald rectangles in the slightly elevated and separated poolroom.

By 9:00 pm most of the regulars and some of the "grotesques" are present. Miss Rose in her accustomed place, muscatel in hand as she composes a slogan or a few lines of "Viona" on pieces of wrapping paper. Now and then the doors open with an attention-getting flourish as someone like "Miss Star" enters. He is a huge—over six feet tall—black and so grossly overweight that he needs no artifice to simulate breasts beneath his tight T-shirt. His lips are the brightest red, his false eyelashes spiky corollas for eyes that move from side to side as, progressing down the length of the room, he makes a preliminary survey of the patrons; already assessing the possibilities and forming impressions, he will move to the end of the bar where he joins a friend, coming upon him unannounced, placing his ample arms around him from behind and pumping his pelvis against the other's backside. The man turns his head casually to look up at Star, and an exchange of scatological badinage ends in laughter as Star, picking up his beer, turns to look over the room more carefully and begins to settle into the scene.

To the straight casual visitor and to homosexuals who patronize more decorous territories but come occasionally to slum at The Columbia, the frequent grotesqueries of appearance, the blue language, and explicit pantomimes of sexual acts are probably the only things they see and take away with them to talk about later. They come—with patronizing attitudes—to be "entertained," and their attention focuses upon the more grossly visible elements of the style. At the peak of the activity, the tavern is a cabaret to which the price of admission is merely a beer. "Yukon Amy" twirling for himself in splendid isolation is worth a second visit, or "Jimmie," an older black man with baggy workman's trousers and a partly drunk but beatific smile, who performs a solo, feet-stomping hoedown to "Dueling Banjos" on the jukebox.

The "entertainment"—which is spiced with a little danger—is also part of the attraction to the tavern's regular customers—an element of "reality" they ascribe to the style. But they do not find Yukon Amy, Jimmie, or Miss Rose grotesque, for their behavior and appearance are accepted components of a world view that is based upon manifold experiences of variance from the normative moral and social order; they are part of a larger "cosmic reality" in which the dominant homosexuality is joined with other "outside" or "castaway" characteristics, and almost everything observed can be contained eventually in a perspective that is "real" in the sense that it expresses and responds to the perceptions and cognitions of a population that is at odds with or excluded from most of the value orientations of middle-class straight society—the society represented by Genet's les justes.

Reading the apologetics of gay organizations, it is difficult to recognize anything similar to the "indigenous order" of the Columbia; but this is not surprising, since most of the activists address themselves to the white middle class in trying to promote the respectability of "the alternative sexual style." The burden of their message is "look, we are really just like you," and perhaps there is nothing basically wrong with this. At the very least, it is politically expedient; but the pursuit of bland respectability inevitably ignores and sometimes denigrates styles that do not fit the more desirable public image, producing a picture that is as out of focus, for the total population, as an aging movie actress who is photographed through gauze and a Vaseline-coated lens. In prosecuting the image of "domesticity in suburbia," there is virtually no mention of the variety of public styles; and if they are given passing recognition, they are more frequently downgraded than approved. In 1974, for example, the Gay Students Association at Port City University published two statements on male homosexuality in the student newspaper. The first merely reproduced familiar evidence supporting the panhuman distribution of the preference, placing, as usual, a heavy emphasis on "the Greek case"; but the second addressed the problem of "coming out," of recognizing one's sexual direction and, thereafter, of finding others who share it. It offered little advice on the latter score, except to join the Association and participate in its organized activities—its discussion groups, picnics, hiking and mountain climbing excursions, and so forth. It made passing reference, however, to homosexual bars and taverns as places that beckoned those newly "come out" and looking for companionship. They were not recommended; rather, they were characterized as "lonely places," and the tone was disapproving.

I suppose that lonely people can be found in any tavern. It is part of tavern folklore that the bartender often serves as a lay analyst for customers with personal problems. The bar—that long, solid demarcation of space—is almost as symbolic as the psychiatrist's couch and adjacent chair; and the anonymity of the bartender not only encourages confessions—and the catharsis of confession—but on occasion also allows him to give the kind of authoritarian advice that would be resented and resisted if it came from someone more personally involved with the "patient."

On almost any night there are "lonely" people in The Columbia— people with a drinking problem, people involved in domestic or other difficulties, and simply people who are new to the city and have no connections there. Certain spatial conventions protect those who are depressed and who want to be alone even while "participating" in the activity of a public place; but the majority of those who come there more or less regularly do so not merely to drink and get drunk, or to find a sexual partner, but to interact with others in a ritualized setting, a setting in which it is possible to find and experience a commonality that contrasts with the world beyond the tavern's doors. It is not a lonely place—though it is a refuge for some lonely people—and the commonality that is sought and found there is not only a positive contribution to the personal economies of its patrons but also represents a structured reality comparable in almost every respect to anything we might be more prejudicially inclined to regard as real.

The ethnographic literature on tavern and bar structure and behavior in the United States is not extensive, but the work of Sherri Cavan is certainly among the best and most readable of it. One of her essays, "The Home Territory Bar" (in her book *Liquor License,* 1966), is particularly relevant to my attempt to delineate the elements of the style of The Columbia.

I have said that The Columbia cannot be called a "neighborhood tavern" because very few of its patrons live in its vicinity. Similarly, Cavan recognizes that residential propinquity is only one of a number of factors contributing to the characteristics of what she calls a "home territory bar." "Territory" refers to the enclosed and physically separated premises and the distinctively patterned behaviors both permitted and expected within them rather than a particular residential location. She does not employ "style" either descriptively or analytically, but I think the concept is implicit in her separation of "home territory bars" from "convenience bars"; and it is crucial in determining why one tavern rather than another may become for some customers a "second home" or a "home away from home."

Physical appearances alone do not generate a style that will result in a "home territory population" whose members will return to the premises again and again. The short and expensive lives of many "sissy" taverns in Port City demonstrate that decorative pretensions are not enough to secure a faithful clientele who are not as captive as the residents of The Port City Plaza and other places catering to tourists and out-of-towners. Visual appearances are, of course, gross indicators of the kinds of people one might expect to find in a particular establishment, of their social and economic positions and of more subtle differences in taste; but ultimately, as Cavan points out, the characteristics of a "home territory" establishment are generated by the regular customers, the "habitués" rather than the management, by people who "create an order of activity indigenous to a particular establishment, to be defended if necessary against the invasion of others."

I am not sure whether The Columbia may properly be called a "home territory" tavern, though it has many of the characteristics that Cavan ascribes to such places. Somewhat surprisingly, given my aesthetic distaste for the tavern, I have often found myself leaving companions in other bars with the remark: "I'm going to *my* tavern." The possessiveness is similar to the way in which anthropologists often refer to an exotic population as "my people." The proprietary implications underscore an investment in time and energy that represents a significant component of one's professional life, but they point to something else as well: to the slow and frequently difficult acquisition of a contextual familiarity with the details of the life observed, a process similar in many ways to learning a second language. There is a unique satisfaction, generating a feeling of identification, when, eventually, you perceive the cues, the grammar and syntax of what you are watching, and become sufficiently sure to experiment with the idioms.

In this sense, I suppose The Columbia constitutes a kind of "home territory" to many of its "regulars" (Cavan's "habitués"). As I have said, some of the regulars (male and female) are straight. Miss Rose is one of them, and her characterization of the tavern as a "kind place" is surely an expression of her "at homeness" there, and she even has her own personal territory within it; the tattered bench where she sits with her back to the sidewalk and her brown-paper shopping bags at her feet, holding a kind of court for those who know her and visit with her. Rose and the other straight regulars are perfectly aware of the tavern's homosexual emphasis, accepting it without any sign of disapproval. When a man sitting at Rose's table picks up his beer and says he is going to the bar, Rose replies: "Go ahead, honey. You might find a friend there," using a common euphemism for a sexual partner.

Excepting Rose, who is there virtually every night, the straight regulars are mostly late-morning and midafternoon visitors, coming at times when the tavern is more subdued and its homosexual tone is less openly expressed. But the straight and gay populations overlap to some extent at all hours. The straights are not spatially separated from the gays. They use precisely the same areas of the tavern and do not necessarily congregate with one another; indeed, at barside (the most "open" space) the populations are interspersed in a more or less random fashion. Who sits where depends primarily on the availability of a stool when entering and only secondarily upon someone with whom you share a sexual preference. The straight regulars (unlike those who enter unwittingly and react with moral outrage) are "neutral" only with respect to their sexual interest, and it isn't always certain that this is as firmly established as they imply. They are, however, only infrequently included in the exaggerated sexual byplay. They are a small minority of all customers, but most of those whom I know share some elements of experience with the gay majority: they are poor; they are (using Cavan's phrase) "biographically blemished"; they have had encounters with bureaucracies whose representatives have questioned their failure to achieve and have frequently implied that they are nonpersons; they are "outsiders" in relationship to the world whose values are represented by the austere brass lettering of Primavera over the doorway to an expensive junk shop. Outside the tavern, some of them are critical of homosexuals (and also of some ethnic groups), but I think that other elements in the experience—the "lore"—of disadvantage and exclusion transcend most moral prejudices. The sexual preference is merely another outcast trait for which you may have to account to the guardians of respectability.

According to Cavan, the habitues of "home territory bars" tend to establish proprietary acts that become routine, acts such as making telephone calls, leaving messages, cashing checks, having mail delivered to the address, and even depositing money with the management against some future need. All of these apply only minimally to The Columbia. My own personal checks have always been cashed there, but this is surely because of the assumption that I have a steady job. Moreover, most of the customers do not have bank accounts, and even checks drawn on state agencies are accepted infrequently. Borrowing money from the bar is even more difficult although, again, my "privileged" position has enabled me to do so on behalf of others. On occasion one of the bartenders has called me at home to say: "So-and-so has asked me to phone you to see if I can give him cab fare. He's drunk and broke." Since the management's rule is that money from the till cannot be loaned to anyone, the exception granted to me seems to indicate my exclusion, which is also apparent in the protectiveness of the owner's wife and others when there is a threatened irruption of violence.

I doubt that the privileges and protectiveness granted by The Columbia's management and many regulars have any connection with possible legal consequences to them if I was physically molested or mistreated. Rather, they reflect a respectability ascribed to me because of my profession, and an ignorance or innocence that might lead me to misconstrue many cues. After many months the bartenders, who see most of what is happening and who are sensitively attuned to recognize when the ritualized limits of behavior are threatened, have sometimes said approvingly: "You handled that well," a remark that is as satisfying as receiving an "A" for an academic course. But the special considerations imply an outsider status, even though it is couched in ways that are substantially different from the "exclusion tactics" used, according to Cavan (1966), on many intruders into home territory bars. Thus:

> [A home territory bar] can be considered as one's "own" bar only insofar as it cannot be considered as "everyone's" bar. Hence the maintenance of proprietary interest in a bar is dependent upon the exclusion of others who, for some reason or other, appear to have no "right" to patronize the establishment. . . . Perhaps the most common form of tacit rebuff that an entering outsider is likely to receive . . . is a conspicuous, questioning look, too long to be taken as a prelude to civil inattention, too intent to be taken as an invitation. . . . Outsiders [in home territory bars] may also be pestered or treated in a purposefully annoying manner. The habitués may attempt to cadge drinks from them or to monopolize the dice boxes, pinball machines, or jukeboxes so that these facilities are not available to the outsider. The habitués may attempt to move past the outsider with a little more roughness than is routinely given to other habitués. They may attempt to bait the outsiders into entering arguments . . . [and] . . . may deliberately engage in routines of behavior that they know will be offensive to the outsider.

I have not seen any of these exclusion tactics used deliberately on casual customers at The Columbia. Straights who enter unwittingly are not subjected to any heightening or exaggeration of customary behavior, and, in any case, it is unprofitable to guess the sexual identifications of strangers. The straights draw their own conclusions from what they see of the tavern's normative behavior, and, depending upon the strength of their moral objections, leave either quietly or with some demeaning and across-the-shoulder remark. References to my customary dress and the beer-pouring incident may seem to follow Cavan's enumeration of tactical ploys. The two blacks, however, were out-of-towners and not known to anyone in the tavern. As to remarks on my jacket and tie, these may have had some hostile implications based upon perceptions of class membership and social privilege; but when I answered the "rude" questions by saying: "Well, this is the way I see myself," the matter was closed.

Cadging drinks, cigarettes, and small change is commonly observed in the tavern, but I can't say that it follows the pattern suggested by Cavan, for it is mostly "intruders" who engage in it—casual, off-the-street down-and-outers for whom sidewalk panhandling is a way of life. I think one must distinguish between "cadging" (panhandling), "borrowing," and "hustling." Borrowing is widely practiced among regulars and has "inside" rather than "outside" connotations. Given the economic status of most of the customers, recurring insolvency is a commonly shared experience, and requests for a drink or a few dollars (seldom more than three) often carry an understanding that they will be repaid and in many cases might be considered a form of insurance, permitting the lender in one transaction to become the borrower from his debtor when their situations are reversed. They are a kind of investment which, to the best of my knowledge, usually pays off, for failure to make repayment will close out future options. The majority of the small loans I have made have been repaid, and even Miss Rose reciprocates by giving me a beer that another person has bought for her or by offering me one loose cigarette from the pocket of her coat.

This kind of credit presupposes that the participants are regulars, that a creditor will be able to locate his debtor in the tavern, for in most cases they have no outside contact with one another. On the other hand, cadging implies no contractual relationship.

There are probably as many differences as similarities between The Columbia and Cavan's model for the "home territory bar." Of course, this does not invalidate the model; all it means is that the tavern does not replicate it precisely. At night, the regulars are never a majority of the customers, and they do not have the kind of proprietary stake in the establishment that leads to deliberate measures to protect their territory against invasion. This kind of possessiveness would be counterproductive for the activities of tricking and hustling.

Patrons of The Columbia do not go there necessarily to pick up a trick or to hustle, but both are indisputably elements of its style. As I have suggested, it is not a very lucrative place for sexual hustlers (male prostitutes) although on one occasion a regular said to me confidentially: "I could show you two guys who come here who are millionaires." It is possible; for the "rough," "western," or "working-class" masculinity presented by the hustlers is sexually attractive to many people whose passing life-styles are privileged. There are also other patrons of modest means who prefer to pay for their trade even if they can do so only once a month, after they have received their paycheck. "Marvin" is one of them. He earns possibly five hundred dollars a month and does not have many personal expenses, living in a hotel room and buying his meals at chain-type all-hours restaurants. His personal belongings fill a single suitcase. But Marvin will pay up to forty-five dollars to a hustler who goes home with him and spends a few hours in his bed; and he explains that he likes to pay, that it is an important element in the gratification he receives. Similarly, some heterosexual males prefer female prostitutes as sexual partners—and such customers, like Marvin, may return again and again to the same woman. Even so, The Columbia is at best a cheap and uncertain locale for prostitution.

There is no separation between the sexual hustlers, their possible clients, and other customers. When I was new to the tavern, people often indicated a man and said, "He's a hustler," sometimes quoting his price. Their remarks were merely informative, not pejorative; and the hustlers join in the full range of The Columbia's activities. I am sure, however, that I missed many nuances of client-related behavior. I did not interview any of the hustlers, and I knew only one of them outside the tavern: "Clint," with the tattooed knee, who came to my house on three occasions with a friend. I was thinking of asking him to allow me to record him when he suddenly disappeared for a whole year. On his reappearance he told me he had been in jail for breaking his parole. I suppose I could have followed up my original intention, but by that time I had had more than enough of the tavern and didn't care if I ever saw it again. Moreover, even in New Guinea I was often unnecessarily reticent about enquiring into sexual practices, a personal attitude probably reflecting my family training that such matters are particularly private. It is an unwarranted inhibition. Populations like the New Guinea Gahuku and the tavern's patrons are often perfectly willing to talk about their sexuality, and over their beers The Columbia's customers often reveal more of their sexual tastes and activities than it seems appropriate to include here.

Sexual hustling, however, is only one form of the "hustling" associated with the tavern. "Miss Debbie's" remark that, "Every mother's hustling something," may be a commonplace appraisal of life from a disadvantaged point of view or a judgment particular to relationships within the setting. It is not precisely correct as a description of many of the patrons, but the tavern's style is steeped in the lore of hustling. People come in from the streets to peddle a wide variety of goods whose ownership is always suspect. Requests for a beer, a cigarette, or a quarter also fit the pattern. "Sonny" is a black man, probably in his early thirties, who dresses in soiled working clothes and has no apparent means of support. He is a familiar figure in the tavern, though he does not qualify as a regular. On a Monday afternoon, around five o'clock, he stood beside me at the bar and asked for a beer, which I bought. He became expansive. "I'm splitting for Miami on the twentieth," he said. "Nonstop to Sun City on United. Baby, I'm gonna have me a ball, get this black ass on the beach! My old lady's down there taking care of five thousand dollars . . ." and he went on and on, embroidering his story while I listened to only one word out of two, watching the clock because of an appointment I had to keep. When I rose from my stool, he placed a restraining hand on my arm. "Hey," he said, "Sonny needs fifty cents. You gonna give it to him?"

Early in the study, I probably would have complied, being unsure of what might happen if I refused. A tyro in the scene suspects that the demands may be a prelude to some sexual advance he does not know how to handle; but you learn gradually through watching and listening and from people who take it upon themselves to instruct and protect you. "Protection," however, is not always as altruistic as someone with a trusting bent might want to believe. Sometimes it is merely self-serving, similar to a warning to other predators to keep away from private property.

Almost inevitably a tyro is "burned" in The Columbia, unless he adopts defenses that isolate him from virtually everyone except the bartender. It is only petty burning as a rule, and there is some consolation in the fact that people far more wise to the scene are sometimes burned more deeply. "Richard," a black man who is "on the streets" and in the tavern almost every night, wanted a television set that was offered to him for twenty dollars. He asked me to hold his coat while he went to view it with the vendor. Returning, he was excited (and also a little drunk) and wanted a favor from me. "You've got your car here," he said. "They'll bring the TV and you can take me home with it." He gave the hustler (also black) the money, and I waited another hour-and-a-half. The man did not return. Richard, who is often accused of ripping off strangers, was a victim of his own style.

Both borrowing and hustling are elements of The Columbia's "indigenous order of activity." The formal distinction between them is often difficult to perceive, for even a beer or a "Logy Flip" may be borrowed, in the sense that one can expect a future return. Borrowing has contractual implications (even when they are not stated) that presuppose some continuing interaction in the tavern; but there is a very fine dividing line between some kinds of hustling and borrowing. The line between cadging and the petty forms of hustling is even finer, but the customers and management seem to have little difficulty in recognizing the nuances. Both activities (as well as borrowing) usually require face-to-face interaction, but the cadge is more blatant, more direct than the petty forms of hustling. The latter, though often involving an explicit request, tend to be embedded in a social context that includes an exchange of first names, extended conversation, and occasionally volunteered biographical information, and, as a rule, granting the request does not terminate the interaction. On the other hand, the "pure" cadge has none of these socializing connotations: a demand is presented, is either refused or granted in a perfunctory and somewhat demeaning fashion, and the cadger knows he isn't welcome.

Everyone in the tavern is liable to be hustled or approached by a cadger, although the better-dressed and more affluent-looking are prime targets. Ethnic identification is also used by the cadger. Black indigents off the streets may pester a white barside patron for a handout, ripping off the "redneck"; but they also exploit their blackness with a "brother." When it is black-to-white, it is legitimized by everything associated with "whitey," who is a nonperson to be used without any reflection on the cadger's self-esteem. In the black-to-black situation, the "brotherhood of color" is invoked as a moral umbrella. It is not a personally demeaning act to cadge and acknowledge your insolvency: a "brother" is presumed to be understanding and supportive. But it doesn't always work. I do not have precise figures, but it seems to me that the black cadger is rejected as frequently by his own ethnic representatives as by whites. Indeed, he is more likely to receive a brotherly homily from the former than the latter.

The point I wish to make, however, is that excepting only borrowing these activities are indiscriminate, not used as protective tactics against intruders by the members of a "territorial collectivity"; rather, they are among the expectations associated with a more inclusive order whose other components are not as highly visible and are generally unnoticed by the casual visitor. The swirling action of the "cabaret" is not entirely extemporized but has an underlying choreography—a basic structure that does not rigidly prescribe the movements of individual performers but prescribes "stage" areas for different kinds of interaction, areas that are mostly a matter of choices that depend upon mood, on short-range objectives, or a preference for and comfortable familiarity with the action associated with a particular space.

Except for the area behind the long bar, the rest rooms, and, to a lesser extent, the poolroom, the stages are not physically separated from one another, and many patrons cross the invisible boundaries throughout the night. Nevertheless, the structure I am about to describe provides a differentiated framework for modes of interaction. It is a floor plan only in the most obvious sense.

The diagram (page 79), Stages in The Columbia Tavern, needs only the briefest explanation. Entering the double doors from the street, the bar and more than a score of stools are immediately to the right. At the far end of the bartender's working area, there is a cubbyhole that serves as an office where the owner's wife (who is there far more frequently than her husband and who seems to make all managerial decisions) interviews prospective employees and takes care of the books. An aisle of bare flooring, no more than five feet wide, separates the "bar stage" from the "table stage," where there are ten tables, an assortment of folding aluminum chairs, an L-shaped vinyl bench beneath the sidewalk windows (Miss Rose's territory) and one that is smaller but equally tattered at the opposite end of the room near the entrance to the urinals. The jukebox stands against the wall near the sidewalk bench, the cigarette machine at the far end of the aisle. From the center of the table stage, moving to the left, three steps lead up to the poolroom through an open archway. There are two pool tables, the usual racks for cues, and vinyl-covered benches against three sides of the room. The wall between the archway entrance and the sidewalk has been opened to provide an uninterrupted view from barside across the entire width of the tavern. The rest rooms (Ladies' and Men's) are at the same elevation as the poolroom. Three steps lead up to them from the far end of the table area. They are side-by-side, and in front of them there is space enough for one table and six chairs.

This is an adequate description of the formal divisions of space. My purpose now is to relate them to the choreography.

The rest rooms are obviously utilitarian, and throughout the night there is a constant back-and-forth procession between them and the other tavern areas. There is, however, a difference between them, one so plainly visible that I don't know why I did not notice it until I had been going to the tavern for several months. The "Ladies' " john has a door that shuts it off from the "public" spaces; the "Men's" is open. One can see into it from almost any place along the bar or at the tables. The cracked enamel trough urinal, with its cakes of disinfectant and floating cigarette butts, is concealed by an angle of the wall, and the single sit-down stall has a door; but the stall faces the open entrance, and, since the door does not extend to the floor, it is relatively easy to see when it is occupied (from the visibility of shoes and dropped trousers) and whether there is more than one person inside it.

The "Men's" john is a smelly place. Even the cakes of crystalline disinfectant do little to obscure the odor of urine in the unflushed trough where disintegrating cigarettes cloud the liquid with meandering yellow and brownish dyes. Against one wall a dirt-encrusted commercial dispenser offers measured shots of the cheapest colognes for those who have the necessary dime. The walls are painted in "institutional green" and badly need a thorough scrubbing. Curiously, however, there is an almost total absence of the sexual graffiti so common in other men's toilets. On one wall someone has scrawled in pencil: "Fuck all Queers." It has been there as long as I have been visiting the tavern; but apart from this single anonymous message, there are no telephone numbers and self-advertisements for the size of one's penis and sexual preferences. The toilets in homosexual taverns seem to have far less of such graffiti than their heterosexual counterparts, far less, for example, than the urinals at Port City University, where among the limericks and terse expletives one may also read anonymous chronicles that begin with someone's expression of sexual need and proceed through reply and counter response to an assignation. Such elliptical advances are not necessary in The Columbia, where the obvious homosexual atmosphere reduces their effectiveness either as a form of erotic catharsis or as clandestine invitations. Quite likely, the single scrawl in the Men's john came from the hand of an outraged straight.

The openness of the "Men's" john is a bow toward police obsession with tearoom activities. It does not stem from the management's moral disapproval of fellatio or masturbation but is, rather, a simple if not entirely successful form of insurance. City police check the tavern frequently, but their presence seems to be prompted by The Columbia's reputation for roughness rather than responding to its known sexuality. Nevertheless, the "police presence" dictates some management precautions. All but one of the bartenders are gay and, as far as I know, do not object to tearoom trading; but they are instructed to discourage it. From their work station they cannot see the trough urinal, but the half-door stall is plainly visible. If it is occupied by two people, the bartenders often go there immediately to end the encounter, standing in front of the entrance until the occupants have rearranged their trousers and leave. But at the peak of activity on crowded nights it is difficult for them to be constantly alert to the enforcement of urinal rules. Occasionally, customers tip them off to violations, not because they disapprove but because they have other proprietary interests in ensuring that the police do not step up their surveillance.

Despite precautions, however, sexual acts occur in the "Men's" rest room. Upon returning to barside from the urinal, companions commonly demand: "What have you been doing in there; what took you so

Stages in The Columbia Tavern

Diagram 1

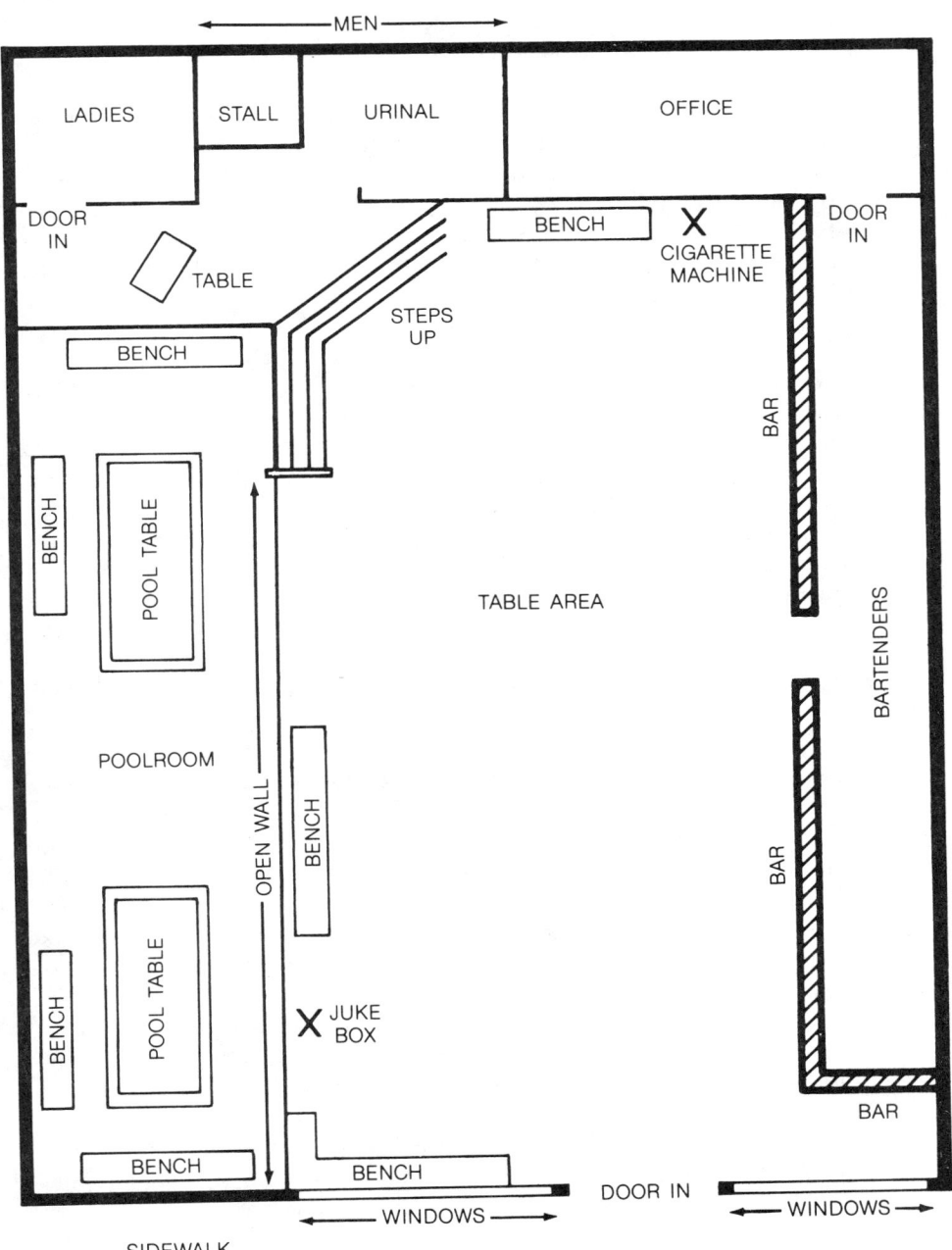

fucking long?," their good-humored quizzing expressing not only the understandings of "tearoom lore" generally but also acknowledging the more limited role of the rest room in the tavern's sexuality. Hustlers use it occasionally to proposition a possible client, usually someone who is not a regular and whose appearance suggests that he may be able and willing to pay for sex. "Denny," who is almost a duplication of Clint—a tall young "cowboy" from the cigarette advertisements—has spent the best part of an hour leaning against the partition between the poolroom and the other tavern stages, a station from where he can view and be viewed by most customers. Denny also displays a gimmick similar to the penis tattooed on Clint's kneecap: a faded, bleached-out circle on the inside of one leg of his jeans which is intended to arouse erotic speculation on the length and thickness of his penis. Having chosen a possible score, he follows the prospective client to the john, stands beside him at the trough, unzips and extends his cock to its full unerect length. "Jeez I'm horny," he says. "Look at this fucking bastard! Man, I've gotta get my rocks off."

It is not unusual for the hustler, at this stage of propositioning, to produce a viewing hard, either alone or by encouraging his prospective score to do it. The likelihood that other customers may interrupt the action does not cause embarrassment or attempts to conceal it; indeed, the "score's" readiness to fondle the hustler does not necessarily imply an intention to make a paying arrangement, for similar trough-side activities are often merely spur-of-the-minute forms of exhibitionism between men who are drunk or "high" on some other substance. People who interrupt the action sometimes stay to watch or to participate—with much ribald commentary—by taking turns in working on an exhibited penis; more rarely—and it seems to be related to the lateness of the hour—the bystanders encourage the principals to go all the way to the climax of orgasm. This, however, is quite unusual in the urinal. It is contrary to management rules, and, since these are more often honored than breached, it is generally understood that sex occurs off the premises. Urinal activities involving exhibitionism and masturbation resemble closely their adolescent group counterparts, and like those that take place in the stall, may be summarily stopped if the management gets wind of them.

The urinal also has a role in the more generalized game of tricking. The small trough—no more than eight feet long—lends itself to voyeurism and to side-by-side attempts to pursue a mutual interest that may have been initiated by the exchange of eye signals in other parts of the tavern. Most men using the urinal, however, tend to move to opposite ends of the trough, preserving a spatial separation that seems to be characteristic of male behavior in rest rooms generally.* The ascription of an asexual bonding to relationships between men contributes to the camaraderie of the locker room, the nude parading and side-by-side showering, and, incidentally, to the customary physical arrangement of urinals, which are not merely biologically functional but also tend to discount any reason for man-to-man modesty. But if anyone wished to take the time, observations of urinal behavior would most likely show that except on crowded occasions men tend to leave one or more spaces between one another when using a public toilet. The chosen distance—and I suspect that urinals, excepting the trough type, are arranged in multiples that tend to respond to it—probably reflects the general uneasiness of Americans when they are forced into close spatial relationships with strangers; but the selected separation may also express the fear of homosexuality that is attributed to American men. The genesis of an anxiety which is virtually a dogma of psychiatry is not important; it is simply enough to note that the "lore of urinals" reinforces the suspicions of those who are threatened by homosexuality, and, obviously, facilities for the general public—where there is nothing similar to the bonding of members of a club or some other fraternal association—present a high probability of sexual affront.

"Urinal anxiety"—to give a label to very diffuse male attitudes and behaviors—is probably not the most important factor behind the observed tendency for The Columbia's patrons to preserve a customary distance between themselves and others who are using the trough. This does not mean that all the members of its population are untroubled by sexual identification. All the "Kings" who refuse to "kiss above the waist" are clearly—like so many young male prostitutes (Lloyd, 1976, p. 11)—attempting to preserve some vestiges of normative sexuality, but the homoerotic possibilities of the urinal aren't basically "threatening." Everyone knows and accepts the fact that the urinal is often used for sexual purposes, and those who keep their distance from one another are probably signalling their present lack of interest or unavailability—because they are already paired—rather than any fear of affront. Men in full drag costume enter it freely, their known masquerade giving them the license to take part in the opportunities for voyeurism and propositioning.

Of all the tavern's stages, the rest room is the most distasteful to me. It isn't only a matter of the smell—the dirty walls and unflushed trough—

---

*See Elliott Oring, "From Uretics to Uremics: A Contribution toward the Ethnography of Peeing," in *Culture, Curers, and Contagion,* ed. Norman Klein, Chandler & Sharp Publishers, Inc., 1979.

nor it is a morally disapproving reaction. I see nothing inherently wrong with tearoom activity or its counterpart in The Columbia. Moreover, possible affront to an unsuspecting public is absolutely minimal, far less than in the tearooms of public parks. Ultimately, my distaste is an aesthetic rather than a moral rejection. The sexuality of the rest room is the keynote of the tavern, but on the other stages it is orchestrated in more richly varied ways, often in a minor key or embedded in a ritualism that qualifies its surface implications.

The barside stage is not only the most open of the tavern's spaces but the action associated with it is also the most fluid and varied. Superficially, it is little different from a multitude of heterosexual bars, and friends who have persuaded me to take them there have often remarked with a hint of disappointment: "It's only a low-class tavern." Their judgment may be justified by a cursory appraisal of the entire setting; but from the beginning I think I may have seen and heard a little more than they perceived.

This is not a claim to a greater degree of sensitivity and perceptiveness; rather, it was due to the fact that when with them we sat invariably on the table stage, a space on which some degree of territorial privacy and exclusiveness is ascribed to those who occupy it. The conspicuous isolation of sitting alone at a table embarrassed me, and I chose the bar as my vantage point, not because I felt there was anything special about it but simply because it was easier to lose myself in the crowd of strangers; and inadvertently I had chosen the place from where it was possible to observe most of the elements in the tavern's style.

The bartenders' space on the stage is organized quite conventionally. The floor behind the bar is raised a few inches above the level of the main room, providing a minimal advantage for viewing the activity within the entire tavern. All but one of those who work the bar (in two shifts extending from 8:00 am to 2:00 am on the following day) are gay. The only straight bartender has a background similar to that of most customers—constant movement from one unskilled or semiskilled blue-collar job to another interspersed with periods of unemployment. He has been schooled in the mores of the streets, and he knows the homosexual scene. Presumably, the management would not employ him if he had any moralistic objections to the style, but his attitude seems to have nothing to do with mere job-keeping acquiescence. When questioned about it outside the tavern, his replies are as matter-of-fact, as accepting and nonjudging as those of most straight regulars, and, while he is on his shift, he uses the same sexually inverted language as the customers, though I have never seen him engage in any more physically familiar interaction.

Contrastively, the younger gay bartenders are not only cruised and propositioned by some customers but on their to-and-fro progress with drinks between the various stages they also respond to passing groping with complementary suggestive action. Occasionally, too, they put on a show behind the bar. The owners' office contains an assortment of funny feminine hats, out-of-style attic relics found in skid-row junk shops. They are tattered and dirty, sad reminders of some brief and distant time when they may have been worn to church, to an Easter Parade, or some other celebration requiring the public exhibition of new finery. In their present archaic state they are a comic commentary on the tavern's lack of social pretensions and on attitudes toward the more serious drag scene. Late in the evening, the gay bartenders may wear them on their job, supplementing the incongruous effect with exaggerated and campy mannerisms.

At barside, the observer is confronted immediately with behavior that requires a reexamination of conventional attitudes. Words like "faggot," "queer," and "whore" are used with a casualness that only only belies their defamatory implications but also runs counter to some of the propaganda of gay activists, who, for example, take particular umbrage at "faggot," citing its etymological derivation from the firebrands used in witch burnings and its connotations of punishment for purportedly unnatural acts. Their crusade is similar, of course, to that of black objections to "nigger" and to those of other ethnic minorities to slurring and demeaning epithets; and to the liberal who tries to be neither racist nor sexist, the tabooed words do not come easily to the tongue or ear. It is startling—even an affront—when a black man commenting on a party he attended remarks: "Jeez, there were a lot of pretty niggers!" And similarly one is caught off-balance when men refer to one another as faggot or queer. In fact, the casual and familiar use of such words is the first introduction to the "outside-inside" understandings of the style.

Putting language aside for the moment, however, the activity on the barside stage encompasses a continuum between extremes of involvement and noninvolvement.

The small, round space of a barstool may become a private territory if its occupant turns his back to the room and faces the bartenders' working area. The position does not prevent attempts at intrusion by those who sit on either side or pass up and down behind him, but it limits interaction and is favored characteristically by drunks and people (also often drunk) who are immersed in some immediate personal crisis. "Manny" is retired and an alcoholic who lives alone in one of the better "Clean Bed" hotels. He appears at the tavern soon after it opens to the public at 8:00 am and is there intermittently throughout the remainder of the day and night, hunched over the bar, withdrawn, his pale blue eyes becoming more watery as he sinks farther into his depression. He is a regular and other regulars sometimes put a hand to his shoulder as they pass, causing him to turn his head and give them a struggling look of recognition; but no one except the daytime bartenders imposes upon his isolation by trying to talk to him. On the other hand, "Chatty Kathy" uses the barside back-to-the-room position when he wishes to unburden himself to a possibly sympathetic ear at an adjacent stool. He is relatively young (early thirties) and seems to proceed from one emotional crisis to another, put-upon both by employers and a family (including a discarded wife and child) which has disinherited him, asking him, for example, not to attend his grandmother's funeral. Kathy's exophthalmic eyes well and his voice begins to break embarrassingly as he says: "She reared me. She looked after me. All I wanted to do was look at her in her coffin. I didn't want to make a scene. I could've scrounged the bus fare, but my elder sister said 'Stay away! No one wants you here.' And there she is—poor grandma laid to rest. Jeez, they're all bastards!" His eyes overflow. "I've never had anyone who cared for me. Only grandma. And that shitty crowd didn't give a fuck. They wouldn't let me say good-bye and tell her I loved her."

Three very simple diagrams illustrate the most commonly observed forms of interaction and communication between barside back-to-the-room customers. The first of them (Diagram 2) refers to the most private and isolating use of barside back-to-the-room space. The prototypical example is the "Manny" case, though people who aren't alcoholics may also use it according to its passing utility as a response to moods of rejection and unworthiness. It tends to limit contact to across-the-bar interaction with the bartenders who, however, are more disposed or able to respond with advice and sympathy during the daytime hours rather than at night. Participation in anything occurring in the remainder of the room is completely minimal, but the chosen isolation is accepted and respected by others; and even while removed from it, the individual is in a familiar place, a place where the background sounds and movements link him to something other than himself, making him, in a curiously paradoxical way, at home. Loneliness is reduced because he is permitted to be alone. He has staked out his right to it either for temporary or more fundamental reasons and knowingly recognizes that he can be both a participant and nonparticipant. The very conventions of the tavern include a nonjudging recognition of the need for personal solitude and cues that indicate when someone does not want to be bothered. Isolation may not only be sought and achieved but is also accepted; and folk-images of the lonely barside lush are minimally applicable to everyone

"Back-to-the-Room" Seated Barside Positions

Diagram 2   SOLO

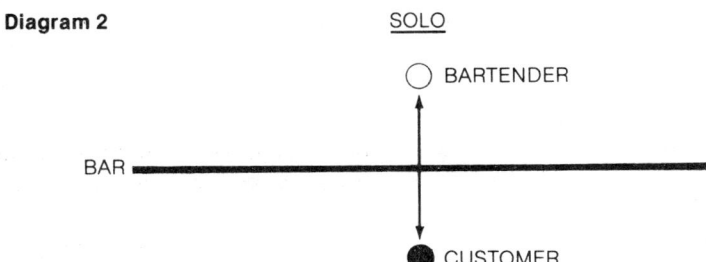

In the "solo," customer interaction tends to be limited to the bartender. It is often a position chosen by those who wish to be alone."

Diagram 3   DYAD

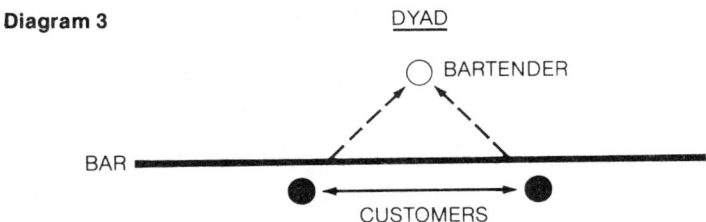

Intensive interaction between two customers that limits "intrusion" from others.

Diagram 4   TRIAD

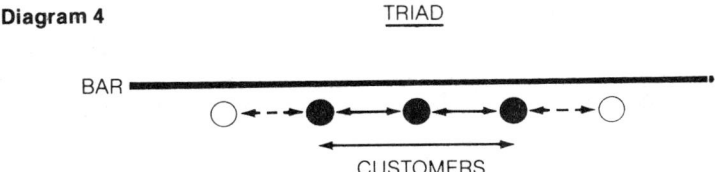

Those who form a "triad" are often less intensively involved with one another than the members of a "dyad." Either of the customers on the "boundaries" of the "triad" may interact with other customers who are seated beside them, perhaps forming a "dyad" or joining another "triad." Members of a "triad are more "open" to various kinds of "intrusion" from other customers than the members of a "dyad."

who on occasion chooses to limit his territorial interaction to the service personnel on the opposite side of the bar. When someone becomes obviously too drunk, the bartenders may protect him and, indirectly, the tavern by refusing further service. Regular patrons rarely object to the denial, which is authoritative but sympathetic, markedly different in quality from the brusque ejection of down-and-outers who stagger in from the street. Indeed, the isolated drinker, enmeshed in his solitary problems, tends to welcome being cut off as a sign that someone cares for him.

Diagram 3 illustrates a back-to-the-room form of interaction in which a dyad of customers is territorially isolated from others on the barside stage. There is minimal across-the-bar communication, merely intermittent requests for service. The casual intrusion of "outsiders" frequently breaches the privacy of those occupying adjacent stools; but such overtures, even when the intruder is a friend or acquaintance, may be rejected merely by maintaining the basic position and responding with an across-the-shoulder remark. The position itself is a cue that privacy is expected, and the need may be underscored by a pointed refusal to introduce a companion to someone who has butted in.

A range of purposes is served. There are people like Chatty Kathy who from time to time need to unburden themselves to a sympathetic ear, not, as a rule, just any convenient stranger but someone who is known to them but not involved in their outside lives. A degree of anonymity is preserved, since the confessing person knows it is most unlikely that he will see his confidant in any extra-tavern situation. For the most part they know one another by first name only and even the most personal revelations remain essentially impersonal. This, however, is a sought-after protection. It allows release while minimizing judgment. Self-esteem is not threatened by the suspicion that what you say will become common knowledge; and even if gossip (which cannot be discounted entirely) does disseminate it more widely, there are few ripples; for no one is supposed to *know* too much about anyone.

Side-by-side privacy suits the advances and subsequent maneuvers of tricking and sexual hustling. If someone looking for a trick or a score notices a vacant stool next to a likely prospect he may use it as his opening gambit, following his move by attempting to begin a conversation or by a direct proposition. Propositioning is often quite bald-faced, but seemingly blatant advances may be misinterpreted through unfamiliarity with the joking and expressive banter of customers who have no sexual interest in one another. Even more subtle approaches such as suggestive positioning to display a basket or a hand whose fingers draw attention to an outlined penis are not the exclusive stock-in-trade of the hustler; they are also used with humorous intent in other contexts. Moreover, any advances, sexual or merely friendly, may be rebuffed if the person approached wants no interaction with anyone except the service personnel.

The members of an established dyad, however, tend to be left alone. Even off-the-street cadgers seldom intrude on them, possibly because the turned backs are themselves a barrier to an activity that requires face-to-face interaction. The cadger must present himself and his request in a more physically intrusive manner than when sidling up to standing patrons, and the risk of rejection is increased by possible irritation at the interruption. The most common response is a curt across-the-shoulder refusal, though the cadger occasionally succeeds when his score, without turning, reaches into his pocket and hands the pesterer a dime. I cannot say whether this perfunctory gesture is more personally demeaning than the questions the cadger may have to endure before a standing customer decides to comply with or to refuse an identical request. Cadgers are inured to the stigma of habitual insolvency, and allowing the potential score to play with them is a fair enough return if it produces the desired result. It is part of the game.

The cues that two people at adjacent stools constitute a dyad proceed from their back-to-the-room position through observations of other behavioral characteristics. Except for those who are close enough to overhear them, it is virtually impossible for anyone to know why they are engrossed in one another. Whether their self-selected separation represents a sexual attraction, is related to some domestic problem, or to one of the many other threads in the tavern's fabric are merely matters of sometimes interested conjecture. The point, however, is that the position is chosen by those who wish to limit their interaction with others within the public space. They use it as an assertion of private territorial rights.

At first glance, Diagram 4 appears to be no more than a variation of this pattern. Once again it depicts a back-to-the-room use of space, but it involves a triad; and the increase in number as well as the inevitable extension of physical boundaries alters the model of Diagram 3 both functionally and qualitatively.

There are some transactions—even sexual ones—that are private but involve more than two people. Most of these, however, are initiated within a dyad: the third person, who may be waiting in some other part of the tavern, is called in only when his particular service or knowledge is needed. Diagram 4 does not include such arrangements. Characteristically, the goals of communication are general rather than specific—an exchange of convivial pleasantries, joking, and innocuous conversation that reflects the basic homosexual tone of the tavern. Confidences of a

more serious and personal kind are generally resisted because they defeat
the aim of keeping it light. The objective is to socialize with strangers or
acquaintances.

The triads are mostly passing and temporary, seldom resulting in relationships that continue or progress outside the setting. The tavern is not
a profitable place in which to seek or pursue the more enduring ends of
friendship. Telephone numbers and addresses are exchanged, but in most
cases the transaction is a formality having little to do with any intent to
follow up with a new acquaintance. "Outside" and "inside" are kept
apart.

The typical seated, barside triad may have peripheral connections
with adjacent groups of the same kind, and on occasion it may split as
one or other of the men on the spatial boundaries becomes more intensively involved with an immediate neighbor, proceeding to establish
with him a relationship similar to Diagram 3. It is usually quite apparent
to other members of the group that one of their number has withdrawn
to pursue more personal or specific ends. They do not resent it. The lore
of tricking legitimizes withdrawal when the opportunity occurs.

The model relationships of Diagrams 3 and 4 overlap in fluctuations
of barside interaction but the interdigitation does not encompass the
entire length of the bar; rather, it produces changing enclaves defined by
spatial proximity. There is, however, a convention that overrides such
territorial boundaries. Drinks may be exchanged from one end of the bar
to the other. For the most part, the practice is little more than a recognition of acquaintance within the tavern. It is a gesture having almost no
relevance to outside interaction and does not necessarily result in any
closer contact, though when strangers are involved it may be employed
as an opening gambit in the game of tricking. At "happy hour" or
"buddy hour" times, when the price of drinks is reduced, unsolicited
glasses of beer multiply in front of the barside customers, their number
testifying to acquaintanceships—and perhaps a degree of popularity—as
well as repayments for prior favors; but it is essentially a distant gesture,
requiring no more than a nod of recognition to the purchaser.

Stool-and-barside sitting takes on an entirely different character if a
customer faces the room rather than the bartenders' area; this is tantamount to a declaration of openness—an invitation to intrusion from any
interested person on the principal stages.

In the room-fronting position, a patron is readily approached by
cadgers, hustlers, and standing drinkers. It suits the sexual hustler who is
hoping to score, providing an opportunity not only to case the company
but also to be seen by potential clients. While many sexual propositions
are quite direct and often initiated by a hustler, some encounters are

arranged with greater indirection. The hustler at the bar presents himself in a way that implies an invitation in the homosexual setting, sitting with parted legs and the toes of his boots tucked under the lower rung of the stool, a position that displays his crotch to best advantage. In some other bars there are special areas—a bench or a section of barside space—where hustlers sit in a similar frontal manner like members of a stag line. The Columbia does not have a "meat rack," as these enclaves are often called; but the end of viewing and of being viewed is served by facing the room; it carries at least a presumption of availability that may be verified by an exchange of eye signals over different stages. Not all of the resulting encounters, however, involve hustler and paying clients, for the position is also suited to the activities of cruising as well as the merely convivial ends of interacting with strangers or tavern acquaintances as they enter from the street or move downstage from poolroom and urinal to the tables or bar.

There are always people on the barside stage who prefer to stand and to move up and down behind the seated customers. The mobility suits the cadger as he bums his way down the line from the door; and since again there is some presumption that those who stand are approachable (not necessarily in parties), movement serves the ends of cruising by allowing strangers to make contact. It isn't always sexually directed, however. Often it is merely visiting—to exchange a few words or to engage in badinage and pantomimes with acquaintances.

On crowded nights, the flux of standing barside interaction contributes greatly to the impression of freewheeling chaos, but even an uninstructed first-time visitor must notice a contrast between the standing action and the more static behavior of those who sit at tables or who front the bar on stools. The ritualized and extended verbal games and tactile pantomimes are generally played by people who stand on the barside stage. For full effectiveness the former require a face-to-face, toe-to-toe standing confrontation as contestants hurl their insults back and forth, and they also need an audience, which is provided by other standees who are close enough to hear and appreciate the verbal ingenuities and who are present at the "kill." Most of the violence—the fisticuffs and wrestling—is also begun by standing patrons, only rarely by people who are sitting side by side. The "genuine" confrontation is easily distinguished from the ritualized contest. A raised level of voice is characteristic of both, but in the "real" argument the subject matter is more personal and private, amounting to an exposure of festering differences and antipathies that may have originated in the tavern setting (and may be confined to it) but that often relate to the details of a deteriorating relationship in outside contexts. The words are harsh. They are meant to

wound, to strike home, to express and to provoke anger, and concomi-
tant attitudes and facial expressions are intensified and emotionally
overheated replications of minor stylistic elements associated with the
ritual games; but the games and the genuine confrontations tend to occur
in the same barside space and commence in the same posture.

There are multiple levels of action and communication on the barside
stage. Certain positions, however, are more congenial for the prosecution of some goals. The goals, both with respect to content and concentration upon a given person or persons, change frequently; and except
for the solitary drinker, people tend to move from one position to
another. Moreover, some of the ends engaging the barside actors are not
peculiar to that stage; yet the choreography is significantly different from
interaction in other parts of the tavern.

Like barstools, the ten tables are spatial subdivisions of a more inclusive area that tend to become the territories of those who occupy them.
They are more noticeably separated from one another than the stools,
their demarcations by little aisles encouraging a groupishness, a cliquish-
ness, that contrasts with the more flexible encounters at the bar. Very
few people seem to choose to sit alone at tables; even when the barside is
crowded and all the stools occupied, empty tables are avoided by customers who enter alone from the sidewalk. Occasionally, having obtained
his beer from the bar, a patron will sit alone at a table observing the
action; but the odds are that he is waiting for someone he has arranged to
meet. Drunks also flop down at tables, where they sit with lowered heads
and arouse themselves now and then to accost some standing or passing
customer. "Hey, fella!" they say thickly. "Wanna suck, wanna fuck?,"
receiving, as a rule, a disparaging across-the-shoulder glance that is
sometimes accompanied by a terse verbal dismissal: "Fuck youself,
man!"

Like all the tavern's stages, the activity of the table area includes
cruising. Men in full drag tend to sit at the tables, possibly because it is
more ladylike and offers a handy place to lay down a purse and to repair
face makeup under the downward glare of the ceiling lights. Some drag
queens favor the table placed between the "Men's" and "Ladies' " rest
rooms where it is necessary for any man to pass them on his way to the
john. It does not seem, however, that the transvestite is often successful
in attracting a sexual partner. Though the impersonation is accepted
without distaste, it tends to provoke a joking response rather than
serious sexual interest.

Cruising on the table stage tends to be less direct than at barside,
where the back-and-forth flow of standing customers encourages close
face-to-face encounters. On the table stage, sexual interest is transmitted

mainly by eye signals from one part of the tavern to another. If the nonverbal advance does not meet with an obvious rebuff, the initiator may move to a chair where his prospective trick is sitting; but an element of uncertainty and the possibility of misinterpretation are always evident. Perhaps there is a degree of inherent ambiguity in the transmission of eye signals even in a setting where the sexual search is an acceptable goal; but there are also other hazards in approaching the members of table-sitting groups.

Table groups tend to be more closed than the barside enclaves. Characteristically, they comprise people who have come to the tavern together or who have been together at some earlier part of the evening and have arranged to meet there later. Some of them are already paired or "married," though the groups usually include some "singles" who may be approachable. From a distance, however, it is difficult for the hustler or person looking who is cruising to know whether the individual who seems to give a positive answer to eye signals is really available or merely flirting. To assume it is the former and to follow through with a direct approach may produce a self-righteous rebuff if the prospective trick does not want his current partner to know he has been showing interest in some other person. Persistence under these circumstances may result in angry injunctions that the intruder "Get lost, man!" or in threats of physical violence.

The stranger who intrudes on a table-sitting group cannot know his precise reception in advance. No invitation is necessary to take an unoccupied barstool or to move among the standing customers; but even where there are empty chairs at a table, it is necessary to receive some sign of acceptance from at least one of those already seated, and even if this is given it does not follow that a relationship is established with other members of the group. Perfunctory introductions (first name only) are usually exchanged, and the lore of cruising sanctions the approach; but there is always the possibility of meeting some resentment, even if it is no more than an aloof withdrawal from those who feel that the privacy of their circle has been violated. Indeed, such subtle forms of exclusion may be used against an intruder although his advances seem to be acceptable to a "single" member of the group. If an individual is sexually unattached, he should be allowed to take advantage of the opportunities presented; there should be no criticism. But the "single" individual who introduces a stranger to a table has, in a sense, destroyed its temporary but visible unity. The newcomer is watched from the sidelines by members of the group who are not directly involved, their inner judgments—sometimes expressed outside the tavern—ranging from dislike for the intruder to reflections on the taste of the friend who

responded positively to his advances. "Doing one's own thing" is qualified when it involves others who because of their chosen seating may be
presumed to have some proprietary interest in one another.

The proprietary interest is not necessarily sexual. As I have said, it
may represent no more than a spur-of-the-moment decision to transfer a
private gathering to a public locale; and there are sometimes ties related
to the illegal activities of selling pills, "grass," and "hot" merchandise.
While all these transactions are accepted components of the style, they
are necessarily undercover, and the relative privacy of a table suits nego-
tiations between vendor and buyer. Some known pushers (sometimes a
heterosexual couple) sit invariably at tables where they may be joined by
an assortment of clients whose purposes range from arranging a sale to
asking for extended credit on an unpaid debt or merely recognizing
someone who is a reliable source for meeting certain needs.

Like the toilets, the poolroom is obviously functional in the sense that
it is a facility offered to those who play the game. The opportunity to
play pool (like the opportunity to dance in other taverns) is an important
attraction for some customers. "Intramural" competitions are held from
time to time, and there is an annual event in which the winners and
runners-up meet in contest with their opposite numbers from a tavern
two blocks from The Columbia. Most of the tavern's patrons, however,
do not play; the activities in the poolroom replicate in a different setting
those observed on other stages.

Pool is a masculine game, almost as closely identified with maleness as
some more violent contact sports. In affluent nineteenth-century homes
the billiard room was virtually a male preserve to which men retreated
after the ladies had withdrawn. This sanctuary, even in highly respectable houses, had a locker-room quality, being a place where men could
discuss together matters that were not supposed to concern the women-
folk upstairs and where, too, polite restrictions on the use of language in
mixed company could be relaxed. Ladies were sometimes admitted in a
patronizing and indulgent manner—allowed to try their skill, under
protective tutelage, at a masculine mystery. But it was no more than
temporary visiting privileges to an exclusive club. Public pool halls also
gathered an unsavory reputation for violence, gambling, and other
probable associations with the underworld.

The Columbia's poolroom is a visual reproduction of many seen in
gangland movies. Its quality is eminently masculine, despite the
transvestites sitting in the gallery—the vinyl benches against the
walls—or playing the tables. Behavior is not modified at all in the
presence of transvestites, whether in the poolroom or on any other stage,
though coarse language and sexual aggressiveness are disapproved and

discouraged in person-to-person interaction with the known straight women who are introduced occasionally by a regular customer. Transvestites don't qualify for any conventional male-to-female niceties of treatment and consideration, not even to the protection of the moral umbrella that is supposed to secure women against physical assault or retaliation.

"Pool hustlers"—including a few in drag—work the poolroom, playing for stakes of a few dollars. It is quite unlikely that The Columbia provides them with any kind of living, but there are always some suckers who are willing to challenge them. Win or lose, it is ego-satisfying to face a known master before an audience, and the pool hustlers take full advantage of the hubris.

The poolroom is probably the closest approximation to a "meat rack" in the tavern. Many members of the gallery are more interested in appraising the players than in the games in progress at the tables. Sexual fantasies are fed by the posturing, cowboy-booted men who bend over the baize rectangles displaying (not always unwittingly) a provocative length of leg and lean asses. Comments in the gallery are similar to those in public heterosexual territories where men who are sitting together cruise the female customers. The display of male flesh is a main attraction, but otherwise the remarks are essentially the same: "Jeez, will you look at that basket!" or "That guy's really hung!" Some players add a deliberate filip to the voyeurism by the conspicuous absence of underclothes or gimmicks similar to the faded spot on the inside thigh of "Denny's" jeans. There is often skepticism, however, that such attention-getting devices represent a discoverable reality. "Oh, shit!" the benchline observers say, "the guy isn't hung that great."

For those who are cruising and those who are hustling, the poolroom has an advantage over the other stages. It is far less crowded than the bar and less groupish than the tables. The players may be viewed from almost all positions in the tavern, and the accepted "manly" interest in the game allows people to leave companions to follow a new interest in a way that is often less threatening than a positive response to a more direct proposition. It is not that sex dominates the activity of the poolroom to the exclusion of any other motives or satisfactions. Sex, however, is the warp of the tavern's style, whether it is expressed in a deliberate search—and this is certainly a motive for some customers on any given night—or in merely being in a "company" where it is unnecessary to dissemble or to conceal a basic ingredient of experience.

The tavern's spatial subdivisions—its "formal structures"—"choreograph" the behavior of its customers at every hour. Even though the boundaries are frequently obscured in the flux of nighttime action, they exist as a paradigm to be used according to need, offering opportunities for different kinds and intensities of interaction. Except for the urinal, the management makes little attempt to enforce any rules; yet there are rules of a kind that are understood and generally respected by most of the clientele. Movement from one stage to another usually signifies a change in immediate goal-direction, replacing a particular kind and quality of interaction with one that is substantially different. It is seldom possible to extrapolate from "stage position" to precise motive, but the positions themselves are cues that either restrict or promote intrusion. The person who "settles nowhere"—who goes from stage to stage throughout the night—is often thought to be "pushy" or "showing off"; for although anyone—excepting off-the-street beggars and drunks—should be allowed the full range of options in using the tavern's stages, those who are conspicuously "rootless" can be accused of "coming on too strong." Their behavior breaches a decorum that includes a willingness to "socialize" and to respect the rights that others have established by the positions they have chosen.

The patterning of interaction by stage location is part of the "reality" the tavern's social order has for its customers; but my description is necessarily oversimplified. Studies of social structure focus principally upon basic rules and abstracted repetitive patterns that are embellished or embroidered differently by different individuals. Even within the boundaries of a single tradition, people always move idiosyncratically, the most conformist of them expressing a persona that isn't reproduced precisely by any other member of the population. The full "reality" of The Columbia's social order has to include the personae of its patrons, and this is at best a risky business better suited to the creative talents of the novelist than to the less vivid and less empathetic reporting of the generalizing disciplines. Yet there is a sense in which the tavern's population share a "collective persona"—a world view that reflects their awareness of their separation or exclusion from the normative value system. Using Durkheimian terminology, they share with one another elements of a "collective consciousness" which, in this case, is the consciousness of stigmatization—of the biographical blemishes associated with the sexual and other variables I noted earlier and of the myths in which they are presented to the straight world: to those who, ultimately, are held responsible for perpetuating the exclusion.

In the tavern, the common understandings of the disvalued "collective persona" are expressed and intensified through the ritualized use of language and exaggerated pantomimes—rituals that adopt the most common elements of the "straight myths" but bend them in ways that are wry and in-group commentaries on the truth values they are supposed to contain. The myth becomes the "myth" that is ritually enacted.

FOUR

The Hall of Mirrors (1)

In *Sexual Politics,* Kate Millet (1971, p. 17) provides me with a useful introduction to the ritualized behaviors of The Columbia when she says of Jean Genet's male homosexual characters:

> Because of the perfection with which they ape the "masculine" and the "feminine" of heterosexual society [they] represent the best contemporary insight into its constitution and beliefs. [They] have unerringly penetrated to the essence of what heterosexual society imagines to be the character of "masculine" and "feminine," and which it mistakes for the nature of male and female, thereby preserving the traditional relation of the sexes.

At first glance, the judgment seems to be supported by many male homosexual behaviors. Homosexual men who adopt the macho costuming of motorcycle gangs and use the "leather" bars and taverns as their public territories are clearly duplicating—though often also exaggerating—a cultural model of "masculinity," asserting a "manliness" that is popularly denied to them because of their basic "gender betrayal." Similarly, the "femmes," the "nellies," the transvestites, and the "drag queens" appear to be replicating cultural stereotypes of "femininity."

Millet's summary judgment also seems to be supported by the attitudes of some gay male organizations that promote people like Sergeant Leonard Matlovich—who felt that he should be allowed to continue his Air Force career even though he had openly admitted his own homosexuality—as their spokesmen while trying to limit their public connections with those who are most obviously "feminine." Their crusade to establish the "masculinity" of homosexual men is an understandable rejoinder to the most popular stereotypes, but, as I noted earlier, the emphasis placed upon "manly identification" tends to reinforce—to

95

"preserve"—the culturally entrenched dichotomy between "male" and "female" in the more inclusive sexual matrix. The displeasure or, at best, the grudging acceptance that "nellies" encounter in the more consciousness-raising organizations reflects the same concern to maintain customary and, therefore, "respectable" "male" and "female" role differentiations in everything except the sexual preference.

Millet's reading, however, is a superficial scanning of Genet, for his treatment of homosexuals is only one telling instance of a far more comprehensive vision of man in relationship to himself, to his society and culture. His *oeuvre*, as Martin Esslin (*The Theatre of the Absurd*, 1969, pp. 167 ff.) has said, is "concerned with [the] feeling of helplessness and solitude when confronted with the despair and loneliness of a man caught in the hall of mirrors of the human condition, inexorably trapped by an endless progression of images that are merely his own distorted reflection—lies covering lies, fantasies battering upon fantasies, nightmares nourished by nightmares within nightmares." (1967, p. 167) Genet's homosexual characters are not merely aping "masculine" and "feminine" role models; rather, they are commenting upon the "absurdity" of the models—ritually enacting and, at the same time, protesting the popular shibboleths of *les justes* and the shackling constraints of their "normative models of reality." The man in "the hall of mirrors" is "alienated man"—man caught in the back-and-forth reflections and refractions of what he *is*, or believes himself to be, and what society says he *is* or *ought* to be. Esslin summarizes Genet's four "prison prose poems"—in which the male homosexual theme is dominant—as "the erotic fantasies of a prisoner, the daydreams of a solitary outcast of society who is resolved to live up to the picture he feels society has imposed upon him." (1969, p. 169) The prison, however, though real enough in these works and in Genet's own experience, is not merely a place of stones and mortar and regimented punishment, for the "prison" is also the "stones and mortar" of cultural stereotypes and role assignments. "Prison" is a metaphor for society's bent to promote a particular definition of "reality" and to consign to "outcast" status those who deviate from its models.

The "hall of mirrors" is the "hall of culture"; for every cultural tradition provides only a selective, "economizing," and, therefore, "distorted" view of "human nature." Culture, as Freud (*The Future of an Illusion*, 1928) recognized, is an "artificial construct," the necessary basis for any viable—more or less self-perpetuating—way of life, but, nevertheless, an "imagined order" in possibly everything except the purely technological realm. Yet the "imagined order" is presented and transmitted as though it is *real*—as a *true* definition of human nature, human relationships, goals, and cosmic values from which one dissents only at some personal peril. "Existential man" is the man who is aware, however dimly, of the contradictions between his persona—his subjective "reality"—and the "prisoning" constraints of the "objective" models of "reality" that are proselytized by cultural tradition.

In Genet's works, it is culture itself that is "absurd," since it is only a shorthand transcription of a reality that escapes any final definition. The complex role exchanges of *The Maids* (Genet, 1954)—the transformations between Claire, Solange, and Madame—are not merely an example of the commonplace theatrical convention of mistaken identity but "a game of mirrors," a "kind of Black Mass," a ritual of alienation, of "frustration become flesh" (Esslin, 1969, p. 175), and the existential metaphor is underscored by Genet's original intention that men should play the female roles. Similarly, it is a superficial reading of his homosexual characters to regard them only as "unerring" reproductions of "masculine" and "feminine" role models, for, like the principals of *The Maids,* they are hieratic figures engaged in an existential ritual, acting out distortions of distortions, playing stereotypes of stereotypes and showing us the final mirror in which we see our own distorted images.

The entrance to the homosexual "hall of mirrors" is through cultural definitions of the nature of "male" and "female." Men and women are considered "unsexed" if they are sexually attracted to members of their own gender. Therefore, it follows—in popular ascription—that the "unsexed" male must be "passively feminine"—the "fairy"—and the "unsexed woman" must be "aggressively masculine"—the "bull dike." And the basic assumptions are extended to those who seem to "cross over" many traditional occupational boundaries. It is fair to say, for example, that most people question or withhold a final judgment on the sexuality of women who have been admitted to the academies of the armed services, as they also question the sexual identity of men who are comfortable in "servicing" and "nurturing" professions such as nursing. The opposed cultural poles of "male" and "female" assign a completely anomalous position to homosexuals of either gender, an anomaly that is "resolved" by attributing to them the characterological traits and interests of the opposite sex. The "cultural myth" of sexuality allows no other alternative.

On any visit to The Columbia, a straight visitor will see many examples of "feminine behavior." Tripp (1975, p. 171) defines effeminacy as: "Any style of male behavior that resembles the gestures, movements, or mannerisms usually associated with women." It is, as he says, "more frequent among homosexual than heterosexual males, [but] is relatively rare even in homosexuality." Despite its relative rareness, however, it is the most popular—the most generalized—heterosexual myth of male homosexuality, and since they expect it, most straight visitors to The Columbia will not only feel that their worst suspicions are confirmed by much of what they see and hear but will also overlook their "masculine" counterparts. There is no easy or ready-made way to accommodate the latter in the oversimplified myths of "gender betrayal" and gender identification.

I do not deny the "feminine motivation" of some homosexual men or that the adoption of some female role models sometimes expresses the dominance of a psychological disposition, but these are mostly errone-ous or at best simplistic explanations for many of the "female-like" behaviors of The Columbia's customers. Relatively few of them —"Tokyo Rose," "Susie Wong," "Marie," and some others—are close approximations of the "fairies" of popular ascriptions. The overriding quality of tavern interactions is "man-to-man," even when it is inter-action between man and transvestite. Male transsexuals—excepting only "Pocahontas," who is "married"—tend to be regarded with the slighting puzzlement they face in the straight world. They have "become" a member of the opposite gender, and certain symbolic elements in the charade of transvestism have been totally erased. The transsexual probably faces as much disapproval and rejection from the homosexual members of the gender he has "left" as from the heterosexual members of the gender he has "joined"; but despite the distaste for transvestites expressed by "Derek"—and more widely distributed in the male homo-sexual population—transvestites are men, a fact that is clearly recog-nized in The Columbia where—following the metaphor of the "hall of mirrors"—the quality of interaction with them is that of men who are playing to men who are playing as women; of men not only playing to reflections of what they themselves are supposed to be but also exaggerating—distorting—conventional elements of heterosexual male-to-female relationships and, thereby, commenting upon these models as well. Straight members of audiences at drag shows—particularly those produced primarily for homosexuals—miss these ritualized understand-ings and appreciations, seeing merely an impersonation that varies in its "faithfulness" (its skill) in reproducing a normative heterosexual model. The symbolic involutions—plainly revealed in the deliberately androgy-nous style of some performing troupes—are often lost to some male homosexuals as well, or if they are understood they are decried; but such disapproval is not a material refutation of my thesis.

Leaving aside for later development the transvestite component of tavern behaviors, the "meaning" I have ascribed to them can be applied to a much wider range of ritualized interactions that include some more or less commonplace linguistic usages and naming practices as well as thoroughly stylized verbal encounters that deserve to be called "rituals of stigmatization"—stylized enactments of and commentaries upon the "normative realities" of the world view of *les justes*. While the heterosexual myth of sexuality is the principal charter of the rituals, they also use other "outside" myths associated with the various additional stigmata that are existential realities for most of The Columbia's population. The following transcription of a verbal ritual serves not only to introduce the general style but will also lead me into a broader consideration of the ritualized use of language. Furthermore, it will allow me to show some ethnic contrasts. While I have left out many passages in the original encounter, the condensed transcription preserves those that are most important.

It is a crowded Saturday night in the tavern. All the stools at the bar are occupied, and most of the tables have been taken. "King" is playing pool with "Witch Hazel," an emaciated man in his late sixties who was a pool hustler in his younger days, earning enough by his trade to keep himself and his older lover—who had brought him out when he was fifteen—as they travelled round the southern and midwestern parts of the country. Because of his recognized skill, "Witch Hazel" is not allowed to play in the tavern's intramural competitions, and he doesn't hustle for money any longer. He is usually dressed in an ambiguous style of drag—black, low-heeled shoes and knee socks and a tartan skirt that could pass as a kilt; a white shirt-blouse and wide-brimmed straw hat or a variety of tam-o'-shanters. When he is on the streets, his long gray hair is coiled under his headgear, but as soon as he enters The Columbia he takes off his hat, shakes his hair loose, and combs it in front of the mirrors behind the bar. The long, gray frame for his yellowed and deeply lined face fits his sobriquet.

The usual gallery are in place in the pool room but are not paying much attention to King or Witch Hazel, who are too well-known to arouse any sexual speculation. Miss Rose is also sitting alone at her table, muscatel at hand, her bulging brown-paper bags at her feet as she plays a game of solitaire with a tattered deck of cards. The jukebox is blaring a currently popular celebration of the brevity of love and the pain of parting.

"Johnny," who is black, handsome, over six feet tall, and probably in his early thirties, is standing at the bar in the "open" room-fronting position, his hands clasping a schooner of beer at waist level, his elbows resting on the counter in a manner that expands his chest to show its striking musculature under a clinging jersey shirt. His trousers are hip-hugging flared corduroys and his feet, casually crossed, are shod in tan ankle boots with polished brass buckles.

The sidewalk doors swing open and "Rudy" enters. He is also black, younger than Johnny and more sharply dressed. His flowered shirt in shades of purple and green has modified leg-o'-mutton sleeves; his acid-yellow pants flare so widely that they almost conceal his parti-colored platform shoes with three-inch heels.

Rudy flaunts his slim hips as he walks down the barside aisle, his alert eyes making preliminary assessments of everyone who comes within their range. Reaching Johnny, he stops beside him with a provocative and exaggerated pelvic thrust.

"Hi, faggot," he says.

"Hi, whore," Johnny replies without changing his casual stance.

"Faggot, you should be as lucky!"

"Lucky's what *you* gotta be, fella. Ain't no stud would give a dime for your black ass."

"Wanna bet on it?"

"You got a dime? You just turned a trick with a drunk in the alley?"

"Man, you somethin' else!"

"Sure ain't no motherfuckin' jive-ass whore gettin' humped in a pissy doorway."

"Shit! You was dragged up in a doorway while your momma got fucked upstairs."

Johnny draws his heels back to the bar and stands to his full height. He is an inch or two taller than Rudy. "Man," he says, "your momma got fucked only once and forgot to douche. You the result."

"All *your* brothers got a different daddy. No telling where you come from, with all them neighbors jiving in and out."

"Man," Johnny says, smiling and enjoying himself, "your momma like to died when she saw you had a cock. Didn't know what it was an' tried to screw it off an' flush it down the john. You never learned what it was for. Thought your ass was the real thing."

"It's real, all right."

"Who wants it? Some redneck lush who don't mind the stink and the clap."

"Nigger faggot, I wouldn't take *your* trade away!"

"Sister, they got your number at the V.D. Clinic, got it all filed under 'Gonorrhea Gertie.' You know what they say any time a redneck wino comes in with a leaking cock? 'You been blowed by Gertie,' they say. 'That's a real dirty motherfucker!' "

"Shit on your black ass! You known in all the tearooms from here to Texas."

"Honey," Johnny says, "honey, I heard 'bout the time the studs tried to blow you in high school. Had to rip off a microscope to find that itty-bitty peter. 'Where the shit is it?' they said. 'We got a broad here?' So they gave up and jacked off."

Obviously bested, Rudy tries a new course. "No secret how you got to be a whore," he says. "Learned it from your momma sellin' her pussy to bring in the bread."

"You kidding? There weren't no bread in your house, nigger. Your momma tried but no one wanted her cunt even for free."

"Your momma's pussy got so wore out she had to put your ass to work."

"Faggot, you simply jealous. You got your shoes wore out walkin' the streets lookin' for a score. All the dudes run when they see you coming. That black ass ain't seen no action since your uncle come home drunk an' thought you was your momma."

Smiling, Rudy places his hand on Johnny's shoulder. "Wanna buy me a beer, brother?" he says in an easy, conversational manner.

"Sure." Johnny turns to place the order and they stand side by side, hips and shoulders touching, forearms resting on the counter as they begin to discuss a party both of them had attended the previous night.

Such verbal encounters are part of the expected order of The Columbia. They have repetitive stylistic elements and some ethnic implications that are not peculiar to the setting—ethnic implications that are far more generalized ways of expressing the "mirror-interface" between inclusion and exclusion. In this instance, the ritual is a slight variation on the dueling that blacks call "the dozens"; but putting this aside for the moment, the exchange introduces verbal conventions that express a far wider range of stigmatized understandings.

The basic anonymity of the tavern is expressed most obviously in the practice of using first names only. Even when telephone numbers are exchanged, surnames are seldom revealed and addresses even less frequently. I am so accustomed to giving out this ordinary biographical data that I made quite innocent mistakes that often prompted a warning from solicitous companions. I was led into making these mistakes by the fact that the tavern is a legitimate public place and by ignorance not only of some of the criminal undercurrents but also of outside attitudes that even today recommend caution in revealing any homoerotic or homosexual interest. The lore of the tavern gives institutionalized protection against the invasion of privacy, and the first names exchanged are often aliases that are altered subsequently to fit a new image. "Ben," for example, was—when I knew him as Ben—a lanky hustler, unemployed and living on the streets. He affected cowboy dress, and his full head of hair was pepper-and-salt in color. After dropping out of sight for two or three months, he reappeared in the tavern, immediately recognizable although he had dyed his hair jet black. "Ben!" I said, confronting him as he lounged against the bar near the cigarette machine. "It's Gary," he replied, offering no explanation for his change of identity.

In many cases, people go by different names in different taverns. "Clyde" in The Columbia is "Joe" in The Rondo. The latter, situated in an old and rather ramshackle public market recently saved from demolition by well-mounted civic protests, is as unpretentious as The Columbia, its clients mostly young and hippie in appearance. Its style is cultish and sexually freewheeling though dominantly heterosexual. On rare occasions one notices a few of The Columbia's patrons in The Rondo, where they pass easily enough in the milieu of casual dishevelment but avoid any blatant display of homosexual interests. "Clyde/Joe" keeps his tavern identities separate and may well be known by other names in other places.

Nicknames are another form of anonymous identification. In some cases they are chosen sobriquets but more frequently appear to be bestowed and thereafter adopted both for reference and address. Many are commonplace female names ("Maria," "Francine," "Della," and so forth), but there are others that are more idiosyncratic.

"Yukon Amy," who refers to himself and answers to either part of the name—"Come and talk to Yukon [or Amy], honey"—had worked in Alaska and Canada before retiring and becoming a regular at The Columbia. Both Susie Wong and Tokyo Rose are Asian-Americans; "Chiquita Banana" is Latino, and, presumably, "Texas Guinan" refers to a past domicile as well as to his prohibition-era appearance and behavior when in drag. Other names are variations on the billings of performers in X-rated pornographic movies and in what remains of burlesque: "Lotta Love," "Honey Buns," "Gail Gorgeous," "Precious," and "Divine."

No one resents or rejects a name he has been given, and they are rarely known by anything except the sobriquet. My own nickname, given by Yukon Amy, is not widely used, possibly because many of the regulars see me as an outsider and also, perhaps, because they may hesitate to treat me with too much familiarity; "Doc" or "Professor" are more appropriate, preserving the implications of social distance in what is known of my background or assumed of my outside life. Nevertheless, "Duchess" replicates the model of most of the nicknames. It is tongue-in-cheek and a reference, in this case, to social and economic class and the customary propriety of my dress as well as my usually reserved behavior. Like "Duchess," many of the names express not only ethnic origins but also quirks of personality, appearance, and, less frequently, sexual tastes.

It is totally wrong, for example, to assume that because the names are feminine those who answer to them are fairies or even occasional transvestites. Sexual roles are not closely related to them. "Miss Debbie's" remark concerning his relationship with his "ex" ("I fucked him as much as he fucked me") applies to most encounters and couples, even to the most masculine studs, though some of the latter reject a passive role in anal sex. Fellatio is frequently performed in the mutual sixty-nine position, though again there are men who will consent only to be blown. I suspect that virtually all sexual possibilities are explored by all partners, with the proviso, however, that some have preferences for a particular role.*

The principal point is that feminine nicknames are not a certain indication of roles assumed in sexual performances; rather, they relate to stylistic elements that are not exclusive to The Columbia.

Like the announced theme (Fairy Tales) of the Empress Ball they are, first of all, an included (in-group) joke, an instance of camp similar to the stage names used by many female impersonators. Such names are often deliberately contrived to reflect the sexuality that press agents have in mind in promoting a public image for a "Rock Hudson." "King," "Ace," and "Butch" are the pseudonymous masculine equivalents of "Lotta Love" and "Klondike Kate."

The remarkable portfolio of photographs of transvestites by Gilles Larrain (Idols) expresses visually many of the understandings contained in naming in The Columbia. None of the tavern's patrons are quite as bizarre as Larrain's subjects, but the manner in which they bend and distort the boundaries of comfortable conventions toward the absurd and shocking is an exaggeration of the intent behind the adoption or bestowal of many nicknames. The clownish face-painting, the variations on "classic" photographic poses, the coy revelation of prominent male genitals in red leotards beneath a music-hall ballet skirt are personal, symbolic reactions to the tastes, pretensions, and prejudices of the outside world. "Tokyo Rose," "Susie Wong," and "Chiquita Banana" might be considered offensive names by those who have become increasingly sensitive to ethnic slurs; but in The Columbia they play upon these very sensitivities and, by exaggeration, eliminate the disparaging implications they have outside. In an important sense they are commentaries upon the multiple stigmata reflected in the straight mirror of reality, commentaries from the inside on other folk-stereotypes that are additional ingredients in the experience of exclusion.

Transpositions of ordinary masculine names are common: Andrew becomes "Andresina," Edward is "Edna," and William is "Willa." Again, almost nothing concerned with sexual roles can be assumed from the

---

*This statement appears to be supported by the data presented by Evelyn Hooker (1965) in her far more systematic study "An Empirical Study of Some Relations Between Sexual Patterns and Gender Identity in Male Homosexuals."

feminine equivalent of the masculine name, and in most cases they are not related to "nelly" mannerisms. The transpositions are commonly used among coteries of male homosexual friends and roommates. They are not equivalent to the cruel and demeaning nicknames of schoolmates often given to a boy who doesn't participate in "manly" pastimes; rather, they reverse the thrust of baiting and obloquy, and are similar— functionally equivalent—to the use of "nigger" by blacks within their own ethnic group.

The use of the kin term "sister" has the same included symbolism. "Brother" is widely used among members of ethnic minorities to express a shared identity and heritage of oppression. It is not merely a recognition of universal humanity but a contraction of the more general usage to convey the experience of an opposed commonality born of exploitation and vilification; and the narrow reference is often resented or interpreted as a threat by those whose origins and backgrounds do not qualify them for inclusion. I recall, for example, a Dean's meeting at my university at the height of nationwide agitation for the development of curricula in Black Studies. The meeting was attended by the chairmen, all white, of academic departments and by spokesmen for the campus Black Caucus, and I was commanded to attend in the former capacity. Possibly because I supported the academic legitimacy of a program in Black Studies, one of the black activists referred to me throughout the debate as "Brother Read," provoking at the end of the meeting an outraged comment from, I think, the chairman of mathematics. "Why," he asked with a visible loss of self-control, "do you refer to Read as 'Brother' and treat the rest of us as enemies?" I confess I was pleased by this honorary inclusion in a group to which I had no visible right to membership, realizing, however, that it represented no more than a nominal bending of the boundaries of identification.

"Sister" is not a precise equivalent of "brother" as the latter is used by members of ethnic groups, but it is commonly used by male homosexuals in referring to one another. Black male homosexuals often refer to each other as "my sister"; and whites also use it, as they may also refer to an older male roommate as "mother." The reversal of gender usages follows the pattern of many nicknames, recognizing and playing upon stereotyped attitudes that homosexuality represents a confusion and betrayal of cultural roles.

The pronoun "she" has similar implications. It is used for transvestites, where it is obviously appropriate for the assumed gender image, but it is also extended more widely. "Oh, she's a bad scene," Miss Debbie says referring to "Rocky," who has absolutely no feminine mannerisms, who is never in drag, who is completely masculine in appearance and employment identification—a construction worker who comes to The Columbia in his laced, heavy boots and yellow hard hat. "She's fucked out of her fucking mind. That baby doesn't know whether her ass is up or down. She thinks she's a big wet dream, the fucking answer to every maiden's prayer. She's *tried* to make me, but you can *have* her, honey. *I* don't need her kind of shit—all that bull-ass 'jock' stuff, that BMOC crap. Jeez, she's a two-bit faggot."

Debbie's characterization of Rocky may have been based upon past experiences of rejection and also reflects a bitchiness that is fairly generally ascribed to male homosexuals when they gossip about one another. The bitchiness is sufficiently evident to confirm the ascription if one ignores the fact that it is also imputed by heterosexual men to women. Men are not supposed to gossip or be verbally vindictive in private situations. It is assumed, however, that it is the very nature of women and a principal pastime among them at organized coffee klatches or simply when neighbors drop in on one another. Possibly, the ascription reflects the limited roles assigned traditionally to women in the larger world—to their relegation by men to domestic chores and the superior assumption that they must have a great deal of time on their hands to be filled with inconsequential backbiting. Whatever the reasons, the stereotype is transferred to males whose sexual preference is associated with a reversal of normative biological roles. In popular belief most male homosexuals are "women" (fairies) by definition and are supposed to have a woman's proclivity for pettiness, for barbed innuendo and elliptical character assassination.

Some male homosexuals (as well as some women) confirm the image. Mostly, however, the bitchy language is an element of the more inclusive style of "camp." The behavior of "camping"—a word current among homosexuals long before it was adopted by the literary media and popular culture—is often a deliberate riposte to the very stereotypes it seems to confirm. "Camp" applies not only to the genre of female impersonators and drag queens but also to behaviors—the "gender fuck"—observed at private gatherings of friends. "Oh, we camp when we're at home, when we're at parties," "Willa" says, referring to adaptations of feminine mannerisms, voice modulations, occasional dressing up, and an exaggerated badinage:

"Honey, if you say that again I'll slap you with my purse!"
"Baby, I *love* your open-toed hook-and-eye wedgies."
"Mary, *can't* you do *something* about those lisle stockings?"
"Dear heart, feather boas went *out* with Mae West."
"Darling, pearls and a little black dress don't *really* suit you."
"Sweetie, let's face it, you're not built for white chiffon."

None of these snippets describe anything worn by members of the particular group assembled for dinner in a private residence. All are conventionally male in appearance and costume and have no "nelly" mannerisms. It is camp, a ritual that also includes the more serious impersonators as well as "Lolita" in his public performances at The Roman Forum. He is overweight, dresses in a flour-sack shift, gaping football boots, and a purposefully stringy and unkempt straw-colored wig with a vermillion paper rose positioned behind one ear, and using an upturned chair as his prop proceeds, with lolling tongue and rolling eyes, to pantomime various positions of intercourse to the jukebox music of "Second Hand Rose."

The bitchy banter is not appreciated by many homosexuals. At the Two-Ten-Four tavern one end of the bar is usually occupied by a number of men who are consummate artists in the style. Though ostensibly talking to one another, their voices are raised so that it is virtually impossible to ignore them. They are very evidently on stage, exchanging witticisms and biting criticisms of mutual acquaintances. Some of the other customers laugh appreciatively and occasionally join in the repartee, but there are also patrons who do not like it. "Shitty bitches!" they say outside the Two-Ten-Four. "Sissy faggots! Those girls need a good kick in the ass." Such disapproval is also expressed more mildly in the "Stage News" section of *Data Boy*, a San Francisco homosexual newsletter (September 25, 1974). Reviewing *Tubstrip*, a play which had opened at the Enterprise Theater on Mason Street, the author remarks:

> Must admit, I didn't anticipate much in way of a fulfilling evening . . .
> I considered that the endlessly pornographic possibilities of a baths setting
> belonged on 16mm film, not on stage to be taken seriously. But the play
> turned out to be a pretty catchy little evening after all. *It's fat with fun and
> filthy sight gags, full of typically bitchy fag chitchat, and is actually pretty
> entertaining if you're not in a mood to take offense at the insistent rein-
> forcement of all the standard gay stereotypes we keep having thrown back
> at us.* One day, I'd like to see a gay play with a hustler who wasn't
> completely retarded, or a not particularly attractive middle-aged gay who
> wasn't a bitch and a lecher, or a black fag who wasn't a bug-eyed darkie, or
> maybe even a leather man with a sense of humor. (Italics added.)

Objections to "fag talk" or "fag chitchat," particularly to its commercialized use in presentations for mostly straight audiences, are similar to the attitudes of many blacks toward Stepin Fetchit and Jack Benny's Rochester, whom they perceived as demeaning stereotypes confirming traditional relationships of superiority and subordination and the "darkie" image associated with the cakewalk and minstrel shows. There is little objection now, however, to Flip Wilson's portrayal of a black minister and his chorus of deacons. The maturity associated with some success in achieving ethnic recognition and dignity often results in a humorous acceptance of the very exaggerations of speech and behavior that were disapproved; but many male homosexuals have not reached this point of objectivity. Fag talk, when it is reproduced for the stage and motion pictures, is often regarded by them as equivalent to "blackface" impersonations.

The linguistic style has no formal correspondence with ethnic dialects. Nevertheless, it is one of the most widely recognized and understood elements of "male homosexual lore." Many gay men slide into it in included situations, as though assuming an Irish brogue or a Jewish-Brooklyn accent. It is seldom an everyday speech pattern; rather, it tends to be party behavior, and in its more extended form it has some of the ritual elements included in the encounter between Johnny and Rudy. The extended form requires almost as much verbal talent as the black "dozens" (a ritualized form of verbal dueling among blacks), and, as with the "dozens," there are individual differences in the artistry of sustaining the banter. Virtuosi of the genre often seek each other out in taverns such as the Two-Ten-Four, or they discover each other at private parties, where a single offhand cue—a bitchy remark—may spark a genre-type response and lead to a verbal competition that threatens to dominate the conversation and to impose a particular quality upon the gathering. The style seems to generate its own internal momentum that tends to exclude those who are less adept or who, even in included situations, do not appreciate it. It is a learned style whose models are presented negatively to all young males, branding as "sissies" those whose accents, choice of words, and vocal emphases are characterized as feminine. Similarly, there is a tendency to question the sexual identification of women whose speech is "manly"—assertive rather than submissive. I doubt that fag talk, however, is reproduced precisely in the included speech of female homosexuals. Female homosexuality (except, perhaps, for the bull-dike figure) is generally treated with less comical exaggeration in public performances and also far less frequently than its male counterpart.

Fag talk, like the transvestite costuming at Port City's Empress Ball, is often taken more seriously by straights than by male homosexuals who use it occasionally. *Newsweek* magazine (issue of March 24, 1975) has a report on the revival of New York discotheques, many of which are said to have begun "as—and continue to be—gay hangouts where outrageous dress styles and sensational dancing now attract straights." The article, quoting the opinion of the manager of one club, offers a four-line explanation for the apparently flourishing "cross-sexual" popularity and frenzy of such places, attributing it to "1930's escapism" from recession and depression—a *la dolce vita* response to social, political, and economic malaise. But the tone is similar to the accounts of the Empress Ball in Port City's newspapers, concluding with a patent misinterpretation of a fairly common example of fag humor: "Yet the heady mix of hetero- and homosexuals inspires disco managers to be prudent . . . A sign near the coatroom at the Gilded Grape primly admonishes, "No fighting, biting or spitting."

The sign is not, of course, a "prim admonishment." It is a joke that recognizes the most popularly accepted images of homosexual men as inverted reproductions of most of the characters in Clare Boothe Luce's *The Women*, a play that is basically a "drag show" and easily transposable to transvestite performers and situations where, however, it would be no more typical of most gay men than the original version is typical of most women.

Bitchy fag talk occurs in The Columbia, though it isn't as obtrusive as it is in the Two-Ten-Four or in Port City's only discotheque—The Cuckoo's Nest—that resembles the New York style described by *Newsweek,* and it seldom provokes any signs of displeasure or rejection similar to those expressed by some patrons of the Two-Ten-Four. As I have said, the style of the tavern is dominantly "man-to-man—masculine." Territories like The Cuckoo's Nest—which is also patronized by many "liberated" or sight-seeing straights—or the Two-Ten-Four are "off limits" to most of The Columbia's customers, either being too expensive for their limited means or because they represent a trendy middle-to-upper-class style that is "unreal." Quite possibly, these differences in class identification and other disadvantaged experiences alter the attitude of The Columbia's patrons toward their own versions of fag talk and other sexually inverted usages and their counterparts in other territories. From the position of an "outside" observer, it is easy to see a common thread of imagery and symbolism in all of them, but people in The Columbia tend to assume that most of those who go to the other places are "real nellies," and their own reproductions of fag talk include an additional mirror-like refraction; for they are not only playing stereotypes of general heterosexual stereotypes of homosexuals but also their own stereotypes of other homosexuals.

The basic "mirror metaphor" is plainly revealed by the fact that none of the linguistic usages I have mentioned have any obvious connection with the "normative" mannerisms, appearance, and other identifications of those who use them or to whom they are applied. Again, I do not want to imply that there are no "nelly"—"femininely motivated"— members of the tavern's population; and, similarly, there are some customers whose "masculine identification" not only causes them to hold the ritualized "femininities" in disrepute but also to extend their objections to some roles assumed in sexual intercourse. Some of them, for example, deride men who prefer to be the passive partner in anal sex. "Dino," who is thoroughly manly though not a "leather" type, recounts three experiences with "X," another manly-looking tavern regular. "Man, he's a real faggot," he says. "All he wants to do is get fucked," and, as he continues, it becomes clear that he makes a moralistic and characterological distinction between fellatio, masturbation, and passive sodomy.

It is only very rarely, however, that any of the inverted usages, epithets, or allegations in the verbal duels are intended to be or are interpreted as personally demeaning. All of them contain a patent element of transformation—or reversal—of their implications in heterosexual speech and characterizations. They are an exaggerated ritual use of heterosexual myths of reality that reflect derisively, if indirectly, upon the myths to produce another mythic charter for those who are excluded; and the symbolism is easily extended to male transvestites in their interactions with other customers in the tavern.

Millet (1971) is obviously correct in saying that many male homosexuals "ape" the roles and characteristics that are culturally assigned to women, and the extreme of "feminine aping" is dressing like women. But as I suggested earlier, she misses the point that male homosexual tranvestism is seldom a simple reproduction of feminine models—varying in its "faithfulness" to the models—but is also a ritual expression of cultural anomaly. The transsexual and the transvestite are completely different. Stating the difference as simply as possible, the transsexual male has entirely "crossed over" the dividing line between "male" and "female," whereas the male homosexual transvestite remains a man, a point that is underscored by many professional impersonators when they conclude their acts by taking off their wigs and stripping to their naked and obviously masculine bodies. They are "playing" women, of course; but they are also commenting upon the ambiguities of the position of those who for various superficial reasons cannot be neatly assigned to one or other of the definitive categories.

An element of "outrageousness"—to use the adjective applied by *Newsweek*—is almost always used to make the point: exaggerations of current and past tastes that remove the performance from the "serious" level to the style of "camp" which celebrates the pervasiveness of cultural schlock and kitsch. The recent (1976) lingerie catalog from Bloomingdale's (New York) Department Store has photographs, by Guy Bourdin, of female models which any male homosexual would recognize as reproductions of the style of "camp" associated with transvestism. A single macabre picture from the catalog (reproduced on page 99 of *Newsweek*, October 4, 1976) could be inserted without comment in Larrain's portfolio of transvestites, and suggests that some of the practitioners of high-fashion art have stolen the conventions—the bizarre hair styles, face makeup, and body postures—that have long been the identifiable hallmark of many male transvestites—a signature, for those who know, that authenticates the charade.

The "distortions" of female costuming, however, which in some instances may simply represent a lapse in personal taste, are not the sole or even most important clue to the mirror-interface between "realities" that characterizes customer interaction with transvestites in The Columbia. Whatever their appearance may imply to the contrary, it is never suggested that the transvestite is anything other than a man.

The verbal interactions between "male" customer and transvestite reported in Chapter Two ("Honey, where'd you get those tits," and so on) are seldom meant to be a pejorative questioning of gender, and the transvestite usually responds in ways that recognize the basic man-to-man quality of the charade. So, "Arlene"—in drag—says, looking casually at his chest: "Jeez, I must be drunk. These tits are slipping." While their content varies, all the verbal exchanges, from the most casual and passing remark to more extended conversations, make several points that underline the "absurd" and in-group understandings. It is clear that the "man" never mistakes the biological identity of the transvestite; rather, he draws attention to it by exaggerated references to the most feminine elements of the impersonation, and, furthermore, responds to them with an exaggerated—and customarily scatological—replication of the sexual interests and fantasies that are components of heterosexual male-to-female lore. The very exaggerations and the explicitness of the sexual references removes the exchanges several stages beyond their heterosexual models while, in a sense, preserving the form—using it, that is, to intensify the experience of anomaly. The transvestite usually responds in the same idiom, not only focusing upon the masculine attributes of his interlocutor but also drawing attention to the falsity of his impersonation—making it clear that he is a man, and thereby, emphasizing the basic man-to-man quality of interaction.

Witch Hazel sits at the bar on a Friday afternoon, dressed in his ambiguous kilt and knee socks. His legs are crossed, revealing—possibly unintentionally—an expanse of sinewy thigh and calf, and Butch, walking down the bar, says: "Sister, you got too much ass showing. Look at this bitch," he says to anyone who wants to listen, "showin' off his ass. Man, you ain't no lady," and, emphasizing the point, he puts his hands inside Witch Hazel's shirt and fondles his breasts. The gesture—modelled after the sexual fantasies of heterosexual men—is basically asexual. Because of his age and unattractiveness, it might be construed as a friendly joke against Witch Hazel, as a form of joshing that plays upon his superficial "nellyness"; but the same gesture is often used by male acquaintances who are not in the least "nelly" in appearance, whose roles in sex aren't "femininely" passive and who have no erotic interest in each other. It is a stylized enactment not only of male heterosexual fantasies but also of heterosexual fantasies of homosexuals.

The included in-group game-playing is equally evident in reactions to customers who appear only occasionally in drag. "You're sure looking lovely tonight" is a common greeting to someone like Susie Wong when he has exchanged his customary jeans for a dress, a stylish wig, and high heels. It is a response that Susie wants and anticipates as he enters the tavern with a flaunting and eye-catching bravado; but the commonplace heterosexual appreciation is lifted out of its customary context because Susie knows he is engaged in an impersonation and others respond to the impersonation on its merits.

There is nothing in these remarks that compares to the snide quality and implications their counterparts often have when male peer groups apply them to those who do not "fit" the acceptable models of masculinity. There are many customers who do not like nellies; but, for the most part, the quality of customer-transvestite interaction in The Columbia is based upon a mutual recognition of an "absurd" charade: the transvestite knows—and wants it recognized—that he is a man, and the bantering customers react as men to women they know aren't women. Even if the transvestite scores with a customer—and I suggested earlier that it seems rare—his success has little to do with his womanly impersonation, for the sexual attraction remains both homosexual and homoerotic. When clothes are removed, it is a man-to-man encounter—a basic characteristic and desirability that does not apply to real women or to male transsexuals who have "gone all the way" to affect a sex change through cosmetic surgery.

The man-to-man quality of the style extends to reactions to arguments between "manly" customer and transvestite as well as those between transvestites. The general response to any threatened physical aggression is a visible but watching withdrawal by those who are nearest to the antagonists. Bystanders seldom intervene. If they do, it is sometimes a response to an obvious mismatching of opponents, but more often it is simply a self-serving reaction, an attempt to "cool" things before anything happens that may bring the unwanted presence of the police. The transvestite receives no special consideration. The remnants of a chivalry that once prescribed a manly protectiveness of women do not apply to the transvestite, who is a man and must take his chances as a man. When it is a confrontation between two transvestites, customer intervention, if it occurs, is generally a reminder that they aren't women. Men tend to assume, however mistakenly, that woman-to-woman arguments are essentially inconsequential, representing a rather comical assumption of masculine behaviors that are easily contained by an authoritarian and patronizing verbal intervention—a "shouting down" that the hyper-masculine and hyper-chauvinistic Gahuku of New Guinea adopted toward the public quarrels of women. Male Gahuku, however, had the cultural license to give a lesson on female decorum by whipping women apart if they became too troublesome, demonstrating with the use of canes that they should not presume to behave like men. In The Columbia, the lesson is reversed: Men should not behave like "women," and the instructive canes are replaced by shouted injunctions to "cut it out, faggots," or "cool it, sissies," injunctions that seem to imply that there are limits to the ritualized assumption of "feminine" roles—a point at which the charade loses its basic symbolism.

Returning, however, to the language of The Columbia, fag talk is never the most striking element of style. The in-group use of customarily demeaning words even by the most "masculine" patrons is a far more impressive indicator of the refractions between myths, and next to it, the sexually explicit banter.

In the context of today's free speech, there is nothing particularly remarkable about the four-letter words sprinkled so liberally through tavern conversations, though they are far more noticeable than anything overheard in "low-class" bars where the clientele is mixed by gender as well as by sexual preference, particularly in those employing female bartenders. Women behind the bar tend to exert a restraining influence on the language and other behaviors of male patrons, but in The Columbia there is usually no reason to observe even the remnants of conventional circumspection. Straight women like Miss Rose—who often "opens and closes" the tavern—do not qualify for any moderation in the locker-room style of the language, and Rose—when she has had too many muscatels—is a match for anyone who has incurred her displeasure.

Certainly, the tavern language takes some getting used to; but word-to-word it is somewhat commonplace. In the context of the verbal duel, however, between "Johnny" and "Rudy"—and in others that follow the same style—the epithets, the insults and the often gross sexuality become important elements in rituals of stigmatization.

I should repeat that these encounters are not ordinary arguments, though an uninitiated observer may think they are and suspect they must surely lead to blows. Personal hostilities or animosities cannot be discounted entirely in every case; but if they are present, they are expressed in and also contained by a mutual recognition of conventional limits. Stylistically, they are easily distinguished from "hard-core" disputes arising out of differences that relate to accusations of ripping off, of jealousy, and to the deterioration of already frayed or fraying interpersonal relationships.

The duels share some characteristics with discursive fag talk, but unlike the performances in the Two-Ten-Four, they are face-to-face encounters, not generalized bitchy gossip but, rather, toe-to-toe confrontations in which the insulted person has an immediate right to reply and, hopefully, the ability to compel his opponent to cap the insults or to announce by withdrawal that he has been bested. People, however, who are familiar with the fag talk of the Two-Ten-Four may decide initially that they are merely low-class variations on "nelly" themes—"street mores" as opposed to "establishment mores." Perceptions of class differences are undoubtedly elements of the reality The Columbia's patrons attribute to their style as opposed to the "artificiality" of the Two-Ten-Four, even though many of the Two-Ten-Four's customers engage in comparable kinds of exploitation and have had comparable experiences with the law. For example, "Rick" was one of the most conspicuous members of the "fag" chorus at the Two-Ten-Four. When I met him, he was under the legal age for being on licensed premises, but he had been going to bars and taverns for a number of years with various kinds of false identification. His parents were more than moderately affluent—civic leaders in the PTA and church organizations—but they showed little interest in Rick's personal life, and whenever he was in trouble, they withdrew entirely, refusing to acknowledge any responsibility to those he had burned or any obligation to assist him with the police. Rick's tastes in furniture and other material things reflected his privileged and well-educated background, and, through bounced checks, forgeries, and stolen credit cards, were commonly the cause of his troubles. His fantasies ran to the alleged ownership of a cabin-cruiser and a classic model of a Lincoln Continental. As I write this, he is in prison in a neighboring state—not a juvenile reformatory this time—for a form of larceny that is merely a repetition of other episodes in his life.

Rick is a hustler, but the image he projected and the trade he sought—mostly older men of respectable station—directed him to places whose styles are several removes from the disadvantaged milieu of The Columbia; and despite a common thread of experience, he would be called an "establishment sissy" by most members of its population, who would carry the contrast further by making a distinction between his faggoty chorus-line gossip and their own "manly" duels. Superficial implications to the contrary, the latter do not apply or refer to any obvious differences in "masculine" identity; rather, their "included" thrust depends upon a patent exaggeration of "outside" ascriptions of male homosexuals generally and of "street" homosexuals in particular.

The principal themes of the rituals are as repetitious as those in pornographic novels published for a male homosexual audience. One publishing house specializing in the market advises hopeful authors that there should be a sexual expletive in every second sentence, that every paragraph should include arousing descriptions of male genitalia and every chapter an explicit account of at least one homosexual act. The publisher's blurb—bowing to the Supreme Court's inability to define obscenity—usually presents the novels as works of "literary merit," and a face-saving justification may be attempted by some initial essays at a "poetic style." But this is soon forgotten, for the audience is not looking for the intellectuality that a different establishment professes to find in the work of de Sade, and, parenthetically, I wonder if anyone, including Simone de Beauvoir, has bothered to read *Les 120 Journées de Sodome* from cover to cover. The purpose of the pulp "pornos" is simply and blatantly the stimulation of prurient interest, yet they do not create a world of pure fantasy. Here is "Cliff," a Columbia patron, recounting an episode in his life:

"Well, you see, man, I'm not a hustler. But sometimes you're really down and a guy comes along and wants to trick. There was this time—a coupla years back—when I was working the wheat in Kansas. Good pay—but I spent it all on booze. Jeez, you'd think I was Rockefeller the way I bought drinks for the house in that two-bit town. Well, it ended, and I had no bread. So I stand out on that shitty road going from nowhere to nowhere. All that sky and stubble and other crap. Stinking black crows. I'm hitching, you know. Wanting to get to hell from that goddam place. Maybe a dozen fuckers passed me 'til this guy—'bout forty, I reckon—pulls up in a blue El Dorado. Gets out an' asks me if I wanna drive. No sweat. I've got his number right off. But what the shit. I stick my stuff in the trunk and get behind the wheel. It feels real good—that fucking road flying away, away behind. Then this faggot—he's real polite, real conversational, asking what I'd been doing, where I come from, was I married or did I have a girl friend—well, he drops his lighter between my legs, an' as he reaches down to pick it up he lays his hand on my crotch. So what the fuck! Sure, I get a hard pretty quick. He unzips me an' goes down, blowing me while I'm sitting there doing about seventy-five. Man, when I came that El Dorado like to break one hundred! The guy wants to go to the coast. It's as good a place as anywhere, so I'll drive him. Took us three days of sucking and fucking. He paid for everything, but I didn't ask him for a cent. So, we get to this motel near Port City, and I split while he was passed out. Sure I used him, but why should I care a fuck? Didn't he get what he wanted—a good hard cock in his bed or up his ass."

There is no reason to doubt the truthfulness of Cliff's narrative. Similar situations recur again and again in the biographies of The Columbia's patrons and are part of the stock-in-trade of many porno novels where the owner of the El Dorado is changed to the driver of a cross-country trucking rig. Similarly, the content of the barside duels is not divorced entirely from experience but relates to an underground lore of sexuality that includes, for example, the assumption that few men are thoroughly "straight," that virtually all of them are available for sexual gratification.

The verbal duels play deliberately upon a shared folklore. Audience appreciation varies with the ingenuity of the players; but the style itself is entertaining to those who listen, and the limited number of themes is a positive advantage to contestants. The opening gambits, the entrances, are immediately familiar, and responses to them are mostly embroideries of "conventional" subjects. Once the basic rules have been learned, almost anyone could try to play, a conclusion I have tested personally on a few occasions. My attempts were brief and I always lost, possibly because the words are not part of my usual vocabulary and also because I have had no experience of the most commonly depicted situations. But in addition to these disadvantages, I simply could not match the original-ity of one contestant who delivered the coup de grace to his opponent by saying: "Fella, if your cock was two inches longer you'd have a two-inch hole between your legs."

While they are related to experience, the language and the situations are hardly everyday for any participant, and they have only a minimal relationship to any verifiable personal knowledge the contestants have of one another. This is one of the reasons why I have referred to the duels continually as rituals. Rituals are symbolic and institutionalized expres-sions of included lores. They are not merely idiosyncratic and extempo-rized exhibitions. They have not only recognizable and repetitive formal properties but they are also enactments of elements of a "collective persona" and of the myths associated with it. In this sense, the chattering chorus in the Two-Ten-Four is also participating in a ritual, though its formal properties are not the same as those that characterize The Columbia's duels. Moreover, The Columbia's rituals have interesting ethnic differences.

To begin with, they are always white-to-white or black-to-black: performers never cross these ethnic boundaries. This could be explained quite easily by the persistence of interethnic uncertainties and animosities even in a setting where most customers are presumably bonded by their homosexuality; but I haven't any ready explanation for the fact that no one belonging to the smaller minorities—the Native Americans, Latinos, Asian Americans and some others—ever play the game with one another or with members of other ethnic groups. The immediate impulse is to fasten on cultural differences to explain why the ritual is only white-to-white or black-to-black. Quite certainly, there are the cultural contrasts in the content of the "black" and "white" varieties; but my data allow no more than a speculation—that someone else may wish to follow up—that different traditions of verbal interaction may be significant variables. Attempts to test this possible correlation in other taverns were unsuccessful. Few of the other territories had the same mixture of minorities as The Columbia. Most were predominantly either white or black. In others, the customers were almost evenly divided between heterosexuals and homosexuals, and the distinctive games did not occur. The Britannia was the only public drinking place patronized mostly by Native Americans; and despite the police warning, I went to it alone on a few occasions—visits that lasted no more than a couple of hours because it was obvious I wasn't wanted there. During this time, I saw as many—but certainly no more—instances of physical violence as I witnessed in a comparable period in The Columbia, but I overheard nothing equivalent to the verbal duels. On the surface, The Britannia is heterosexual only, and for this reason alone the explicit homosexual content of the games may be out of place; but since I noticed some homosexuals there—known to me because they also visited The Columbia—it is possible that the traditional acceptance of transsexualism—the *berdache*—in many Native American cultures tempers attitudes toward homosexuality to the point where the symbolic bite of the rituals is irrelevant.

While it isn't precisely to my point, it is a matter of record that only blacks, whites, and Asian Americans appear at The Columbia in drag. Pocahontas—"the Indian broad"—is the sole exception, but Pocahontas is a transsexual, not a transvestite. Population for population, I don't think there are significant differences in the incidence of homosexual motivation. When I began my study, colleagues suggested that I would find fewer black than white homosexuals and that straight blacks would be more opposed to gays of their own color than whites to deviant members of their ethnic group. None of my observations support a view that seems merely to reflect white folklores of the "black stud"—of the hyper-masculinity attributed to black males and supposedly fostered by the values of black culture. The "jock," the "superstud," however, is also a white model for masculinity, and there isn't much difference in the folk-images. Only color. Similarly, I saw no obvious differences in the levels of tolerance or intolerance for homosexuals within the two populations. If anything, gay blacks seem to be accepted more easily by their straight ethnic brothers than white homosexuals are accepted by straight whites. My only evidence for this is that in The Chop House, a bar and restaurant that is mixed black and white and heterosexual and homosexual, the straight blacks seemed to make no difference in interacting with gay blacks whereas straight whites tended to keep apart from gay whites or, when they were forced into brief associations, responded to them with belittling emphasis. The contrast may support a point I made much earlier, namely, that the "brotherhood" of color—and the more generalized discriminations associated with it—is a bond that transcends sexual preferences.

I have no explanation for the fact that none of the members of the smaller minorities—the Latinos, the Eskimos, and the Native Americans—ever appear in drag in The Columbia. It is likely that my observation does not hold outside the tavern, in other public or private settings to which I have not had access; but it is certainly an oversimplification to try to account for it by gross contrasts in cultural definitions of masculinity.

There is firmer ground, however, for suggesting that culture is a variable in accounting for some of the differences between the white-to-white and black-to-black duels. Here is a duel between Cliff (mentioned above) and "Harry," who is also white.

Both men are tavern regulars; both are manly and are approximately the same age—nearing thirty. Neither lives anywhere near Occidental Square; and though each knows something of the other's background, they have no mutual friends outside. If they meet beyond the tavern, it is merely an unplanned street or bus-stop encounter or because they find each other in another tavern when they are on their separate rounds.

Cliff, leaning against the bar and fronting the room, is wearing a plaid shirt, blue jeans, and mud-stained loafers. Harry's dress, as he comes down the aisle toward the cigarette machine, is item-for-item the same except that his jeans are tucked into the calf-high boots worn by lumberjacks and telephone linesmen.

"Hey, bitch!" Cliff calls, raising his voice in a way that alerts customers who are standing or sitting near him.

Harry, who hasn't seen Cliff, stops abruptly, turns, and responds belligerently, "Who the fuck's calling me a bitch?" Then recognizing Cliff, who is smiling, he adds: "Sure knew it had to be some faggot hustler!"

Cliff: "You answered, didn't you?"

Harry, abandoning his trip to the cigarette machine, stands at arm's length from Cliff. "You been busted lately?" he asks. "Haven't seen you on your beat for 'bout a week."

Cliff (gesturing to Harry's boots, which he knows are costume rather than employment identification): "Your old man get tired of your ass and let you out of the lumber camp for a coupla days?"

Harry: "Sure didn't come lookin' for you, man. There's more meat in a sissy joint than in that phony basket."

Cliff (reaching out and groping Harry): "Who the fuck's talking. You got a roll of toilet paper stashed in your crotch?"

Harry spreads his legs in ostentatious invitation. "Get your kicks, man," he says, "but you won't raise a hard if you tried all day."

Cliff: "You impotent or somethin'?"

Harry: "Asshole faggots don't turn me on."

Cliff: "That's not what the guys say, honey." He accentuates the final word, giving it a derogatory implication.

Harry: "You call me 'honey' again an' I'll bust your cunt."

Cliff: "Turn round fella an' I'll do the same for you. But you won't get the toe of my shoe. Not any way, man. I'll give you the real bastard," and overemphasizing his point, he runs one hand upward from his knee along his thigh and rests his fingers on his fly.

Harry: "Shit! You couldn't tell it from a mosquito bite!"

Cliff was not bested immediately, though at the end of the game, lasting perhaps a minute longer, I think that Harry won when, eventually, they changed their confronting positions and stood side by side at the bar.

I have not bothered to report the final minute of the game partly because there seem to be limits to the inventions of the erotic imagination and, ultimately, one example serves as the prototype for a style. Certain elements of style are common to all the games, whether they are white-to-white or black-to-black. All of them proceed from exaggeration to exaggeration and have only a slight content of any biographical knowledge shared by the players, for, like Cliff and Harry, they are usually not "friends" but merely "acquaintances"—and most certainly *not* "lovers"—who seldom see each other outside the tavern, or in some similar public territory, and know very little about the details of their respective private lives. Even the most commonly repeated sexual descriptions have rarely any visible justification. There isn't any obvious difference in the manliness of Rudy and Johnny or Cliff and Harry, though each of them uses heterosexual myths—particularly the myth of "femininity"—to score in-group points. Similarly, references to genital size not only reflect a male homosexual lore but also connect the duels to the more generalized heterosexual myth that masculinity and sexual performances vary with penis size.

Male homosexual fantasies are stimulated by penis length and thickness as male heterosexual fantasies often focus upon the size of a woman's breasts. The sexual fantasies of women are also stimulated by speculation about the size of male genitals, and the centerfolds of magazines such as *Playgirl* and *Cosmopolitan* are well-turned responses to the custom of using women only as erotic symbols. Yet both liberated women's magazines and male "girlie" publications are tarred with the same brush of sexual exploitation; both continue to promote the fantasy that sexual desirability and satisfaction can be measured anatomically.

The anatomically based expectations of erotic gratification are repeated again and again in messages in the "personal columns" of male homosexual newsletters and other periodicals. Entries under "modelling" commonly include:

"White male, thick, thick, thick. Available for photography, etc. Private appointment only."

"Black stud, 6'4", very butch. Long and thick. Modelling of all kinds."

The expectations promote voyeurism and the anticipation of obtaining a memorable lay. In one of my recorded sessions with him, "Joe" recounted his meeting with a casual customer in The Columbia:

"Man," he said, "I saw this guy sitting at the bar, spreading his legs and showing off his basket. Well, I joined him, feeling horny and wanting to get a closer look. He said his name was Jack. He wasn't wearing shorts under his jeans, and his cock almost reached his knee. Well, maybe not as long as that; but it sure was a thick bastard. He was ready to score, so after rapping a bit we went to my place. When I got his pants off, I like to come just by looking at all that meat. But jeez it was a real bummer. That guy couldn't have come whatever you did to him."

Such discrepancies between visual expectations and performance may be fairly common; but like beliefs in magic, one success tends to outweigh several failures, and, as a rule, informants recount only the episodes that confirm the folklore.

Penis size, sexual potency, and masculinity are also correlated with one another by male heterosexuals, and the obsession with them in The Columbia's duels may seem to be little more than a ribald play upon interests often expressed in adolescent competition and exhibitionism. Generally, however, adult heterosexual males do not confront one another with deliberately belittling comparisons of their sex organs. In most heterosexual situations, the allegations hurled back and forth in the tavern contexts would cause a physically aggressive response; and where there is mutual hostility, they are often intended to produce it, since they question the "manliness" of other men. But in the tavern, the patent exaggeration of the insults not only removes them from these other contexts but also uses the genital-based heterosexual folklores of masculinity to comment, in a reversed fashion, on heterosexual folklores of male homosexuals, who are assumed to be "womanly."

While themes of sexual deviance dominate the rituals, they also include materials related to other outcast experiences. As far as I know, neither Cliff or Harry has been busted, but being busted is accepted as an ever-present probability by the tavern's clientele. Themes that are based upon various forms of hustling, of living by one's wits, of taking advantage of those who are respectable and ignorant, are interwoven with the sexual banter, all of them adding up to a delineation of a disadvantaged and "put upon" collective persona that transcends differences in ethnic origin. Yet despite the shared elements of an alienated world view, ethnic differences are responsible for some contrasts in the content of the "black" and "white" rituals.

Perhaps the least conspicuous difference is duration. The encounter between Rudy and Johnny lasted far longer than it takes to read in my edited version. I have tried to preserve the essence of their contest, but, as with the game between Cliff and Harry, there seemed to be little profit in reproducing all of it. Very few players, white or black, can sustain a high level or originality throughout an entire set. There are always periods when the insults are merely commonplace: "Get fucked, man!" "Go fuck yourself, fella!" And so on—the interspersion of conventional epithets indicating either an inability to continue with the ritualized expectations or providing a pause in which one player may think of a response that will bring the game out of the doldrums and set it sailing again on its initial course.

None of the white games, however, approach the median duration of their black counterparts. Two to three minutes as compared to six to eight minutes is a reasonable estimate of maximum difference, and I have no certain answer to the question "why?"—only the suggestion that it may reflect some differences in the oral styles and traditions of the ethnic groups.

There is an enormously rich oral tradition associated with black-American culture. Throughout the greater part of their historical experience in the United States, most blacks were excluded from the literary values and goals of the white establishment. There were notable exceptions who overcame the caste barriers and gave eloquent literary expression to the black experience, but they were not discovered by their own people or by many whites until quite recently. Though he had many predecessors, Richard Wright's *Native Son*, published in 1940, was probably the first contemporary work by an American black to receive wide critical acclaim and to generate an enthusiastic audience of white liberals. But even he was relatively unknown among his own people. Historically, the experience of being black in America has been transmitted orally or communicated in musical forms that were ultimately usurped by whites.

Since I am not a linguist, perhaps I shouldn't touch the debate concerning the legitimacy of "black-American English" as contrasted with "standard white-American English." In any case, the purely scholarly issues are irrelevant to my present point; but there are a few observations that may not be entirely peripheral to it.

Most white Americans for whom English is their native tongue are more ready to accept the bilingual rights of ethnic minorities other than blacks, generally assuming that black Americans have no other recent and different linguistic heritage. The assumption is relatively valid. Swahili for blacks is not the cultural equivalent of Spanish for Latinos and seems to be a rather useless focus for trying to retrieve or reconstruct a linguistic component for a pre-American and African identity. This does not mean, however, that the English language forcibly imposed upon blacks and subsequently developed by them through the centuries of their separation is easily transposable to situations in which "standard white-American English" is the only acceptable instrument of verbal and written communication. The school classroom and the universities are situations of this kind. Of course, the languages of scholarship are specialized instruments that must be learned by all students whatever their ethnic origins; but in my experience, non-English-speaking foreigners as well as members of American ethnic minorities with a living but different linguistic heritage are granted a greater latitude for verbal and written imperfections in English expression than is usually given to American blacks. Though the majority of classroom instructors are white, I don't think the difference in tolerance necessarily reflects a continuation of racial biases; rather, it expresses the still prevailing ignorance of whites concerning black culture, and the frequently unconscious supposition that since blacks have received their schooling in a "standard" and nationwide institutional system, speaking, reading, and writing English from their earliest years, there are fewer excuses for awkwardness in using and understanding their "mother" tongue.

The standard English of classroom instruction, however, is often a cultural barrier that blacks—particularly those from highly disadvantaged backgrounds—have to surmount in addition to assimilating the arcane methods of academic scholarship. It is not unusual for black graduate students to express a preference for oral rather than written examinations, whereas their white peers tend to regard the former as particularly threatening. I have heard colleagues dismiss the black preference as a not-too-subtle attempt to con their way through the program of examinations, either because orals are characteristically less exhaustive tests of knowledge or because of a lingering suspicion that there is a little of "Sportin' Life" in the majority of blacks. A more reasonable and less cynical explanation—disregarding any substantial differences in literacy—may be that it is always easier to try speaking a foreign or unfamiliar language than committing it to writing. Errors in speech tend to be indulged or may be corrected or qualified by face-to-face question and answer, whereas it is difficult to retract the written word. And there is the additional possibility that many blacks are more adept at oral rather than written communication.

I am not suggesting that the majority of blacks are oral virtuosi and that the majority of whites, by contrast, are relatively inarticulate. In both populations there may be little difference in the range of oral facility. But more blacks than whites have not completed high school, and far more whites than blacks have been exposed to the literary values of a college education. The tradition of communicating the shared ethnic experience orally continues to be more important as a focus of inclusion among blacks than among the more heterogeneous white population. The distinctive idioms, the value placed upon using them with ingenuity, and some folkloristic styles are still lively components of black culture that may contribute to the noticeable differences in versatility and duration between the black and white rituals at barside in the tavern.

Many of the formal styles of black oral folklore have been studied and reproduced by Roger Abrahams in *Deep Down In The Jungle,* a work that seemed to require at its first publication (1964) an apology for some of its sexual content. Apart from dialect, many of the forms are not exclusively black. For example, the oral tale of "The Signifying Monkey" belongs to a more inclusive genre of folk humor concerning the trickster. There is an understandable disposition to find racial overtones in the encounter between the lion and the monkey, identifying the animal protagonists, respectively, as stereotypes of the white man and the black man, but many blacks do not regard it as an interracial commentary. Rather, it reproduces the verbal smartness and ingenuity that white folklore also ascribes to the traveling salesman, the con man, and the carny barker—the individual whose livelihood and survival depend upon manipulating a gullible public, using his wits to exploit their avarice, their anxieties, and their conceptions of social status. Similar themes are found in coyote tales in the oral literature of many Native American tribes and in the animated cartoon adventures of *The Road Runner* and *Sylvester* (the cat) and *Tweetie* (the canary).

In Abrahams' anthology, the style most closely resembling the duels in The Columbia in the trading of insults between contestants is the ritual of "the dozens"; but once again, the form is not unique to black culture. Similar games are played by British cockneys and are reproduced in more literate and sophisticated guise in most comedies of manners. In academia, the form sometimes appears in interpersonal exchanges in the deliberate situation of faculty meetings, where, however, the thrusts are supposedly tempered by objectivity and veiled in a mannered politeness. Content and expression are the principal differences between the versions: gross differences similar to the colors of the squares on the game board and the carving of the players' pieces rather than basic moves and responses.

All the games require verbal talent. Black informants recount that in their growing-up years in urban ghettos there were recognized experts in "the dozens" and that it was common practice for the members of one street-corner group to pit their champion against his opposite number in a rival group. Sponsored contests do not occur in The Columbia. The encounters are spontaneous and individualistic in the sense that the contestants are not the chosen representatives of larger followings outside or inside the tavern. Strictly speaking, there are no recognized champions, though regular patrons tend to expect more in entertainment from some players than from others.

The prize for audience appreciation must be awarded to the blacks. Games between blacks draw an audience of as many whites as ethnic brothers, whereas blacks tend to stand aside from the white-to-white versions, watching and listening from a slight distance and with a hint of condescension reminiscent of professional actors judging a commencement play staged by a high school senior class.

Differences in audience response may be linked with interracial attitudes. Black aloofness from the white games may not be condescension for amateurs as much as a reflection of a more general tendency to "leave the man alone," not to interfere in the relationships and pastimes of whites. I am sure blacks would never intervene in hard-core altercations between whites; and although the style of the games is both different from emotionally engendered quarrels and also basically the same in the two ethnic versions, there is possible a residue of racial feelings that is very rarely expressed openly in the tavern but is sometimes announced outside it.

For whites, the black games have several qualities that set them apart from their own versions. The idioms are obviously different, not precisely a novelty (for everyone is familiar with them) but adding an element of dialect humor to essentially similar themes, an embroidery that whites—responding to racial attitudes and stereotyping—find amusing in itself. Like the blacks observing the white encounters, they are outsiders; but the music-hall images of blacks have predisposed them to find their routines amusing.

Many black games also include a content that is alien to white conventions and has a curiosity value in itself, though the laughter it provokes often has an underlying uneasiness because it seems to breach sexual taboos and definitions of ideal domestic relationships that are cornerstones of a morality to which even a majority of The Columbia's white customers subscribe.

The contest between Rudy and Johnny—and most other black-to-black duels—not only emhasizes homosexual stigmata but also includes defamatory allegations about mothers that are lifted from many examples of "the dozens." Mothers are often principal characters in "the dozens," but they are not shown in the traditional role of the staunch church-going matriarch heroically keeping her family together through innumerable vicissitudes and teaching her children, by precept and example, the basic virtues to sustain them in a hostile and discriminating world. Rather, they are often characterized as neglectful, as promiscuous, as ready to prostitute themselves, and even as incestuous. The family life presented is sometimes one of disarray, though the mother remains the only center it may be said to have, for fathers seldom enter into the picture. In short, the mother is demeaned. Her sexual life is treated scatologically and an important element of the form is to find increasingly higher levels of insult directed at an opponent through his maternal parentage.

The inclusion of this "dozens" content in many of the black contests separates them completely from all the white versions I have overheard. The black confrontations attract by far the largest audience; yet, as I said, white reaction to them has an undercurrent of discomfort, perhaps not only because mothers are ideally sacrosanct and may even be said to have no sexual life to their children—at least not one to joke about in public—but also because this component of the black rituals is such a clear revelation of cultural differences that go beyond anything that may be assumed from the "common bonding" of homosexuality and other disadvantages.

Giving a brief summary of this chapter—and leaving some final interpretations until later—I do not want any reader to think that the various linguistic conventions and styles I have described are the only ways in which the tavern's customers communicate with one another. On any given night, a great deal of the conversation isn't much different from anything overheard in many lower-class heterosexual taverns, and similar themes of "making it," couched in a far more privileged and, therefore, respectable guise, can be heard in places like The Library of The Port City Plaza. Even the anonymity of first names only is not exclusive to the tavern. The convention is often used to signify membership in fellowships and brotherhoods that have no taint of stigma, and in some—like Alcoholics Anonymous—that are respectable but where social disapproval and a lingering degree of suspicion may be encountered by someone if his past history gets generally known. Perhaps the fairly common use of aliases is a more critical indication of the sexual and social stigmata that stamp the collective persona of the clientele. Similarly, the distinctively homosexual usages are not exclusively "Columbian." As I said, they are not characteristic of the total homosexual population, but their forms—including the extended verbal rituals—are distributed more widely through the population, suggesting that their basic symbolism, turning upon the poles of inclusion and exclusion, reflects more generalized experiences of cultural anomaly and antinomy.

At the beginning of the chapter, I suggested that virtually none of The Columbia's "impersonations" can be viewed simply as more or less "faithful" reproductions of heterosexual models of "the masculine" and "the feminine." I think they have a far more important point to make, and they make it by deliberate, ritualized distortions of heterosexual models of men, women, and homosexual men. The behaviors described so far express the cultural alienation of men whose sexual preferences brand all of them as "unmanly," and they intensify the shared experience of alienation by exaggerating the characteristics generally ascribed to "unmanly men." They are enactments of the myth of what homosexual men are supposed to be rather than true depictions of what they are—refractions in "the hall of mirrors" that have their tactile counterparts in the ritual pantomimes that are the principal focus of the following chapter.

FIVE

The Hall of Mirrors (2)

Toward the end of my study, I went to The Columbia less and less frequently, often staying away from it for days or as much as a week at a time. The long hours had exhausted me, and it had lost its initial gloss, which may seem a strange word to apply to its bare wooden floors, its aluminum and formica tables—where the brown rings from last night's glasses of beer had not been wiped clean by twelve the following morning—and its day and nighttime population of transients, "grotesques," and underprivileged. At first, however, it had seemed to be almost as exotic as the life I had studied in New Guinea, so far removed from any familiar context that I had felt a highly strung and refreshing awareness of discovery—a mental and sensory excitement based upon the knowledge that there is so much to learn, and that while you are learning it you have to maneuver warily through rocks and shoals that aren't indicated on the charts by which your own "outside" life has been coursed. But in time—provided you are temperamentally equipped to persevere—the "extraordinary" becomes so ordinary that you cease to notice it and a suspended subjectivity begins to assert itself. After almost two years, I could say truthfully to myself that I did not like The Columbia, without, however, implying any fundamental value judgments of its patrons. Yet even when I had decided I did not want to see it again, it was with me day and night—a palpable presence not only just a few miles away but also in my house as I began to order my notes and to put the first words of this book on paper.

Sitting at my desk one night, my thoughts were blocked suddenly by a bending recollection of Miss Rose, and I was moved to see her—to reassure myself that nothing had happened to her in the weeks since I had sat across from her at her table in the tavern. I dressed quickly and drove to Occidental Square, parking my car at curbside near The Two-Ten-Four.

It was Saturday, and standing at the corner, waiting for the traffic lights to change, I saw that the Silver Star—separated from The Columbia by a small commercial building—was packed to its doors. Wayne's was to my left, catercorner from the Star. Every now and then the doors of the three taverns opened. Yellow shafts of light flicked on and off like the picture on a defective television set; jukebox music and a cacophony of voices erupted as though projected through a bullhorn, to be silenced abruptly as the doors swung shut again. Men, alone or in small groups—some of them walking unsteadily—made a semicircular progress from one tavern to another. A few of them recognized me and called my name from across the street and I began to feel at home again.

Rose wasn't in her living room when I entered The Columbia. Four men who were unfamiliar to me sat at her table under the sidewalk window, and momentarily I wondered if she might be ill and how I could find her, for she had never given me her address. I knew only that social security was her sole source of regular income and that she had a room in a "Clean Bed" hotel where she did not trust the cleaning women, the reason why, she explained to me once, she always carried her shopping bags of manuscripts, old newspapers, tins of Copenhagen snuff, and personal trinkets whenever she went to the tavern. Then the crowd in front of me parted and I saw her sitting with a youngish man at a table against the wall near the cigarette machine.

I was making my way toward her when "Yukon Amy," standing sideways at the bar, saw me, caught my arm and exclaimed: "Duchess! Where the fuckin' shit you been?" I did not want to talk to Amy, but I had to stop. He had returned recently from a short visit to his daughter and two grandchildren in the Middle West and insisted that I hear about it.

Amy is still physically trim for his age and is always neatly groomed and conventionally dressed. His eyes are rather small and dark, like shiny currents set in yellowing whites, but his face, which is almost as round as a ball, has fewer lines than mine, though this impression is probably helped along by his pancake makeup and powder. His mouth is a bow in the round face, and, with the little eyes and short nose set above it, he often reminds me of Humpty-Dumpty. He always wears some kind of jewelry: a necklace with a pendent medallion, a few rings, and bracelets on both wrists. His hair, cut short, is obviously dyed and his thin eyelashes are augmented with mascara which he applies unself-consciously in public, as he also takes out his compact from time to time when he thinks his makeup needs repairing.

He was doing this now as he spoke to me, peering into the oval mirror and turning his head from side to side as he powdered his cheeks. Perhaps he guessed what I was thinking, for, snapping the compact closed and putting it in the pocket of his jacket, he said:

"Honey, she tells me to leave this crap at home when I visit her. Guess it wouldn't be too smart for the kids and neighbors to know she's got a faggot father. She wants me to live there, to keep an eye on me, but, shit, I'd have to be too fuckin' careful."

I gained Miss Rose's table.

"Oh hi, honey," she said, looking up at me and smiling. "Where you been? I thought you musta left town. Sit down, take a seat," she added, indicating a folding chair in front of her. "Let me give you a beer. This fella just bought me a pitcher."

As she filled a glass for me, I thought I recognized the "fella" as the young man who had brought her the sweet rolls from The Lighthouse.

Rose slid my glass toward me across the table, relaxed against the vinyl wall-bench like a grande dame who has offered tea and cucumber sandwiches to a guest at her afternoon salon, and, continuing with the social niceties, introduced me to the "fella." I can't remember his name, but Rose, having explained my own professional background to him, said he was a "friend" of "X," naming a nationally and internationally known stage and television actor then completing an appearance with the Port City Repertory Theater. He nodded an acknowledgment and turned to Rose.

"You're looking really good," he said.

Rose demurred. "Oh no, honey. I've been sick with the flu."

Perhaps, I thought, watching her while they continued talking to each other, for I had noticed a gradual deterioration in Rose over the past eighteen months. Always overweight, with a shapeless sack-like figure, she had nevertheless maintained a semblance of the gentility of most of the characters in her handwritten short—very short—stories. Her only footwear was either a pair of saddle shoes or tennis shoes, but her Goodwill clothing and knitted turbans were usually clean. Her heavily powdered face and the enormous gash of red lipstick reminded me of a circus clown, but in their own way they indicated some care for appearances when she left her hotel for her Columbia living room. Recently, and with increasing frequency, she had often seemed to be giving up, and on this night there was every visible justification for turning aside the young man's compliment. She had applied her lipstick only to the center of her mouth, which looked like a bright red Charlie Chaplin moustache positioned under her nose in an otherwise empty space. Her powder was unevenly applied, revealing pink blotches of skin, and her face, lacking any muscle tone, reminded me of the chalky, molded milk desserts called

strawberry blancmange that my mother had forced upon me as a child.
A large safety pin fastened her coat in the region approximating a normal
chest; her brown turban was slightly askew and needed washing. Yet
there were some small touches that seemed to indicate that the slide
downhill had not yet reached the bottom of the slope: several colored
plastic bangles on her right wrist; a necklace of white plastic daisies, and
a wilted rose pinned to the lapel of her stained coat.

The actor's friend was clearly only visiting for a short while. As they
talked, he turned his head to make quick glancing appraisals of the
barside and table customers. Finally, he placed both hands palm
downwards on the table and asked Rose if she'd like a muscatel.

"Honey," she said in the tone of an economy-minded housewife, "they
charge you fifty cents for a glass. If you've got a dollar, you can get a
half-pint bottle."

He returned from the bar with her bottle in a paper sack. "That's real
good of you," she said, stowing it into one of her shopping bags, and,
knowing he was leaving as he placed his hand on her shoulder, asked if
he was going "some place special."

"Just looking around," he said.

"That's good, honey," Rose replied like a mother approving an innocent excursion planned by a son. "You have yourself a good time."

After he had left, she tapped the shopping bag where she had stowed
the bottle. "This flu hasn't been so good to me," she said. "My chest and
throat have been actin' up real bad. Wine's the best thing for it." And
brightening visibly at the thought, she changed the subject. "You wanna
see my new story? You'll like this one."

Digging into a shopping bag, she passed me two sheets of ruled paper
covered with writing in a large hand that began precisely, keeping to the
lines, but gradually seemed to lose direction, zigzagging erratically over
the pages. As I read it, I felt Rose watching me with the mixture of diffi-
dence, hope, and anxiety most authors know when they submit their
work to criticism.

The title "LOVE" had been placed between two squiggly, ornamental
flourishes. Two lines below, the story began:

> Colleen came to the bar one Saturday night looking very nice. She had
> lovely dark hair and eyes and she wore a golden velvet skirt and yellow silk
> blouse.
> Colleen had a bird at home. He was a black bird with yellow eyes. She
> kept him in a cage. When she dressed up to go out Colleen sometimes
> showed off to Bird. "Bird," she said, "do I look nice?" Bird said "awwak,"
> flipped his tail around and jigged on his perch. Bird always thought Colleen
> was lovely.
> Tony was sitting at the bar. He was very handsome. Nice blond hair,

blue eyes and a moustache. He was young and looked very good in an open shirt and flared checked pants.

Colleen and Tony hadn't met but they saw each other across the room and Colleen went to him.

"What's your name?" Colleen said.

"Tony. What's yours?"

"Colleen."

"Hi, Colleen."

"Hi, Tony."

"Colleen, I think I love you."

At home Bird drooped his head in his cage and said "AAAWWWAKK."

"Love?" Colleen said.

"Yes love, Colleen. I know I love you."

"I love you Tony."

At home Bird fell from his perch to the bottom of his cage.

When Colleen got back she found him lying there. His yellow eyes were closed and his feet stuck up in the air. He was dead.

"Poor, poor Bird," Colleen said. She wrapped him in newspaper, put him in the garbage can and went to bed thinking "Tony, Tony, Tony."

As I finished reading, Rose smiled as though she guessed that I had liked her story. "I knew you'd go for that bird," she said.

Rose tells fortunes with cards and claims to be clairvoyant, and, since I hadn't said anything, I assumed that, like most authors, she was asking for approval or demonstrating her psychic intuition. I replied truthfully that I had liked the bird; but I had also been moved by the whole story in ways I could not explain to her, seeing her, as I read it, sitting alone at her table on some afternoon when there were only a few desultory drinkers at the bar. With the jukebox silent and the chilly autumn light of the street behind her, she would have had her shopping bags at her feet and her tin of snuff and a glass of muscatel at hand as she laboriously summoned Colleen, Tony, and Bird from her fantasy that she was gifted; for Rose had confided to me that she hadn't been published only because she couldn't find an agent. "You gotta have one," she said. "No one looks at anything if you just put it in the mail. Honey, you gotta have influence."

Providentially, someone took the chair vacated by the actor's friend and asked her to tell his fortune, allowing me to turn away and watch the action in other parts of the tavern. I had no intention of joining in, but for a few minutes I recaptured the role of the aware but detached observer I had assumed so frequently facing the room from a barside stool.

Perhaps it wasn't quite the same as it had been at the beginning. I did not expect to see anything new, only variations on familiar activities; but ordering my notes, sorting impressions and information and condensing them to generalizations had generated doubts concerning the correspondence between my relatively unfleshed formal statements and the "reality" The Columbia's patrons attributed to and apparently found in the tavern. I have always found it difficult to move from the particular to the general—from "subjective" to "objective"—from the purely personal dimensions of experience to the statistical perspective of the social sciences. The kaleidoscope of individual differences has interested me more than the charts that summarize them—the carousel rather than the stationary image. Yet I know that the "stationary image" is a necessary device; and while Miss Rose arranged her sticky playing cards on the table, I used her distraction to test my image of the tavern—still not completely formed or brought to final rest—against the current scene.

Most of the tables were fully occupied—it was one of the tavern's more crowded nights—and, as usual there were many strangers as well as regular customers. "Susie Wong," "Tokyo Rose," "Chiquita Banana," and "Miss Debbie" were sitting at a table in the center of the room, Debbie at the end facing the bar. A youngish man with a four-day stubble of dark beard, a soiled and crumpled shirt, and tattered jeans had claimed the end of the table opposite Debbie. He was very drunk. His hands were clasped round a schooner of beer in his lap; his head sagged and nodded on his chest in stupor from which he roused himself spasmodically, lifting his face to stare blearily in the direction of the other four and to make a remark which I guessed was probably something akin to "Hey, hey! You girls wanna be fucked?"

Obviously, he wasn't their type, and they were trying to ignore him, even refusing to look—except perhaps surreptitiously—when on one occasion he lifted his glass to the table—almost missing the edge—and tilting his chair, spread his legs, cupped his crotch in his hands, made suggestive pumping movements.

Debbie seldom entered the conversation. His blondish hair was drawn back from his forehead and fastened in a pony tail at the nape of his neck, an ordinary enough convention if it had not been for the penciled butterfly eyebrows, arching above his movie-star glasses, and the light glossy color on his lips. His contrived detachment fitted the controlled hauteur of his hollow-cheeked Marlene Dietrich mask, but I was sure that his eyes were constantly moving behind his glasses, roving up and down the bar and appraising the anatomical exhibition. The other three chattered back and forth across the table, not, however, so completely absorbed in one another that they were mssing the surrounding action.

It was impossible to overhear any part of their conversation or, for that matter, anything said by anyone farther away from me than Miss Rose. The music of the jukebox overwhelmed the human voices, but this did not matter; for I was presently more interested in tactile components of the style.

From where I sat, I could see one-half of the poolroom through the open entrance: a portion of a bench against the far wall and the green rectangle of a single table glowing brightly under the illumination of an unshaded electric bulb. The bench seemed to be crowded with spectators, but shadows cast by the light—hanging low above the table— obscured the upper parts of their bodies, virtually cutting them off at the waist, so that from a distance they looked like an array of jeaned and booted legs similar, except for their movement and the occasional appearance of a hand and forearm lifting a glass from the floor, to a storage rack of parts for window dressers' mannequins.

"King" and "Ace" were playing, moving round the table to make their shots or standing aside with their cues positioned vertically between their legs as they waited their turn. My eyes followed King. I had not seen him since asking him to leave my house, and I had been troubled by wondering what had happened to him. Knowing he was broke and jobless, I had given him a little money—enough to tide him over for a day—but I had felt guilty for having turned him out, a guilt that was quite unwarranted in the opinion of other tavern regulars. "Man," they had said, "the guy's been running the streets for thirty years. He can take better care of himself than you can." And they were probably right, for King—whatever he had been doing—looked far cleaner and neater than when he had stayed with me.

As I watched King, "Richy"—glass in hand—mounted the steps to the poolroom. He was blond, dressed in the tavern's customary uniform, and possibly high; but then Richy is almost always high on something, perpetually strung out and intruding his sexual jokes and suggestions on anyone. "Fella," he said to me once, "if I can't make out in any fuckin' joint I go to there's gotta be something wrong with the other guys. You can take it from me, it isn't Richy."

Richy stood at the entrance to the poolroom, watching the players. It was King's turn to shoot. He came to the end of the table near Richy, studied the lie of the balls for half a minute, then bent from the waist to make his play. Richy stepped forward quickly. With his back toward King, he straddled the cue, held the end in one hand, and pumped back and forth along the shaft. Disconcerted, King swung round, pulling the cue from Richy's grasp; but Richy had not finished his performance. Saying something across his shoulder, he adopted a bending position and placed his hands on his knees, presenting his rear to King who, laughing good-naturedly, prodded it several times before returning to the game.

The brief pantomime is typical of many others played in the poolroom or at barside. People on the table stage are generally less demonstrative. They kiss occasionally and grope a crotch here and there, or they sit with arms around each other; but the touching has a quality entirely different from the byplay of the pantomimes. It is mostly serious—expressing either an established sexual partnership or announcing sexual attraction and availability—whereas the mimed games are as stylized as the verbal duels, and, like the duels, imply very little in the way of sexual interest.

The pantomimes are not as obtrusive as the duels. Virtually everyone uses some components of the linguistic style, but only a few of them use their mimed equivalents. Some, such as Richy, seem to have adopted them as their special forte in much the same way that others have fastened on the duels as vehicles for expressing their wit and originality, and both share a common symbolism.

Lores of male homosexuality are the hub of the rituals, as they also dominate all the most visible elements of the style. Other understandings and experiences—shared with many heterosexuals—contribute importantly to the total composition, but they are like an underglaze or, perhaps more appropriately, like a completed work that has not been removed from a canvas but overpainted with a second one. The former is still there, intact; but the gallery goer sees only the one displayed for public viewing. For example, I do not know how "Lucille" and his lover were going to obtain the color television set for me. Almost certainly they weren't going to lift it from Blumenfields, but were suggesting I use the store as a showcase, picking out a model they would acquire elsewhere, perhaps from a private home, a warehouse, or a shipment reaching one of Port City's wharves. Naturally enough, I suppose, such criminally sanctioned knowledge isn't shared, though most customers know the person to go to when they need a particular illegal service; but there is no attempt to conceal the sexual understandings.

Like the verbal rituals, the pantomimes depend upon exaggeration for effect. Since they mimic the most common male homosexual acts— sodomy, fellatio, and mutual masturbation—there is probably less room for original embroideries, but, at first sight, they are as startling as examples of sexual pathology lifted from Krafft-Ebing or de Sade. Very few males are unaware that men can and do obtain sexual gratification from one another. At some time in their lives, a probable majority have watched others of their sex masturbating. A smaller number have brought another male to orgasm by masturbatory techniques, and there are assuredly few who haven't experimented with themselves. Until quite recently, however, even this most common form of sexual stimulation was proscribed by Judeo-Christian morality and folkloristic warnings that it could cause such disparate conditions as acne and insanity. As a consequence of the contemporary "sexual revolution"—and an example of the excesses that frequently accompany revolutions—masturbation is now such a commonplace topic that *The Hite Report* (Shere Hite, 1976) seems to recommend it as the best technique for women to achieve sexual climax. I do not object to the popular "unveiling" of elements of human sexuality that used to be described in Latin or indicated by a row of asterisks in scholarly and literary works. Yet the sexual explicitness of The Columbia's pantomimes produces initially a wary fascination similar to watching someone tear away the wrappings of a package you have been forbidden to touch.

But this wears off, and the seemingly endless repetition of the same acts suggests that it needs a highly original imagination to find new ways of using the limited erotic vocabularly. Ultimately, the behaviors are as standardized as male homosexual movies, which are only minor variations on a few stock situations. The characters—or, rather, the performers, for there is no attempt to portray anything except the sexual acts—alternate between sailors, college men, hitchhikers, truck drivers, and "western" or "leather" types. The settings differ, but they are limited by conventional and easily recognizable notions of what is appropriate for the selected situation; and in at least one respect, The Columbia's rituals are more entertaining than the porno movies. The players are not characterless men chosen only for their physiques—they are fleshed individuals with distinctive personalities. Yet the themes of the pantomimes are even more limited than the movies, and, unlike the movies, they are not intended to be sexually arousing.

Contrary to anything that might be assumed from their person-to-person explicitness, they are not sexual invitations or advances. Direct invitations are often involved in the exhibitionism of the urinal and, more discreetly, in the suggestiveness of some clothing styles—the absence of underwear or a bleached spot on the inside thigh of a hustler's trousers. Other barside and table behaviors—groping or standing so close to someone that two bodies are deliberately placed in touch—also transmit messages that are not intended to be pantomimes. These carry only the shared understandings of a generalized lore of homosexual behavior.

Like the fleeting lapses into "fag talk" by otherwise "masculine" men, vestiges of the game occur at private parties when, for example, someone underscores a point by pantomiming masturbation or uses the gesture as a humorous response to bitchy innuendo. It doesn't have the hostile and demeaning implications that are often intended when young heterosexual males use it in confronting one another; rather, it is cognate with the use of feminine sobriquets and pronouns—a playing with cultural stereotypes of male homosexuals and sexual morality that turns insult and obloquy into an "included virtue" that is similar, again, to the inside usage of resented epithets by many members of ethnic minorities.

The pantomimes, despite their portrayal of so-called "unnatural" sex, are not obscene, unless the word is used in its most conventional and, nowadays, largely discredited sense. I have not seen anything like them in more decorous taverns such as Spiffy's or in "leather" bars where the style favors a macho immobility, a quality of menacing self-control; but in The Columbia they are as easily accepted and expected as the verbal duels. Players, however, unlike exhibitionists in steam baths, are not allowed a free rein to embellish the standardized material as they wish.

"Mike" and "Jerry" are tavern regulars who almost always play a game when they meet. Mike is white and probably in his late forties, Jerry late thirties and black. Mike is short and stout, with thinning sandy-colored hair and small pale blue eyes that seem to have been pinched into a puffy face latticed with fine red veins. He is always seated at the bar with his back to the room, and, except for his games with Jerry, shows little interest in other people. Jerry, on the other hand, is always in motion, usurping the barside stage as his personal playing area, moving from one seated acquaintance to another and introducing himself to strangers by saying: "Hi, I'm Jerry. What's your name?" His voice is loud even when he is only slightly drunk. Despite the tavern's noise on crowded nights, you can't miss Jerry from the moment he enters. He is on stage as soon as he opens the doors, hesitating for no more than a second as his alert eyes search for someone to use in his act.

Jerry has a checkered personal history, moving from one job to another with intervening periods of welfare and unemployment assistance. He is, however, seldom out of work for more than a few months at a time. His native wit and intelligence are impressive, but he is easily bored by routine. At first, each job seems to be the one he has been looking for, the one that will take him off the streets, but, after a while, he generally concludes he already knows more than the people to whom he is responsible and he resigns—to go back to the "real" world of the streets and taverns. Yet I don't think he is completely happy there. Just beneath his bravado, he realizes that he has squandered his talents and that it is rapidly becoming too late to recoup the loss. The "reality" he ascribes to The Columbia, and, by extension, to other tavern scenes, is mainly a rationale for failure and habituation, similar to the rationalizations of alcoholics who realize where their habit is taking them but haven't the will to break it, even, perhaps, preferring the downhill slide from responsibility to the difficulties of commitment to others. The many people he calls "friends" are merely "acquaintances" with whom he has to maintain the pretence of always being "with it," of always being "on top" of everything that touches him. But in the privacy of his rather bare room in a deteriorating duplex in the black ghetto of Port City, the armor of his public facade is sometimes pierced by sudden inward doubts. His eyes cloud as though he is struggling to reconcile two different perspectives, and speaking to himself, he says: "Oh, jeez man. I think I gotta fucking see a shrink."

I was sitting near Mike at the bar, and I noticed Jerry as soon as he came in from the street. There had been numerous occasions on which I had walked with him from one tavern to another in the quarter of Occidental Square and had felt the way in which his step and posture changed—tightened—at the moment of entering a place where he felt he had to be "on stage." I hadn't said a word to Mike, yet I knew he was fully aware that Jerry had come in and was making his way toward us down the barside stage, stopping here and there to banter with seated or standing customers but always moving on his customary progress.

Jerry was only a few stools distance from us when Mike, not even turning his head, flung a challenge across his shoulder. "FUCK OFF, JERRY," he said so loudly that no one near him could miss it. Jerry hesitated for only the second it took him to recognize and accept the signal. He was already committed to the game as he covered the few remaining paces separating him from Mike, and Mike, knowing the encounter had been joined, said once more across his shoulder: "FUCK OFF, JERRY. Get yourself fuckin' lost man."

Jerry interrupted his progress at Mike's stool, halted there with his legs assertively spread, thrust his pelvis forward and pressed it hard against Mike's thigh.

"Fella, you *are* lucky," he said, beginning to pump vigorously. "How's that turn you on?"

Mike, falling into his expected role, tried to show even less concern than someone who has been bumped accidentally in a crowded subway station.

Jerry ignored Mike's lack of interest, moved behind his stool, and continued to pump so heavily that Mike, to avoid toppling from his seat, had to grasp the edge of the bar.

"Man, you sure look horny tonight," Jerry said. "Looks like you haven't been fed for a coupla days. You want a bit of gourmet ass?"

And turning aside, he unzipped his pants, dropped them to the floor and offered his ass to Mike.

"Here," he said, "take a good look before you eat it. This ain't no 'house special' going for a lousy dollar."

Jerry was wearing shorts under his trousers, and his gesture had none of the invitational qualities of men who unzip and ostentatiously display and fondle themselves in the urinal; but one of the on-duty bartenders stopped the show. "Cut it Jerry," he said. "Pick up your fuckin' pants or you'll find that fucking ass out there on the street."

Jerry's only solecism was dropping his trousers in this very open section of the tavern; otherwise, his performance contains most of the standardized elements of all the pantomimes and illustrates one radical difference between them and the verbal duels, namely, the crossing of ethnic boundaries. Some of the games are black-to-black and some are white-to-white, but this seems to depend upon conventions that have nothing to do with color. I have not, however, seen any members of the smaller minorities—the Asian and Native Americans, Latinos, or Eskimos—playing the "aggressive role"; they are always the foil for either a black or white performer. I do not know if this has any cultural significance. The Asian Americans are the most "ladylike" of the tavern's regulars, those who appear most frequently in drag, and even out of drag, generally project a "womanly" reserve—sitting mostly at the tables—which contrasts with the overriding assertiveness and masculinity of the style. Yet the appearance of "masculinity" and "femininity" are not decisive factors in determining the roles enacted in the black and white or the ethnically mixed versions between members of these minorities.

It is possible that the crossing of ethnic boundaries in the pantomimes reflects the fact that they are not contests. While the insults in the verbal duels are thoroughly stylized, they are, nevertheless, a competition. Even though they always end on a note of friendship, they aim to lead an opponent to the point where he is ambushed, bested, and unable to extricate himself from a trap. It is always clear who has won, whereas in the pantomimes there is no attempt to establish supremacy.

Despite the physical contact, the pantomimes are more impersonal than the verbal duels. It isn't possible to exclude a component of interpersonal animosity in all the duels, even though it is contained by and expressed in a ritualized form that is very different from "hard-core" arguments. As far as I can tell, however, there is not the slightest hint of hostility in the tactile games. The sole exception may be the "passive" and "womanly" role always assigned to Asian Americans, but this isn't necessarily a personal "putting down"; rather, it seems to reflect generalized homosexual stereotypes of Asians. For reasons I cannot explain, there does not seem to be any Asian American equivalent of the black or white stud, at least not in the ethnic perspective of The Columbia's patrons, who tend to assume that members of this minority are "girls" and always interact with them on the basis of a "male-to-female" model.

I do not think it is because the Asian American regulars are more frequently in drag then other members of the tavern's population; rather, it reflects very generalized intercultural stereotypes. Someone else may want to ask why there isn't any equivalent to the black or white stud in homosexual folklores of Asian Americans. The "masculinity" of *bushido* has its cultural equivalents in various Western styles of machismo, and certainly—using only the Japanese case as an example—there are "masculine" and "feminine" male homosexuals in traditional Asian cultures. Yet *all* Asian American homosexuals seem to be assigned to the "nelly"—to the passive and "feminine"—category by whites and blacks.

The pantomimes contain very few formal elements of fencing—of thrust and response and the scoring of points. Mike knew that his opening remark would produce Jerry's act, but thereafter he remained completely passive and feigned indifference. Most of the games are cut to the same pattern. They need two players, but one of them merely acts as the other's foil. Occasionally the foil responds with a shoulder-glancing look, runs an indifferent hand over the performer's ass, or gropes his crotch—ploys intended only to prolong the game. Mostly, however, even these casual responses aren't necessary.

If the absence of competition—of "winners" and "losers"—contributes to the ethnic mixture of the players, particularly the mixture of blacks and whites, there may also be another factor, namely, that the idioms of the pantomimes are not ethnically bound. The basic homosexual material of the verbal duels is understood by everyone, but it is presented and embellished differently by blacks and whites, whereas the repertoire of pantomimed acts is precisely the same for both groups. Moreover, linguistic virtuosity is the crux of the duels and isn't necessary at all in the pantomimes. Like Jerry, many performers use dialogue as an adjunct to their act, but that is all it is—an "adjunct" that requires no response in kind. There is room for wit—but little scope for real innovation—in the postures chosen from a limited number of possibilities, in the exaggeration of those chosen, and in the rapid change from one to another, including reversals of invitations to active or passive sexual roles. A fairly commonplace comedy seems to be modeled on the stock vaudeville routine in which a muscular and overweight man in tutu and leotards plays ballerina to a smaller male partner. In The Columbia's pantomimes, the comic incongruity is expressed when a small man plays the assertive stud against a "butch" foil.

Unlike contestants in the verbal duels, there are some pantomime performers—such as Richy—who play against strangers. These games, however, are by no means as common as those between acquaintances. Once again, I make a distinction between "acquaintances" and "friends," and those who are lovers are excluded because they don't perform to one another in the public style. "Acquaintanceship" distinguishes a relatively limited bond from others having far more varied and more intense ingredients of affect and interaction. Mike and Jerry are "friends" in the sense that they apparently like each other well enough, but they seldom meet outside the tavern. Being regulars, they have many mutual acquaintances among the tavern's clientele, but they do not go to the same parties honoring birthdays and other anniversaries or to spur-of-the-moment and after-hours gatherings. Jerry has a greater knowledge of Mike's outside life. Mike has been steadily employed for many years in a travel agency. He often talks about his work and his colleagues, whereas Jerry is secretive about his past and present life. Most regulars know he has a prison record, that he is mostly indigent and lives by his street-side wits, but he won't talk about his private life. His many failures are not compatible with the sharp and self-assured image he has adopted as his stock-in-trade.

Jerry performs against other people, but his act with Mike is a characteristic part of their acquaintanceship. It is invariably the way in which their tavern meetings begin. Its details change only slightly from one occasion to another, but its quality is different from games that are played with strangers. The latter often seem to be merely forms of exhibitionism—attention-getting responses to a "high" of one kind or another—that, paradoxically, can be construed more personally than those between acquaintances.

The difference between "friendship" and "acquaintanceship" isn't simply a quibbling with terms. "Friends" share far more with one another than "acquaintances." They exchange confidences, meet outside the tavern, and have been party to other exploits. A few of them have had sex with each other in a comradely way that hasn't any of the emotional investment of a "lover" relationship and is different, too, from the anonymity of steam-bath sex, pickups, and casual one-night stands. But "friendship" is basically asexual, and the byplay of the pantomimes does not fit the pattern of a bond in which sex is discounted as a reason for sharing a far wider and more varied range of tastes and interests. Similarly, the comedy of the pantomimes—with their underlying bite—is not suited to the serious involvement of "lovers." One member of a pair of "lovers" may act against an "acquaintance" but never against his recognized sexual partner, and, as a rule, the partner is not offended. It is only when their relationship is already strained—when the excluded person is angry with his partner or suspects he may be losing him—that the game may be used as an excuse for a public confrontation.

The pantomimes never reach the minimum duration of the verbal duels and do not attract an audience of comparable size. Unlike the duels, there is seldom an alerting signal. Most duels begin on a note of challenge; and although people prefer not to interfere in "hard-core" arguments, they are warily interested and listening. A couple of exchanges is generally all that is necessary to establish the form, to show that they aren't confrontations leading up to possible physical aggression, and at this point the contest in verbal virtuosity is enough to keep a sideline audience together and to attract customers from other stages.

Most pantomime players do not seem to be seeking any audience other than their chosen foil. The Richy-type of perfomer is often disparaged. Richy is always on the move, going down the bar and from one stage area to another and offering himself to every second or third customer. His indiscriminate exhibitionism draws an acid comment from Miss Debbie. "That faggot's gonna get himself fucked to death," he says, adding that Richy should know he "isn't worth a shit."

It is obvious that Debbie doesn't like Richy, and Richy's games may have more personal overtones than many other examples of the pantomimes. By his own account, he was "brought out" at fourteen when he was sodomized by an older member of his high school football team. "I guess you can say he seduced me," Richy says. "But, shit, I'd watched guys jack off and I always got a hard-on. Man, I knew what I wanted, and it didn't take much to get me down on my back." He laughs. "I've been sucking and fucking ever since."

Richy's self-admitted promiscuity isn't a sufficient reason for disparaging his act, since the search for sexual partners is a recognized motive for going to the tavern, only one among many, and not the most important one for many customers, but nevertheless, a motive that is accepted without prejudice. Yet there are many people who don't know Richy personally but who put him down, suggesting that he is "coming on too strong." They do not criticize Mike and Jerry or similar couples—such as "Dale" and "Greg"—who use the form less indiscriminately. Dale and Greg are both whites, both in their mid-thirties and conventionally masculine. Dale works in a warehouse on the waterfront; Greg is a part-time driver of a Yellow Cab. Greg uses Dale as his foil. When Dale is standing at the bar, back to the room, Greg approaches him from behind, circles his waist with his arms, and pumps against him or fondles his breasts in a patently exaggerated male-to-female fashion. If Dale is facing the room at barside, Greg drops to his knees in front of him or backs against him, miming the appropriate sexual act. They have never had a sexual relationship with each other. "Shit, *no!*" Greg said when I asked him. "Man, I don't even see him outside this joint. Maybe just passing on the street when I'm driving, and I give a blast to make him jump on the sidewalk—letting him know I've got his number. Caught him peddling his ass to the sissies."

It is difficult to pinpoint the reason why Richy's act is less well received than those of other couples. There isn't any noticeable difference in the sexual elements of any of the pantomimes. Richy probably isn't much liked by anyone. He doesn't seem to have any "friends" in the tavern and few relationships that qualify for the less intensive bond of "acquaintance." He may well have some personal qualities that are fairly generally disliked; but from most conventional standpoints he is physically more attractive than many customers and, from the same standpoints, more acceptable than those I have called "the grotesques." Some people may resent his bragging about his sexual successes, either because they are jealous or because they don't take seriously the stereotype of "the stud who can always make it with anyone." But I think there is a less obvious reason why people react differently to Richy's use of a common form.

The Jerry-and-Mike and Dale-and-Greg type of pantomimes are rituals that share some basic properties with the verbal duels. The pantomimes require a physical contact that is only minimally present or entirely absent in the duels, and the duels use a wider range of in-group and stigmatized lores. The central motif, however, of both forms is a heightened embroidery of many commonplace heterosexual myths of homosexuals. I do not mean that the sexual acts portrayed have no relevance to what occurs sexually between male homosexuals. Obviously, fellatio, sodomy, and mutual masturbation are among the ways in which men find sexual gratification with one another. The images in the "mirror" of the pantomimes reflect some basic sexual realities, but their essence is a deliberately distorted manipulation of folkloristic themes of gender identification and betrayal and of a life-style that is perceived from "outside" as a constant hustle. Hustling of various kinds is undoubtedly a part of the experience of most customers, whether they are regulars or transients. Miss Debbie's remark that "every mother's hustling something" applies, in the broadest sense, to the way in which a majority of the tavern's population perceive relationships between people, not only interpersonal relationships but also the gamut of their connections with the institutions of society—and their representatives—with which the circumstances of their lives bring them into a dependent situation where their failures tend to be suspect.

Themes of manipulation and exploitation run through both rituals, but they are at least a four-way "mirror" reflecting, first, the "outcast" images les justes ascribe to those who are separated from the normative social, economic, and sexual values. Second, they reflect the shared awareness of "outcast" status by those whose modes of life are generally disparaged. Third, they reflect some of the realities of a life-style that is regarded as "outcast," and, last, they transform the first, second, and third dimensions into a satirical commentary upon all of them.

The final refraction is the one that most straight observers do not see, but it is the crux of both styles—the quality that separates them from everyday, run-of-the-mill encounters and raises them to the status of rituals. The transformation from the "ordinary" to the ritual level is underscored by the joking quality of the bond of "acquaintanceship." The intent of the rituals is not "personalized"; rather, the rituals project, play with, and comment upon the "collective consciousness" of those who share a stigmatized and excluded world view. Possibly, Richy confuses form with intent. Others see his indiscriminate advances as personal approaches that are better suited to the steam baths, where fantasies are usually fulfilled in the context of an unhinhibited and anonymous reality. Unlike the steam baths—with their "barracks" of double-tiered bunks, their "glory holes" and jacuzzi pools—the sexuality expressed in both duels and pantomimes touches a different level of understandings.

Conclusion

Before concluding, I think it may be useful to respond to some questions concerning the relevance of my material to the total population of male homosexuals in the United States—questions that have been raised by some gay activists who have either read the manuscript or have heard me present some of the materials at public meetings. Their objections—disregarding arguments concerning the concepts of "culture" and "community"—usually fall into one or other—or all—of the following categories. First, that the behaviors described are not typical of homosexuals; second, that I have overemphasized the importance of public territories as "social mechanisms"; and, last, that the descriptions—and even the choice of the locale—are a disservice to the activist cause by reenforcing the most commonplace heterosexual stereotypes of male homosexuals.

There is a simple rejoinder to the first question, namely, that neither the personae nor the behaviors of my population are typical of homosexuals because there isn't "a typical homosexual" any more than there is "a typical heterosexual." But I detect in this criticism an echo and also a confirmation of my earlier statement that homosexuals are a highly fragmented minority. Those who have complained most have been members of dominantly white middle-to-upper-middle-class organizations. Their sexuality aside, they conform to and seek all the values and aspirations that are customarily ascribed to "middle-class and white America," including most of those associated with traditional cultural definitions of what it is to be "male."

What they are saying, in effect, is that they are no less "manly" in the *cultural* sense simply because of a sexual preference for members of their own gender. Millet (1971) might have used them to better effect rather than Genet's symbolic characters in trying to demonstrate her thesis concerning male homosexual perpetuations of cultural myths of "masculinity" and "femininity."

As I have said earlier, I can understand the political strategy of promulgating a middle-of-the-road image in trying to secure the civil rights of those who have "chosen" what is nowadays often referred to as "the alternative sexual life-style," and the image is not off-center if you compare the total population of male homosexuals with its heterosexual counterpart. I have a strong objection to it, however, and it is an objection I extend to all fundamentalists, namely that the pursuit of purity is often accompanied by a totalitarian rejection of all the styles that do not replicate the ideal model. Though I am not a political scientist—and do not wish to engage in polemics—it would seem to be politic for the activists to recognize the diversity within their "constituency" and to reach out to as many of them as possible rather than erecting barriers of disapproval between themselves and those who participate in styles that are perfectly innocuous but are not regarded as suitable.

The public "drag scene"—and even occasional public transvestism—is one of these frequently disparaged styles; and since I have mentioned (Chapter One) Port City's Empress Ball and the Court it represents, it may be useful to record what happened when I invited the 1975 and 1976 Empresses to visit my Port City University class on "Culture and Homosexuality in the United States."

The class had a student enrollment of fifty-six. Slightly over half were women; of the remaining men, most were homosexual, and a few of these were members of the Gay Students Association which has, in any case, a small membership, using the "Kinsey ratio" of approximately one in ten of the probable 3,000 homosexual students in the campus population. My guests were invited to see and to comment upon and answer questions related to a film called The Queen, a documentary that follows a number of male homosexual contestants through the routines of a transvestite "beauty competition" modelled on the "Miss America" or "Miss Universe" pageants (and I should emphasize that the Empress Ball is not this kind of competition).

I was aware of an attitude of censure—even one of censorship— among the few male activist members of the class, and not only took pains, a day or two before the screening, to point out that the style depicted in the film was not typical of male homosexuals but also to note that it was often derided. Further, I suggested that whatever personal objections anyone may have to the style itself, my guests were entitled to the consideration that ought to be given to anyone with whom we may differ on relatively minor matters of taste.

As I had expected, the Empresses appeared as completely conventional males, no different in appearance from any of the other men in the class; but at question time it was the male activists who subjected them to an obviously agreed-upon barrage of questions that were implicitly—and sometimes explicitly—pejorative and demeaning, to the extent that I felt I had to cut them off. I did so only because I did not think it fitting to subject my guests to the hostility of a few people who, in a more inclusive sense, might have been expected to regard them as "brothers."

When I took my guests to lunch following the class, they said they had been quite aware of what had been happening. They had expected it from those I have referred to as "the fundamentalists," and their admission points up two things I have said already: namely, that the total population of male homosexuals in the United States can be said to be "bonded" only by a sexual preference and a generalized awareness that the preference is stigmatized.

The "fundamentalists" also take exception to what they believe to be my unwarranted emphasis upon public territories. Again, the answer to this criticism is a simple one, though it has several dimensions. I have not suggested that the public territories are either the sole mechanisms for expressing homosexual motivation or that they are used by all male homosexuals. Other mechanisms exist, including Port City's variety of activist groups and even more discreet networks that are no different— except for the dominant sexual understandings—from similar networks of acquaintanceship and reference groups that help to produce enclaves of association among members of the heterosexual population. To announce that large numbers of homosexual men do not use the public territories and even find them distasteful does not eliminate their significance to those who do resort to them; and their sheer numbers and economic survival in all major American cities seem to be positive indices of their institutionalized role.

The public territories are not only the most "visible" and most easily accessible of the social mechanisms but many of them, particularly the bars and taverns, are also the closest approximation to anything that may be called "homosexual institutions." I have a personal dislike for the styles of some of them, such as the steam baths and public urinals; but the urinals, by my prior definition, are "homoerotic" rather than homosexual, often used by men who identify as heterosexual. For example, my study brought me into contact with hundreds of male homosexuals and I found only one who admitted to visiting Port City's tearooms. Of course, some of the things that occur in The Columbia's urinal—and in the rest rooms of some other taverns—might be labeled "tearoom activities," but their quality is very different from the encounters studied by Laud Humphreys (1970). They are not as furtive, as silent, or as thoroughly anonymous; rather they might be viewed as an extension —though one that is often disapproved—of some of the socializing elements of the tavern's order of activities.

While I have justifiably stressed the sexuality of the tavern—it is, after all, a recognized male homosexual territory—I have also emphasized that the pursuit of sex is only one thread in its fabric. It serves a far wider range of goals, interests, and needs, and this is more generally true of most homosexual bars and taverns than the heterosexual public suspects. There are "cruising bars," in which the search for sexual partners is a dominant motivation, and there are others—mostly those that might be called "home territories"—where any sexual advances are regarded as an intolerable social solecism. Most of them, however, seem to lie on the median between these extremes. On any given night, a majority of The Columbia's patrons are not "searching for sexual partners." Undoubtedly some of them are, and there are others who will take advantage of such an opportunity when it is offered; but most of them are there to pursue goals of fraternization that are little different—*except for the public setting and the nonsexual variables of socioeconomic class*—from those that are promoted for members in many formally constituted and identified gay male organizations.

I think there is a warrant for the emphasis I have placed on the qualifying clause in the last sentence. Even though it is either discounted or not even mentioned as a reason for joining them, gay organizations, by their very identification, are "mechanisms" through which some members may develop sexually approved relationships. Recognition of this possibility does not subtract anything from the legal and political goals of the organizations, for sexual relationships may also develop between some members of any organized heterosexual interest group. I do not think that the sexuality of The Columbia is the reason why my descriptions of its style have produced such strong expressions of disapproval from some activists; their opposition reflects class-based antinomies.

Most of The Columbia's patrons are "failures" if their lives are judged against ideal standards of achievement in American culture. They are poor, and the poor—particularly the urban poor—tend to be regarded as a bar sinister on a national coat of arms whose other emblematic devices emphasize upward mobility and material success. The patrons of The Columbia are marked with stigmata that are additional to their sexuality, and these additional stigmata give a negative coloration or value to a sexuality they share with members of a far more numerous population.

These activists object not only to the themes and language of the verbal duels I have recorded but also to the more commonplace, more widespread, linguistic style of "fag chitchat" and the essentially facetious and anarchic behaviors of the "gender fuck." Generally, they are also as moralistically opposed to Genet's *Nôtre Dame des Fleurs* (1964) as the censors who originally banned its distribution in the United States. To them Genet's characters represent everything that is undesirable and counterproductive for their goals. Their attitude is similar, though far more acerbic, to the protest against the public reproduction of stereotypes included in the *Data Boy* review of *Tubstrip*. Their objection to Genet's characters, however, is not simply because they see them only as stereotypes but also because they are criminals in the conventional sense, and they fear that these other outcast traits—through a process similar to guilt by association—may be extended to all male homosexuals.

Conventional criminality is no more characteristic or more frequent among the total homosexual population than it is among the heterosexual population. Indeed, given the ratio of one population to another, it is probably far less frequent. Contrary to Anita Bryant's relatively recent (March, 1977) opposition to the Dade County (Florida) ordinance rescinding discrimination against homosexuals in housing and employment, the vast majority of homosexuals do not recruit new and innocent members to perpetuate their own life-style. In fact, they are less interested in recruitment than the pimps and higher echelon members of the heterosexual prostitution marketplace.

This does not mean that the recruitment of teenage boys for homosexual or homoerotic activities does not occur. Robin Lloyd in his investigative report of boy prostitution in America (1976) gives a concise account of some recent scandals of this kind; but he is scrupulously fair in rejecting the commonplace heterosexual tendency to brand all homosexual men as "child recruiters." Indeed, most of the men involved in the most notorious cases were not homosexual as I have defined them earlier.

Again, this observation does not deny the existence of adult males—the "chicken hawks" or "chicken queens"—who seek young boys for sex. It would be quite as foolish to deny it as to deny that there are some adult males who seek teenage girls for the same purpose. Prostitution, irrespective of the ages and the genders of those involved, is an element of American society—and so is pedophilia—and to extend the tastes or aberrations of some male homosexuals to the total population is as ridiculous as assuming that because many whites are violent *all* whites are violent, or because a numerous population of heterosexual males patronize female prostitutes *all* heterosexual males are potential customers. In any case, Lloyd points out that many boy prostitutes are recruited into the existing marketplace by teenage peers.

The most widely held stereotypes of male homosexuals are as gratui-
tously demeaning as stereotypes of all minorities, and they share with
these others a common foundation in the definitions of "reality" that suit
and help to preserve the cultural hegemony and historical privileges of
les justes. Male homosexuals are as justified as blacks and Native
Americans in protesting the perpetuation of grotesque stereotypes in the
popular media, but occasionally they seem to be oversensitive, criticizing
not only the conventional distortions of vaudeville and the characters
and relationships shown in *The Boys in the Band* but also the homosexual theme in some of the works of Tennessee Williams, such as
Suddenly Last Summer and *Cat on a Hot Tin Roof*. They object to the
latter—and to films like *The Sergeant, Midnight Cowboy,* and *Death in
Venice*—on several grounds; but there are two criticisms that are used
most frequently, namely, that they portray the homosexual as being
unable to express affection and "love" for another man, and, secondly,
that the relationship always ends tragically—in death or suicide.

For several reasons, these are spurious arguments. It is necessary to
remember, first of all, that the portrayal of homosexuality in "serious"
drama and films is only a recent development in popular American
culture. Not so many years ago, for example, it would have been prohib-
ited under the code of ethics governing the film industry, a code that also
banned scenes of heterosexual lovers in completely horizontal positions.
Disregarding trifles such as *The Ritz* and *Norman, Is That You?'* the
better entries in the homosexual genre use homosexuality as an example
of a more generalized tension and discomfort with traditional role assignments and a more generalized inability for human beings to form open
relationships with each other in a conventionally structured world. The
better plays and films should be placed side by side with others that
depict the writhing of the human spirit straitjacketed in a "cultural shirt
of Nessus"—a shirt emblazoned with the imperative "this is what you
are, so this is what you *will be!"* The shirt fits members of both genders
and large numbers of heterosexuals as well as homosexuals. For every
reputable homosexual film or book there are probably ten that portray
heterosexuals in situations of comparable dilemma. Most certainly, the
dilemma of the homosexual has been exacerbated, and still is, by cultural
anathema and civil and criminal sanctions that—requiring a great deal of
circumspection or dissembling for mere survival—added a quality of
tentativeness or furtiveness to many encounters and relationships. The
knowledge that a homosexual relationship was not only disapproved but
could also lead to personal destruction has been part of the homosexual's
tragic experience.

The final tragedy of suicide is probably no more frequent among homosexuals than among heterosexuals; yet the homosexual's lot remains potentially tragic in contemporary American culture. Sixteen states have repealed criminal statutes against sodomy in private between consenting adults, but as yet (March, 1977) no *state* has enacted legislation to secure the civil liberties of homosexuals in such areas as housing and employment. Some local—city or county—bodies have done so, including the City Council of Port City, but this represents only a limited and localized legal protection that does not extend to state and federal agencies; and it only needs another law or the repeal of existing ordinances to erase the little that has been gained.

Because of the virulence of the entrenched, socially misinformed, and moralizing opposition, the condition of the homosexual may qualify as a special case of disjunction with the normative order; but it is not, of course, a unique experience. The experience of disjunction—"the writhing of the human spirit in the cultural shirt of Nessus"—is a theme whose lineage is as old as oral and written literature, and the homosexual has a rainbow-colored company of heterosexual brothers and sisters who have resisted or suffered in the confining straps of the straitjacket in which they have been placed, and whose lives have been destroyed either by small erosions or by open rebellion. Perhaps *The Boys in the Band* and *The Sergeant* and others in the homosexual genre do not portray the "typical" homosexual, but Nora in *A Doll's House* is not a "typical" housewife.

Placing these three works together in the same sentence may seem to be bending the canons of art, yet they have a common denominator in focusing upon persons whose subjective reality is at odds with the definition of reality imposed upon them from "outside," and this is a generalized element of the human condition of homosexuals. Most of them presently have to cope with varying degrees of tension that is a product of a culturally imposed disjunction with a normative order whose guardians, by and large, continue to regard them with suspicion and brand their sexuality variously as "unnatural," as "immoral" (a sin), or, at the very least, as prima facie evidence of unreliability—evidence that something is "wrong" with them and, therefore, that they can't be trusted.

Recognizing that there is an underlying tension in the homosexual's world view lends no support to the classical psychoanalytical diagnosis that he or she is "mentally ill." This automatic diagnosis should have been discarded ever since Evelyn Hooker (1956) published her groundbreaking study of two matched control groups of homosexuals and heterosexuals. Old ideas and their justifications, however, are consigned to a very slow death that seems to be prolonged beyond conscience by some of the "shamans" (the psychoanalysts) to whom we have entrusted —on entirely inadequate theoretical grounds—the task of defining what is "normal." Most frequently, the "normal" turns out to be only replication of cultural assumptions of "normalcy," and the therapeutic process is designed to produce a population of conformists—a population that can be made comfortable in its straitjackets. Even the 1974 position adopted by the American Psychiatric Association represents only a minimal advance. Its wording remains ambiguous, an ambiguity probably forced by compromising with "traditionalists" such as Irvin Bieber and Albert Goodman (a social critic), whose contribution to a 1967 CBS television documentary *(The Homosexuals)* is a litany of vilification and misinformation.

Almost nothing is known about the etiology of homosexuality, but this is, ultimately, beside the point for even if it can be proved, for example, that the sexual preference is positively related to a chromosomal imbalance (over which one has no control), the findings will do little to dispel the homosexual's awareness that he is an alienated person in a cultural system whose basic premises concerning what is "right," what is "proper," what is "normatively expected" are not at all related to etiology.

The culturally induced feelings and experiences of alienation that homosexuals share with members of other stigmatized minorities may and sometimes do lead to the development of anxiety neuroses, and the classical psychoanalytical position that homosexuality is an "illness" tends to be a self-fulfilling diagnosis. When all the members of a given group, homosexuals in this case, are branded as "ill," some will accept the diagnosis as the cause of their feelings of alienation and inadequacy and some of these will seek the "curing" help of those who have said they are ill, thereby providing "confirmation" for the diagnosis that they *are* ill. Psychoanalytic thereapy, however, has a singularly poor record in effecting "cures" for homosexuality, and labeling the sexual preference as an illness per se may intensify feelings of "unworthiness."

This possibility is recognized by the private or publicly funded "Gay Counseling Services" or "Counseling Services for Sexual Minorities" that have arisen since the "Stonewall Riots" of 1969, an event that is frequently cited as the precipitator of the contemporary gay movement. Though the number of such specialized services is still quite small—and when they are publicly funded they are often the last to be approved and the first to be discontinued under general budget reductions—they attempt to provide an alternative support system for those who are troubled by their sexuality. It is estimated that Port City's Counseling Service for Sexual Minorities receives 2,000 telephone and in-person inquiries a year. Not all of the callers are homosexual, and a relatively small number of the self-identified homosexuals either appear or return for counseling. The total number of inquiries doesn't support the indiscriminate labeling of a population as "mentally ill"; but by the same token, the relatively small number who seek the help of the Service does not mean that the remainder do not have to make some personal adjustments to the cultural stigma of unworthiness.

While it is only an intuition—for I have not researched the question and do not know of anyone who has—it is possible that social, economic, and other cultural variables contribute importantly to the homosexual's personal adjustment to the experience of alienation. For example, homosexuals who are highly gifted and successful in any of the arts tend to receive support from a heterosexual audience that often affects a moral neutrality concerning the sexuality of those whom they admire. The case of Oscar Wilde might seem to refute this suggestion but Wilde's folly lay in challenging an aristocratic establishment whose members customarily winked at the sexual peccadillos of their class and joined ranks to protect "birthright" members from the consequences of acts that were not appreciably different from those that destroyed him. The tacit sexual latitude extended to members of privileged establishments of birth, wealth, talent, or, sometimes, a combination of all three often seems to be replicated at the lowest social and economic extreme, in the "establishments of outcasts" for whom many proscribed sexual acts—excluding child molestation—may be accepted and accommodated in a system of mutual support and identification against the "enemy" of entrenched civil and moral authority. If the extremes of this continuum have any validity at all, they suggest that people in the middle range tend to have most difficulty in adjusting to their outcast status, people, that is, whose backgrounds, occupations, and day-to-day associations emphasize conformity to the traditional "sexual verities" of moral respectability. It is certainly this middle population who are most threatened and most easily destroyed by excessively discriminating statutory proscriptions.

Some degree of disjunction with the world view of *les justes*, however, is a component of the homosexual condition, and those who object to the portrayal of its consequences in the popular genre I have mentioned might be accused of wanting to censor a perfectly legitimate dramatic theme that rather than serving to further entrench heterosexual stereotypes of homosexuals may help to advance heterosexual awareness of the way in which a multitude of lives are damaged by their misinformed moralizing and their tenacious grip on privilege and power.

Objections to Genet's homosexual characters on the ground that they are only literary replications of disapproved stereotypes is a serious misreading of the intellectual and thoroughly humanistic thrust of his art. The members of his various "casts" are not "characters" in the conventional literary sense (Esslin, 1969, pp. 196–197); rather, they are symbols—hieratic figures—that are used to explore the human condition. His theatre, as Esslin has said (1969, p. 197), ". . . is, profoundly, a theatre of social protest"; and the fact that his "characters" are mainly "outcasts" underscores a more comprehensive vision of "the alienation of man, his solitude, his search for meaning and reality" in a world in which his subjective persona is sharply at odds with the definitions of "reality" imposed upon him from "outside."

There is, of course, a major difference between Genet's dramatis personae and the "cast" of The Columbia. The former are the creation of a guiding intellect, abstractions that are used to convey the philosophy of their creator, whereas the latter are fleshed individuals, the raw material which the alchemy of the artist transmutes to symbolic incarnations. In their transmuted form, they move to self-consciously constructed ritual measures like figures in a temple frieze—stylized emanations of a world of fantasy and myth (Esslin, 1969, p. 196). Both Esslin and Sartre (1964) emphasize that this world is a private one. For example, Esslin (1969, p. 169) refers to the prison narratives as "the erotic fantasies . . . the daydreams of a solitary outcast of society"; and while acknowledging that Genet's theatre "undoubtedly has psychological truth," he seems less certain that it has "social truth" as well. Yet if it is, as he says a little later, "profoundly a theatre of social protest"—and I think it is—then it has a social relevance that transcends the private vision. Esslin himself seems to imply this in summarizing the intent of Genet's drama:

> It is clear that in confronting *society itself* in the theatre, rather than as solitary readers of his narrative prose, Genet comes far closer to his objective. Here a group of living people constituting a collectivity—the audience—is confronted with the secret dreams and fantasies of the outcast. What is more, the audience, *by experiencing the impact of what they see . . . is forced to recognize its own psychological predicament,* monstrously heightened and magnified though it be, there in front of them on the stage. (1969, p. 196; italics added)

Genet presents this social and psychological predicament through highly involuted images that are like the Chinese puzzles, carved in ivory, in which a series of spheres of diminishing size repeat and reflect the designs engraved on the one that encloses them. His vision, however, is even more tortuous than this, as Sartre (1964, pp. 654–669) reveals in his unsurpassed exegesis of Genet's The Maids (1954), in which the audience, society, is propelled into a seemingly endless maze of reflections and refractions of reflections. Probably, most of the audience are little more than voyeurs, similar to the hooting crowds watching Stilitano—the pimp—who was unable to find an exit from the hall of mirrors in an amusement park (Genet, 1967). But in Genet, the audience—though perhaps they do not know it—is an essential member of the cast. In a sense, they, representing society, are the "movers" behind the action unfolding in front of them; and in the final mirror, they are looking at themselves—at the fakery and lies and the dissembling that are associated with all establishments.

The "play" observed on the stage of The Columbia lacks the self-conscious intellectualizing and introspection of Genet's work, and one cannot make a full transposition from one to the other; but there are points at which his prose and formal theater illuminate many of the tavern's ritualized behaviors. Many members of his casts are homosexual men—Sartre (1964, pp. 628 ff) insists that Genet's homosexuality is the base of all his work—and, for the most part, they are otherwise separated from the mainstream of conforming expectations. No member of the "cast" of The Columbia is a murderer. The biographies of some of them duplicate some of the events in Genet's own life, but the criminality of those with official records is conventional in the sense that it far more widely distributed through all strata of the population whether heterosexual or homosexual, and most of The Columbia's customers have no "official records" at all. Yet they are "others" in the eyes of those observing them across the footlights of conventional rectitude. "We 'normal' people," as Sartre (1964, p. 630) has said, "know delinquents only from the outside, and if we are ever 'in a situation' with respect to them, it is as judges or entomologists . . . [considering] them from outside and as species . . . The homosexual must remain an object, a flower, an insect, an inhabitant of ancient Sodom or the planet Uranus, an automaton that hops about in the limelight, anything you like except my fellow man, except my image, except myself. For a choice must be made: if every man is all of man, this black sheep must be only a pebble or must be me . . . [And] Genet refuses to be a pebble; he never sides with the public prosecutor; he never speaks to us about the homosexual, about the thief, but always as a thief and as a homosexual. Hs voice is one we never wanted to hear; it is not meant for analyzing disturbance but for communicating it."

The final sentence in this passage can be adapted almost word for word to the ritualized behaviors of The Columbia, recognizing, however, that "disturbance" is not a synonym for "mental illness"; for in Sartre it stands for the experience of disjunction between "being" and "otherness," between the self and the social and cultural medium in which all lives are steeped, an experience that is intensified for those who have been assigned to "outcast" status but that also reaches deeply into the ranks of "normal" people, all of whom are "compelled" to effect some resolution between the "subject-object" poles of human existence. For Genet, the resolution leads to the self-conscious embracing of "an impossible nullity" (Sartre, 1964, p. 637). He makes no excuses, offers no apologies to those who have made him an "object"; rather, he embraces the status and says—flying in the face of "normal" expectations—"yes, this is what I *am!*" He demands his right to be "a pure thing" (1964, p. 641) and, thereby, presents himself as "an insolent mockery" and "absolute opponent" of a "society of subject-objects."

I do not imply that any of The Columbia's customers have consciously chosen Genet's resolution of the subject-object dichotomy—which in his case is the product of both genius and ruthless self-analysis—but they share with each other an awareness of their "otherness," of their common status as "delinquents," as members of an "entomological species," and there is definitely a component of Genet's "insolent mockery" in the rituals I have described. While they touch a base in the real-life fantasies and experiences of many male homosexuals, they are essentially stylized and exaggerated enactments of the "characteristics" assigned to the "species"—an audible and visible echo of Genet's decision to *be* the "object" others say he *is*. The mockery of the rituals removes them from the "ordinary"—I hesitate to say "profane"—realm of day-to-day life, and I think there is a warrant for including them in the category of "rites of intensification," comparable, that is to the "communion ceremonies" of a multitude of other "believers." The Columbia's rituals, however, include a patent element of irony which is not characteristic of their more respectable secular and sacred counterparts. The ironic twist escapes most heterosexual and many homosexual observers, yet I think it is one of the most important ingredients in the communication and intensification of included and excluded understandings, for it plays with the "otherness" of a stigmatized species, not only the assumed "characteristics" of "the homosexual species" but also the "characteristics" of the urban poor and others who are "outcasts."

I shall return to this a little later, for I do not think it is possible to appreciate these highly exaggerated stylized behaviors unless they are viewed as "rituals of stigmatization," as the apotheosis of the several relational, perceptual, and cognitive levels included in the "reality" the tavern's customers attribute to its style.

Some of the "attributes" of "reality" are obvious but not unimportant because they are manifest and easily extrapolated from observation. For example, in contrast to the circumspection required of The Columbia's customers in their relationships with the "outside," the "order" of the tavern is "real" in the sense that homosexuality is not only accepted but also has a positive value. There is no need to dissemble, not even in front of the straights who, entering the scene unwittingly, react to what they see with expressions of rejection and distaste. A degree of dissembling may be necessary or prudent—and is also understood—where some biographical information is concerned, but not in the case of "deviant" sexuality. The disgust and moral outrage expressed by the straights— their demeaning gestures and frequently deliberately loud verbal disassociations from and condemnations of what they see—do not provoke any comparable vocal or physical response; rather, their obvious discomfort and self-righteousness are answered with an amusement that may well be more devastating that a rejoinder in kind. In more open and outside contexts the barbed words flung across a departing shoulder may hurt and produce a defensive reaction, but in the tavern they can be disregarded. The group of "believers"—the homosexual customers—with their obvious strength in numbers, faces the "heretic"—if only temporarily—from a position of advantage, and the rejection can not only be taken lightly but also serves to intensify the generalized experience of "otherness," that is, the "reality" of exclusion from the sexual hemispheres of a conventionally depicted world. For the time being, the cultural polarities are reversed. Those who would make an "other" of the homosexual in relation to their own "subject" become in turn an "other" to the homosexual's "subject."

The "community of believers," however, share far more than deviant sexuality. Their experiences of stigma also encompass marginal economic survival, the suspicion frequently encountered by those receiving public assistance, the blemishes of prison records in some cases, and the more diffuse opprobrium directed at social failures. The cumulative experiences of numerous stigmata bond them in ways that transcend the differences of individual biographies, such that the person who does not steal or hustle shares far more with those who do than he does with the relatively privileged patrons of Spiffy's. Homosexuality is one element of the "reality" The Columbia's customers ascribe to the style, but "real" also subsumes the world view of those who are associated in a more inclusive commonality of exclusion from and opposition to the values and expectations of the normative order. To some extent the normative order is always "unreal" to those whose behaviors fall outside its permitted and expected range of variance; it is "unreal" to them because they cannot be "whole" in their contacts with it. The commonality of The Columbia exorcises this frequently lonely experience of disjunction and incompleteness. Of course I do not mean that The Columbia's patrons are any less alone is an existential sense—or any less subject and object to

one another—when they are in the tavern than in their "outside" relationships; but the conventional cartography of the world changes radically. Submerged continents rise and others are pushed closer to or
beyond the edge of the horizon. Paradoxically, "reality" corresponds to a
heightening and intensification of the awareness of disjunction.

The paradox is not unusual, however. The same effect, for example, is
deliberately sought by many religious sects whose members emphasize
their separateness from—their disjunction with—the established social-
ecclesiastical order through institutionalized rejection of many of its
values: its schools, its technology, and its political control over many
aspects of the lives of its citizens. In The Columbia, the verbal and tactile
rituals are the closest approach to such institutionalized ways of expressing and communicating disjunction and thereby intensifying the "reality"
of a separate commonality.

But the "reality" ascribed to the tavern's order also encompasses the
structure described in Chapter Three. The division of the space into
"stages" or "performing areas" is closely related to the full range of ends
sought by the patrons. These are as varied as the desire to be solitary yet
not completely alone, pursuing sexual goals, getting drunk, or merely
socializing; and while many are only commonplace, all are presented in
the colors of a palette that distinguishes them from heterosexual taverns
and many homosexual taverns. Moreover, the relationship between
stage and activity provides not only a set of directions for accomplishing
different ends but also permits almost everyone to make general assessments of the motives of others. While it is impossible to know the precise
details of the scores of engagements, the behavior is coded by location
and by cues of dress and posture. For anyone familiar with the basic
directions, a quick glance round the room is sufficient to make a preliminary sorting of possibilities which can be refined as the customer settles
into the action. Impressions of randomness and disorder are relative to
knowledge of the code, which shares some of its signals with those associated with other bars and taverns but which also includes many that are
particular rather than general, that reflect an order which has sufficient
distinctions to enhance the view that it has a lien on definitions of
"reality."

Viewed against the total range of public male homosexual territories,
this is a parochial definition of "reality"; yet its warrant comes from the
very diversity of the styles. Other than the two commonalities I have
mentioned, the frames of reference that connect homosexuals to the
"outside" world are as different and numerous as those within the heterosexual population. The "reality" of The Columbia's style lies in its relationship to and expression of its population's view of their own social

universe, a universe in which the stigma of homosexuality is one among many other bonding stigmata. Both the generalized population-wide sexual stigma and the additional stigmatized characteristics of the tavern's clientele are enacted in the ritualized behaviors described in Chapters Four and Five, and all of them are communicated to members of the commonality by the same forms of symbolic manipulation, forms which I suggested are more widely used to communicate stigma within the total population but which also have additional embroideries associated with a particular frame of reference to "the others," including many homosexual "others."

In Chapter Four I noted some similarities between The Columbia's verbal dueling and "the dozens" among lower-class urban blacks, a population that is also stigmatized and alienated. "The dozens" has been studied by a number of sociologists and psychologists and I think it is useful to look briefly at some of the meanings and functions ascribed to it. I shall disregard, however, the differences in ethnic content noted in the black and white tavern versions, concentrating on the properties they share as members of a single category. I should also point out that my understanding of "the dozens"—and thereby my understanding of its Columbia counterparts—has been helped considerably by an as yet unpublished paper, "Mamas and Motherfuckers: Another Look at the Dozens," by two anthropologists, Michael D. Lieber and Mary Agnes Lewis.

Lieber and Lewis point out that "the dozens" is one form of verbal contests "characteristic of social interaction in black communities." They subsume the various forms under the generic label of "capping" and make a distinction between "capping" and the verbal style of "rapping." They identify two styles of rapping, "running it down," and "shucking and jiving." Both kinds of rap, however, differ from capping. Though it is certainly an oversimplification of the materials presented by Lieber and Lewis, one may say that rapping conveys information either about a given subject or event or about some personal intent such as a man indicating his desire for a sexual relationship with a member of the opposite sex. Rapping generally lacks overt competitiveness and aggressiveness and is not necessarily person-oriented. It may also concern general issues and ideas, employed as a way to explain them or to convert others to them. On the other hand, the various forms of capping are "highly competitive, highly personal and offensive, involving direct insults to an individual about some visible aspect of his person (appearance and character), his associates, his family, and his relationships with other people." (Lieber and Lewis) To cap is to try to "put down" or to "low rate" an individual and to evoke laughter from listeners. Lieber and

Lewis remark that "one's success or failure in a capping duel is measured by the laughter [evoked] from the audience. The presence of more than two people is characteristic of capping duels; the audience functions to give or withhold approval of the protagonists' efforts and to keep the duel going."

If these may be accepted as characteristics of capping, then the verbal rituals of The Columbia seem to share many of them. They are person to person, overtly insulting and offensive, and require an audience, the presence of more than two people, although unlike some examples of "the dozens" the audience does not enter the verbal competition, which always remains a two-way—two-person—contest. Recognizing the similarities, however, one may ask if any of the sociological and psychological explanations of the insulting form of capping provide adequate theoretical frameworks for analyzing The Columbia's duels, and if they do not then what other meta-messages are conveyed through them.

Perhaps the most common functionalist explanation views "the dozens" as a socially valuable mechanism for releasing and displacing aggression from the dominant and stigmatizing (white) population to the relative safety of one's group. "Frustrated out-group aggression is safely channeled into the in-group. In this way the formalized game of 'The Dozens' has social value to a group subjected to suppression, discrimination and humiliation." (Sperling, 1953, p. 470) Lieber and Lewis accept this proposition as one latent function of "the dozens" and point out that the verbal jousting frequently ends in physical combat. To the best of my knowledge the insulting duels of The Columbia never end this way, but that does not mean that they have no cathartic value. All homosexuals, but particularly those who carry the additional stigmata of The Columbia's population, belong to a group whose members have been—and still are—punished and suppressed. The "latent" explanation assumes that it is a psychoanalytical truism that experiences of suppression must find some outlet, some way of venting frustration, and the hypothesis then assumes that since it is dangerous to release the frustration overtly against those who cause it a surrogate object is sought and, finally, that the object chosen may be the one that is most handy, the person or the group of persons who share one's own frustrations. As Lieber and Lewis point out, the aggression is not always "safely displaced" in "the dozens," but they agree that the game is an aggressive act and I would not entirely eliminate aggression as a component of The Columbia's rituals, though the relationships between the persons involved are characteristically quite different from those between the duelists in their black counterparts. In the latter, for example, the duelists are connected to one another in a far wider range of interpersonal contexts and share a far greater knowledge of one another. Being more than simply "acquaintances," their encounters are more personal, more "vicious" than those associated with the tavern. Yet the "impersonality" I have ascribed to the tavern duels does not eliminate a cathartic value, for they certainly express—and in a "safe" way—shared experiences of stigma and cultural alienation.

Those who have written about black capping have also given considerable attention to the character and direction of the insults which have to strike the "outside" observer as being contrary to the brotherhood and mutual protectiveness that is frequently ascribed to members of outcast groups. Lieber and Lewis summarize this dimension of black capping:

> The subject matter which forms the raw material of capping is or is closely related to highly visible aspects of the person being capped on. One's clothes, shoes, hair and hair form, nose form, lips, skin color, personality, presumed intelligence, economic situation (his or his family's), his house, his friends, his dating partners, and his family are all observable aspects of the person which can be used to put him down. The very criteria for occupancy of the restrictive and oppressive environment of the black ghetto are often the raw material for the games of insult. . . . Many other characteristics of persons forming referents for capping also reflect a relative valuation based on white, middle-class standards . . . Always implicit in such invidious comparisons is a relative scale of rich-poor, good-bad, ugly-beautiful, human-sub-human, black-white.

There are similarities between this summary of the content of black capping games and the rituals of The Columbia. Perhaps the latter are not as explicitly personal as capping encounters. Physical appearances, except for demeaning genital references, are not often used to score a point against an opponent, and dress is referred to only occasionally. Both games use distortion and exaggeration as the basis of their humor, however, and in both of them the distortions are distortions of the undesirable characteristics assigned to the respective species by those responsible for stigmatizing them—the "black species" and the "homosexual species." Thus, the duels of The Columbia employ themes of "personal disorder," or "whoring" and "hustling," or "mendaciousness" and "shiftlessness" and other "unworthy" characteristics of poverty and unreliability as the black duels seems to be obsessed with the "unworthiness" of blacks in a white-dominated world. The very "standards" that are used to stigmatize them are used in exaggerated ways to "stigmatize" those who share the stigmata. Referring to this aspect of black capping (particularly "the dozens"), H. "Rap" Brown has said: "That's why they call me Rap, 'cause I could rap . . . But for dudes who couldn't, it was like they were humiliated because they were born Black and then they turned round and got humiliated by their own people, which was really all they had left. But that's the way it is. Those who feel most humiliated humiliate others." (Rap Brown, 1971, p. 196) And one informant remarked to Lieber and Lewis: "You laugh just to keep from crying."

In both cases, the epithets and demeaning remarks connect the duels to the "excluded" social universes of the two populations; and if one accepts Rap Brown's statement (1971) that *"the real aim of the Dozens was to get a dude so mad that he'd cry or get mad enough to fight,"* it is not difficult to appreciate the strategy of a "double humiliation." Of course, the tactic is used far more widely in verbal contests of one-upmanship and in what I have called "hard-core arguments." It is usually particularly telling and also hurting to accuse a person of being the object he is said to be by those who live in a different social universe. He becomes a twofold object. Moreover, the person who uses the tactic and those (the audience) who laugh at it may be said to be doing so for their own benefit, disassociating themselves from their object status. James Herndon (1969, pp. 70–71) makes this point in summarizing the behavior of his pupils in a ghetto high school, in their incessant and fanatic use among themselves of all the abusive epithets applied to them by "others": "If I had supposed that the students . . . would present a united front on the question of their own (relative) blackness, it was a mistake. . . . They weren't interested in degrees of liberal white attitudes like they spozed to be. No, just let the cry of watermelon-head! ring out through the classroom of the Tribe and you knew that somebody was making a poster, painting himself white . . . painting himself into the good, white side like any other artist."

The interplay between two social universes is an important element of The Columbia's rituals of stigmatization, and superficially it may seem that those who exchange such epithets as "whore" and "faggot," who question the attractiveness of another person, or who derogate his economic situation are "painting themselves" into the "white"—that is, "good heterosexual"—picture. Though the descriptive range of the insults in the black games is wider, the tavern's verbal duels—by implication if not directly—always seem to imply a relative scale of comparison, a comparison between two different "realities," one of which is "good" (normal and heterosexual) and one of which is "bad" (abnormal and homosexual). Yet I do not think that the meta-messages and the functions of the two versions are the same. If this is so, it may simply be because most explanations (mostly by white investigators) of black capping have focused upon either their "social value" as mechanisms for displacing aggression or upon their function as a means of achieving interpersonal status.

It seems to be clear that the immediate purpose of capping is to put someone down and thereby demonstrate superiority over him. Writers such as Abrahams (1964), Kochman (1969), and Lieber and Lewis recognize that the manipulation of language has important status implications. Power accrues to the winner of a verbal duel, to the person who is particularly adept at discomforting his opponent, at maneuvering him into a position where his back is against a wall and he cannot extricate himself from the trap that was laid with the opening gambit, with the recognized verbal signal—invitation and challenge—of what is afoot. Kochman (1969, p. 34, quoted by Lieber and Lewis) remarks: "The function of the 'dozens' or 'sounding' is to borrow status from an opponent through an exercise of verbal power. The opponent feels compelled to regain his status by 'sounding' back on the speaker or other group member whom he regards as more vulnerable."

Lieber and Lewis accept the proposition that capping involves a competition for status, but quite rightly they point out that other writers do not "elaborate on the reasons for the status implications nor the kinds of status for which people compete nor the criteria of eligibility for the statuses." In their development of these points they carry their analysis of capping and our understanding of the form and the meaning of its content several stages beyond the explanations of their predecessors. I cannot summarize either their thesis or their supporting materials adequately and I do not think it is applicable point for point to the rituals, verbal and tactile, that are part of the order of the tavern, and, needlessly perhaps, this observation does not invalidate its applicability to the milieu they have chosen to investigate. The social universes (the milieus) of disadvantaged ghetto blacks and the disadvantaged homosexuals of The Columbia intersect at some points but do not correspond completely. The relative "richness" of black capping and the tavern's duels possibly reflect relative intensities in the experience of stigma as well as more basic components of social organization. But the hypothesis of Lieber and Lewis corresponds to my own starting point in trying to understand the meaning (what is communicated) and the function of the tavern rituals; and since they state it clearly and succinctly, I reproduce it with their permission:

> To discover the meaning of capping, we must ask what people are communicating to each other in these verbal messages and how the messages relate to the speakers' world. The meaning of capping is not inherent in a single jibe or even in a sequence of jibes but in the pattern of information encoded on these verbal messages. We know that capping involves insulting someone in a face-to-face encounter. We know that the insult is couched in specific terms—statements about the person being insulted. [And we know these terms mean] the stigmatization of the person

being insulted. Our hypothesis is that the implicit information conveyed about the person, the meta-message of each verbal message (following Bateson and Ruesch, 1951) is about the relationship between the person being insulted and all other persons. To be more precise, the meta-message of capping is that the person being insulted is ineligible for normal social relationships with people.

The meanings and functions of the tavern rituals also need to be sought through the characteristics of the social universe of players and audience, a social universe chartered by outside myths that question the "wholeness" and the right to be "whole" of those who belong to it. Since blacks have also been denied "wholeness," my explanation of the tavern rituals may shed some light on capping behaviors. The absence, however, of some of the qualities that have been important for functional interpretations of capping suggests that additional meanings and messages need consideration. Neither interpersonal aggression nor competition for interpersonal status are major components of the tavern duels. Of all the forms of capping, "the dozens" is the most overtly aggressive and is primarily a preadolescent game often called "kid stuff" by black adults. But adult capping is also aggressive, and the situations in which it occurs are often fraught with interpersonal rivalries— precipitated by quarrels and conflicts of interest. Rivalry of any kind (other than demonstrating skill) does not seem to instigate the tavern duels. The protagonists are always acquaintances only. I am not ready to eliminate "hostility" entirely. There may be elements of dislike and sometimes envy that are masked by the comradeship shown by winner and loser at the end of the encounter, but players always reject the suggestion that they may have some personal axe to grind in belittling their opponents. Since I do not know how to demonstrate that "latent hostility" may be present, I think it needs no more than a nod of recognition.

I am also uneasy with the "displacement-of-aggression" hypothesis. Abrahams (1964) rejects it as "too simple," yet of course it is not "simple" at all. It is generated from complex theories concerning the components and interrelationships of the human psyche and involves notions of "suppression," "deprivation," "frustration," "projection," and so on and the manner in which such experiences are expressed in the social behavior of individuals and groups. Perhaps I do not have to point out that the generative theories are largely intuitive, but my uneasiness with the hypothesis is not because of this or because of its "simplicity"; rather, it does not explain why the "aggression" is displaced in some ways rather than others, and I do not think it helps very much in trying to understand the messages that are being communicated.

There cannot be any serious questioning of the alienated status of homosexuals in the United States, and "the gay movement," even though nonviolent, is a direct ("aggressive") protest against it. Moreover, if Rap Brown's statement that "those who feel most humiliated humiliate others" is recognized as a rephrasing of the "displacement-of-aggression" hypothesis, it may seem to be easily transposable to the tavern rituals. "Humiliation" seems to be the goal of the protagonists in confronting each other and their audience; and as with capping, the humiliations are highly stylized. Protest is involved; but the interesting questions are what kind of protest and what ends are served by it. For example, the aggressiveness of capping may be a "safer" way of releasing frustration than violently confronting those whose attitudes and institutions have caused it; yet according to all observers the immediate interpersonal consequences of the duels are destructive. But this, too, is commonly provided with a positive function. The very destructiveness of the duels is said to be a useful "school of toughening" for those who are reared in the social environment of the ghetto. This may be so. I do not wish to debate the procedural elisions through which negatives are frequently transformed into positives by some theoretical positions in sociology, social psychology, and anthropology. I am simply suggesting that there are meanings to the tavern rituals that these particular functionalist interpretations do not reach.

Status, like protest, is involved in the rituals; but echoing Lieber and Lewis, the question is "what kind of status?" The encounters are competitive and interpersonal, but are they primarily or even significantly strategies through which one person "borrow[s] status from an opponent through an exercise of verbal power"? I suppose one must grant that there is some personal satisfaction and personal enhancement in winning a duel and also in being a recognized master of the form, but this kind of "achieved status" is quite fleeting and has no implications for other relational contexts. The *quality* of an individual's relationships with others is frequently a subject for insults. They are characterized as transitory, sexually obsessed (promiscuous), and predatory, the opposites of the "meaningful" and "lasting" relationships that are most highly valued, promoted, and sought in the normative order. Given that the latter are criteria for "normalcy," attributing their opposites to another person's relationships impugns his eligibility for "normal status," his status as a "worthwhile" person.

Lieber and Lewis, noting that "what the ghetto Black is most concerned about, other than making a living, is the quality, quantity, and stability of his personal relationships with others," demonstrate convincingly that the content of capping is implicitly an attack upon or questioning of an individual's "resources for personal relationships," an attack upon his "personhood," his persona, within the ghetto context, being defined ultimately by the kinds and amounts of relationships an individual has and his manner of handling them. I do not think that "personhood" is perceived and judged in the same ways by ghetto blacks and male homosexuals, if for no other reason than that members of the latter population are connected with the normative order through more numerous and diverse frames of reference, experiences, and identifications; yet it is "normative personhood" and, therefore, "status" that is the butt of the insults.

The messages encoded on or transmitted through the ritualized behaviors speak to the cultural "myths" that deny personhood to the homosexual per se. Such myths cast the homosexual as an "object." They deny him eligibility for a wide range of "normal" relationships and statuses, indeed, virtually all of those that are dependent upon the basic, culturally ascribed definitions of gender and gender roles. The initial "betrayal of gender" turns the homosexual into a "nonperson," a challenge and affront to the values placed upon "masculinity" and "femininity" and most of the institutions and institutionalized relationships in which they are embodied: family, husband-wife, parent-child, teacher-student, political leader, and so on. The list of statuses for which the homosexual is ineligible, or for which his eligibility is very questionable, is almost endless, and his ineligibility is "justified" by other myths, one after another, that embroider upon the fundamental myth of gender and its notions of natural complements and oppositions.

This is the context in which the meaning of the rituals must be sought and in which their messages can be understood. It is also the context in which it is possible to appreciate the strategy of distorting and exaggerating stigma, a strategy that is not peculiar to the verbal and tactile behaviors observed in The Columbia but is present also in the more widely distributed behaviors of "fag chitchat," the "gender fuck," and deliberately androgynous forms of self-presentation. There are similarities in all these behaviors to the racial slurs that are so prominent in black capping. Lieber and Lewis point out that most writers see the ingroup racial slurs—"watermelon head," "liver lips," and so on—as evidence that blacks "have accepted white evaluations of them as true." They reject this explanation as "ethnocentric"—a "projection of Whites' views of Blacks onto Blacks"—and conclude that "the racial slurs are simply prognostications about one's career chances based upon a long and monotonous history. The so-called racial slurs . . . are just another way of talking about the implications of poverty for one's personal relationships and about the relation between poverty and Blackness." Similarly, the "racial" (homosexual) slurs in the tavern rituals and other

stylized behaviors do not mean that the homosexual has accepted heterosexual views of homosexuals as true. This is also an "ethnocentric" interpretation. The slurs do comment upon a "long and monotonous history"
of discrimination and exclusion and upon the object status of the homosexual. They use and distort the cultural myths of what homosexuals are
—the myths that "justify" their exclusion from normative personhood—
and through distortion they intensify the commonality of those who
have been "objectified" by distortion. Stigma is manipulated not only to
intensify the shared experience of those who are stigmatized but also to
mock the cultural straitjacketing responsible for stigma.

It is time to return to the derealization of appearances in "the hall of
mirrors." Sartre has said (1964) that "in Genet's plays every character
must play the role of a character who plays a role." He (Genet) is the
master of fraud and fakery, and time and time again he warns his reader
and his audience that this is what he is about. Reader and spectator must
not be allowed to become caught up in the illusions presented to them,
mistaking them for reality; rather, they must be forced constantly to
recognize that the "reality" of appearance is profoundly unreal. Femininity and masculinity, for example, are only categories of the imagination.
"Anything can be a woman: a flower, an animal, an inkwell." (Sartre,
1964, p. 655)

The "reciprocal derealization of matter by form and of form by
matter" (Sartre, 1964, p. 657) is conveyed most explicitly by performers
with their beards, their gowns and feminine makeup, their male genitals
and voices, and their feminine gestures; but the same message is
transmitted by the "glamorous ladies" of the Empress Ball. "We know,"
Sartre (1964, p. 656) says, "that Genet values above all the labor of
derealization. The thing that attracts him in *Our Lady of the Flowers* is
the spectacle of a man being worked upon by femininity: 'Our Lady
raised his bare arm and—it's astonishing—this murderer made the very
same gesture, though a trifle more brutal, that Emilienne d'Alençon
would certainly have made to rumple her chignon.' " The "labor of
derealization" is present in the "gender fuck" between friends, in the
"bitchiness" of the "girls" in The Two-Ten-Four and in "Arlene" drawing
attention to his fake breasts; and it is also present, though not as
immediately recognizable, in the apparel and posturing of the "Marlboro
Men" and "leather" swashbucklers who emphasize the *appearance* of a
masculinity that is culturally denied to them as homosexuals.

There is an "insolent mockery" in all these behaviors, a mockery
directed at the myths of gender and the myths of the homosexual—
that is, to the *appearance* of the homosexual. The appearance of the
homosexual is the product of the appearance of masculinity and the

appearance of femininity which are ultimately—biological differences notwithstanding—categories of the imagination, as virtually all the categories of culture are imaginary. Simply as human beings, all of us are locked into categories of the imagination, and in our culture the "locking into" the opposites of gender begins at birth with the color coding of "blue for boys and pink for girls" and from then on gathers to it almost endless accretions of appearances: reason-emotionality, aggressiveness-passivity, hardness-softness, competition-cooperation, active bread-winner-domesticated nurturer, and on and on. The homosexual betrays the fundamental *appearances* of sexuality and sexual attraction, and therefore, in the male case, the fundamental appearance of "masculinity." Thus, he betrays all the other "appearances of masculinity" and must be assigned one of his own. He becomes a symbol in the cultural myth of gender, gender roles, and gender identifications—the hieratic figure of the outcast who is used as an exemplary warning to those who may question the veracity of the myth. "Look out; for this is what you will be if you don't accept our categories as real."

The whirligig of appearances and imagination (that is, myth) is the basic message transmitted through all the stylized behaviors I have recorded: from the reversed use of pronouns signifying gender through drag-costuming ("feminine" and "masculine"), "bitchy" gossip, the insults of the verbal duels, and the affronts to "normal" sexuality in the tactile pantomimes. As in Genet's work, every character is playing the role of a character who is playing a role: men playing the role of "men" to men who are playing the role of "women" to men who are playing as "men" to "men" as "women," and homosexuals playing to homosexuals—who are neither "men" or "women"—as homosexuals are thought to be by "men" and "women."

Validation of my thesis is not dependent upon a precise confirmation from the actors that this is the purpose of their script, any more than the performers of *The Maids* and the audience observing them would be consciously, intellectually aware of the final betrayal being perpetrated on all of them had not Genet given instructions—never, to the best of my knowledge, executed—that the females should be played by males *and* that this deception should be brought to their attention by a placard "nailed to the right or left of the sets during the entire performance." Certainly, the deceptions of the androgynous performing troupes and of Arlene and the gorgeous "stars" of the Empress Court are consciously assumed. The "Empresses" who visited my class described their public style as an "art," but I do not think they have made the symbolic transformations between the "myth of appearances" and the "appear-ances of myth" that I have done. Thus, I suppose that the meta-messages

I ascribe to the rituals are "latent" messages, but this is also true of the majority of messages encoded on patterned behavior.

I have not been interested in the possibility that some male homosexuals may be "femininely motivated." It is entirely beside the point if "male" and "female," beyond the purely biological differentiation, are recognized as cultural categories, that is, categories of the imagination, for it is not necessary to assume "psychological motivation" in order to understand the symbolism of the behaviors—their playing with the symbols of masculinity and femininity and the symbol of the homosexual. Genet on symbolism is instructive. In *The Child Criminal* (quoted by Sartre, 1964, p. 656), he refers to the director of a children's home who has given the inmates *tin* knives and justifies his action by saying "they can't kill anyone with that," to which Genet comments: "Was he aware that by departing from its practical destination the object is transformed, that it becomes a symbol?" And Sartre adds, explicating the passage in which the question is embedded: "As the material grows poorer—steel knife, tin knife, hazel twig—as the distance increases between itself and what it signifies, the symbolic nature of the sign is heightened. . . . [Genet's] maids are fake women, 'women of no gynaeceum,' who make men dream not of possessing *a* woman but of being lit up by a woman-sun, queen of a feminine heaven, and finally of being themselves the matter for the heraldic symbol of femininity. Genet is trying to present to us femininity without women."

That it is the appearance (the symbol) of femininity and of the male homosexual as "feminine" that is being manipulated is obvious in the deportment and costumes of the "ladies" at the Empress Ball, whose very exaggerations are equivalent to the placard Genet would have placed "to the left or right of the sets" and the "placard" he places in his description of *Our Lady of the Flowers:* the gesture that was "a trifle more brutal" than that of Emilienne d'Alençon. This is possibly why many feminists, including some lesbians, object strongly to the "drag queen" style, for the impersonators are announcing, though it may not be their conscious intent, that anything can be a "woman," that is, the "imagined woman" of the cultural myth of womanhood. Similarly, it is the myth of masculinity that is being manipulated and exaggerated by the posturing studs in their tight pants, cowboy boots, and hats. They are "fake men"—playing a role that is itself a "fake." And since in both instances the performances are clearly fake—consciously distorted—they are a commentary upon the myths of masculinity and femininity that characterize the homosexual as a fake.

The myth of the homosexual, that is, the incomplete and fake "man," is also the charter for the verbal insults and the indiscriminate, aggressive

sexual advances in the tactile pantomimes. In Chapter Four, I said that
the traded allegations in the verbal duels have virtually no foundation in
biographical truth or, at least, little foundation in any truth that is
unequivocally known to the protagonists, excepting only their homosexuality and otherwise disadvantaged station. This does not mean, as I
also pointed out, that they are entirely divorced from the fantasies and
experiences of many homosexuals or have no foundation at all in the
private activities of some of those involved in the encounters. It isn't
possible to deny that, excepting recruitment, child molestation, and the
indiscriminate imputation of feminine motivation, the behaviors of some
male homosexuals replicate some of the characteristics assigned to the
"species" by heterosexuals. There are sexual hustlers. There is a good
deal of impersonal and anonymous sex, quite apart from "homosexual"
encounters I have called "homoerotic," that is, many that occur in public
rest rooms, some parks, peep shows, and some movie houses (and,
incidentally, in Port City these encounters—"homosexual" by dictionary
definition—apparently occur far more frequently in movie houses
showing pornographic films for ostensibly heterosexual audiences than
in the far smaller number exhibiting homosexual pornography). And
there also seems to be some factual basis for the instability of the "lover
relationship" between male homosexuals (particularly when compared to
the lesbian population) provided, of course, it is possible to define what
is meant by "lover" in the context of the homosexual universe, something
that has not been done by the investigators with whom I am familiar, all
of whom seem to approach the problem from a "heterosexually ethnocentric" point of view.

Granting, however, that there is some correspondence, at some
points, between the heterosexual myth of homosexual behaviors and the
behaviors of some homosexuals does not place a serious question mark
against my thesis that it is the myth of the homosexual—the nonman,
nonwoman, the "fake" and outcast—that is being enacted in the rituals
of The Columbia. Very few, if any, male homosexuals are unaware of
the appearance the entire population has in the eyes of heterosexuals who
have been conditioned to accept as real the basic gender myths of our
culture, and it is this appearance that is being enacted. The fact that some
of the allegations in the verbal duels may touch a base in the real-life
activities and proclivities of some protagonists is not important, for
the message conveyed is one of generalized stigma: the image of the male
homosexual as outcast and unworthy. The actors are playing the roles
of homosexuals as written by "normal people" (by *les justes*), but they
are not playing them "straight." Every narrative distortion, every exaggerated gesture is a "placard" that announces the game-play, which is

essentially the communication of stigma and a shared "object" status. Thus, the rituals may be characterized as "rites of intensification" not intended for analyzing "disturbance" but for communicating it, that is for communicating the appearance of the homosexual in the cultural hall of mirrors.

Afterword

As I write these last words (in 1978), The Columbia remains open for business, but I do not think it will endure much longer. For many months now, its neighbor, The Silver Star, has been vacant during obviously expensive remodeling and renovations. Smaller than The Columbia, the Star used to be almost as unpretentious though a little "higher class." It wasn't a "sissy" tavern, but its customers were generally younger and cleaner than a cross section of The Columbia's regulars and transients. Miss Rose has never been inside it. She often asked me about it; but once when I offered to take her there, she put her hand to the safety pin fastening her Goodwill coat and said: "Some other time, honey. When I get some new things." I never repeated the suggestion, for I felt she was happier in her living room at The Columbia than among a younger crowd.

If Rose felt some class consciousness in intruding on the Star at that time, it would be completely off limits to her now, judging from what can be seen of the planned remodeling—linen-fold, antiqued paneling on the street-side facade and rose-red brick arches and high-backed booths inside. No one on the street seems to know if it will be a gay place. Probably not. The refurbishing of the environs of the Square culminated not long ago in the opening of a monstrous domed stadium. Land values, rents, and taxes skyrocketed, and the present owners of the Star are probably hoping to attract the tens of thousands who pass through the Square to stadium events.

But Miss Rose will not be there to see the opening of the new place or the end of The Columbia.

Five months ago as I skimmed the morning newspaper over my coffee,

171

I saw a headline above a half-column story: "Gallant Lady Is Taken to Hospital." It was not a story I was likely to read while getting myself together for the day, but there—in the first line of the report—was Miss Rose's name, not the pseudonym I have given her but her own identity. The account said that some of the regulars in the tavern had noticed her absence for several days and had called the police, who went to her hotel room and found her on the floor, comatose and suffering from malnutrition and bed sores. The reporter described the disarray of her room, the stack after stack of old newspapers, the bulging brown-paper shopping bags, and scattered and empty muscatel bottles, and I thought: "Oh, no! Rose shouldn't have her private life exposed so publicly and clinically," and I wondered if anyone had found the stained manuscripts of "Viona" and "Love," which were more like the Rose I remembered than this case history of an outcast, eccentric, and derelict old woman.

I went to the huge, federally supported hospital where she had been taken, going from one floor to another, from one busy and impersonal desk to another until someone realized that Rose and I shared the same last name and assumed I must be a relative.

So they took me to a seemingly endless ward of curtained cubicles and stood me at the foot of her bed. I am sure Rose recognized me, but I stayed for less than a minute—only long enough to give her a five-dollar bill and to run, literally, from the stench to the closest men's room.

Later, the people at the desk told me I should not have given her any money. "Those others in there," they said, "will rip it off of her."

I don't know where Rose is now, and I wasn't pleased with myself as I left the hospital, feeling I had done something demeaning to her, not only by seeing her totally bereft of all her little pretenses but also by giving her my token charity. And I thought that those who had noticed her absence from The Columbia and had alerted the police had been more kind and more concerned. They wouldn't visit her. Most of them would not want their names or their connections known, but they had known her as one of them and I had seen her primarily as a "grotesque"—as someone to use in trying to describe the quality of a style that is a whole world removed from everything I have known and have tried to be comfortable with.

If anyone finds The Columbia—and it is not difficult to do so—and goes there now, they will not see Rose, and they will not see much of what I have described. Physically, it is essentially the same—bare, dirty, tattered, and still announcing its counterculture pride in the absence of wall-to-wall carpets. But the poolroom is hardly ever used now, and even at the height of the holiday season there are many empty tables and vacant stools along the bar. On the few occasions I have been there recently, I have rarely seen a familiar face. The customers seem to be mostly transients, still impoverished, unkempt, and ethnically diverse but with a conspicuously larger number of Native Americans, who may have begun to gravitate there since The Britannia was demolished. It is not the same place in which I invested so much time, and the difference suggests some final comments.

There are a few gay taverns in Port City—Spiffy's, for example—that have more than twenty years' continuous identity. They are not "neighborhood" or even "home territory" bars, but over the decades they seem to have attracted a population sharing the same characteristics of class, age, and relative economic advantage. Their longevity is exceptional, however; for gay bars and taverns seem to come and go, being "in" for a while then suddenly "out." Many of my Columbia informants do not go to the tavern now, and when I ask them "why?" they usually say "well it was different when so-and-so was tending bar." Bartenders seem to be more important in setting or reflecting a style and making patrons comfortable than anything that may be suggested by their service roles of drawing beer and pouring wine. They are liked or disliked according to what they allow or disallow and according to the customers' perception of their empathy and understandings. The owners are rarely a visible presence, being even more anonymous than the patrons; and while they are accountable for the physical setting, it is the bartenders who bring everything together and are largely responsible for the quality of the final composition.

During my study of The Columbia, there were noticeable differences in atmosphere when the bartenders changed, a perceptible drop in the feeling of "at homeness" among the regulars, as though some stabilizing linchpin had been removed. Most customers, even the regulars, know as little about the private lives of the bartenders as they know about the outside lives of a majority of other patrons. On the other hand, the bartenders, often functioning as lay analysts, have a greater knowledge of the circumstances of many of those they serve night after night, knowing when to cut off drink, when to give a warning that a new face should not be trusted, when to decline a check—because it is too late in the month—and when to eject a stranger who is too obviously hustling the style of the establishment. The authority of the bartenders is more often welcomed than resented. They are a *presence* that *presides,* and they are often the first contact sought by many customers, not simply to be served a drink but to "settle in" with someone they know—who seems to provide a sense of security—before exploring other opportunities.

At the present time, none of The Columbia's bartenders were employed there when I was a regular. Some of those I knew seem to have disappeared, no one knowing where they have gone; but a few of the old hands work in neighboring taverns and have been followed there by former customers.

Yet the imminent demise of The Columbia can't be attributed solely to managerial disputes, dismissals, and changes in personnel. The city-sponsored upgrading of Occidental Square has proceeded apace since I began my study. Almost every week, it seems, new restaurants and expensive shops open in renovated buildings. The character of the square has changed remarkably. The police cars are far less visible now, and I do not think their departure is merely a reflection of more tolerant policies toward homosexuals. For one thing, most of the new gay bars and taverns have opened in scattered locations farther downtown; but more importantly, the engineered changes have dispossessed most of those who found some kind of haven there for the end of their lives and the transients—young or old—who had gravitated to a section of the city where they had expected to find others who shared the experiences and understandings of disadvantaged and submerged lives. A majority of the thousands who visit the Square today are transients, but they are "respectable," with money to spend, and an obvious police presence might be intimidating, suggesting dangers and suspicions of undesirability that are counter to "cultural" and commercial promotions.

On a few occasions recently, I have stood outside The Columbia and watched the crowds flowing to a Billy Graham Crusade, to a convention of Jehovah's Witnesses, or to a National Football League contest in the domed stadium. These are now the clientele that most businessmen hope to attract. Perhaps the bars and taverns do not expect much custom from the hordes gathering for some religious event, but they certainly have an eye on the sports fans who want to celebrate either defeat or victory. The streams of people are like an inundation that is contained only by police barricades that proclaim "No Entry," "Sidewalk Closed," or "Sidewalk Unsafe," and The Columbia is merely a spit of land preserving its precarious identity behind a temporary levee.

I do not know where most of the tavern's former patrons take their custom now. Some of the older regulars have probably died or, like Miss Rose, have suffered some kind of physical collapse. The younger ones have almost certainly found a place whose style is similar to the one I have described, for the style itself will persist as long as the population of any city contains a sizeable minority whose lives are stamped by the same experiences as those that characterized my sample. On any given night, most of The Columbia's customers were transients—"rootless" from some moralistic points of view—moving from one state and one city to another as though carried along by some underground river and always, wherever they interrupted their journey, finding their own level.

Despite their regional differences, the cities of America are essentially the same, so similar that a mobile population—drawn from any social strata—can always find others who are infected by the same virus.

Cities are not the lonely places depicted in many classical studies in urban sociology. The models used in these studies generally harkened back in a nostalgic fashion to the idealized and romanticized conception of the rural (primitive?) community whose members were supposedly bound to one another by day-to-day personal ties within a matrix of homogeneous values. Many contemporary efforts to foster and to create "neighborhoods" in urban centers are nothing more than a romantic perpetuation of this lost but ideal image, and they are doomed to failure, for one cannot return to conditions that may have existed a couple of centuries ago—conditions that have been formalized and reified as the ideal state of man in much the same way that Rousseau and other philosophers of the Enlightenment fastened upon the "noble savage" in searching for an ideal contrast to the social ills of their time.

Of course there are "lonely faces in the crowd" (Riesman, 1952). Many of them are old people who are infirm or isolated because they have been discarded by the pervasive values of "youth culture"; others probably would be lonely in any setting, either by personal choice by because of personal inability to make any meaningful contact with their fellows: the "fault is often in themselves" and not in the characteristics of urban life itself.

At a gross descriptive level cities are "impersonal" if you contrast them with the idealized small town (Plains, Georgia?), but American literature is rife with examples of those who suffered under the constrictions of homogeneous values and the overpowering expectations to conform to them. The "sore thumbs" lived lives as desperate as many urban dwellers.

The virtue of cities lies in their very diversity. In a mass population comprising many different patterns of life and experience, it is far easier to find others with whom you can be "at home" than in the monolithic and self-contained small community. Cities have been misjudged. Public attention has focused upon crime, violence, slums, and all the other evils that are unquestionably a part of urban life and more manifest in cities than elsewhere simply because they contain the highest concentrations of population. But there is another side to the life of cities. If there is no longer a monolithic structure of American values, if that ideal has been shattered by over a hundred years of constant change and the failure of enculturative institutions to reproduce generation after generation of people who have internalized the same verities, cities are places where all the fragments can be found, where, rather than being lost in the faceless crowd, it is possible to find a reassuring and mutually supportive place with others in the kaleidoscope.

This statement has nothing to do with moral judgments. I am sure that from some points of view, there are many people who would attach little if any moral worth to the lives of most of The Columbia's customers, but I have tried to eschew anything of this quality in my relationships with them and in reporting about them, and I have not been interested in questions of what "made them what they are" or in remedial social programs. Possibly there are some who would blame the anomie of city life itself for some of the "flaws" in personality and world view that appear if placed against some normative standard; but many of those with whom I have been involved are not children of the city, having childhood and youthful backgrounds in "Main Street" rural communities. Many of these consider themselves the lucky ones who have "made it" into a world where there is a far greater opportunity to find a comfortable and sharing company.

Finally, the fact that no one who may be moved to look for The Columbia now will find it as I knew it raises some questions concerning virtually all ethnographies, the method of participant observation, and the social sciences versus the experimental sciences.

The problem of eliminating subjectivity in research that relies solely or largely upon participant observation has been recognized for a long time by anthropologists and continues to be a focus of contention. Laymen and professionals alike can gain a great deal from an Appendix to a paperback reissue of E. E. Evans-Pritchard's *Witchcraft, Oracles and Magic Among the Azande* (1976), which, in my view, is the best exposition of the ambiguities of fieldwork that I referred to briefly in the Foreword to this book. Addressing the question of subjectivity in fieldwork, Margaret Mead is said to have suggested that every anthropologist should submit to the self-revealing instrument of psychoanalysis before being "let loose" in situations where he or she is both recorder and judge. It is probably an apocryphal attribution, but it touches a basic problem that more formalist investigators often raise. Stated briefly, the problem is how to control for the personal world view of the investigator, and for the likes and dislikes that are part of his persona and the filtering effects his persona has not only upon what he sees and records but also upon the very problems he chooses to research. A classic example, frequently cited by those who suspect the "personal approach," is the two ethnographies of Tepoztlán, a village in Mexico, one by Robert Redfield (1930) and the other by Oscar Lewis (1951). The Tepoztlán described by Redfield is almost an idyllic peasant community characterized by close and harmonious interpersonal ties and a virtual absence of the conflicts and factionalism that Redfield associated with industrialized urban life. On the other hand, Lewis' Tepoztlán is a community that is rife with conflict and factionalism. Lewis' study was made seventeen years after the publication of Redfield's book, but it is almost inconceivable that this relatively short interval of time could have wrought such dramatic changes in the quality of life in a small community, and the question, then, is which is "true." The answer is quite probably that *both* are "true" but that *neither* of them depicts the total "reality" of life in Tepoztlán.

Redfield was interested primarily in questions of order and the contrast between the relatively self-contained and personalized life of rural—peasant—communities and the mass populations of urban centers. On the other hand, Lewis was interested in conflict and disorder. Redfield had a bias toward a particular ideology and its frame of reference and Lewis had a bias toward a different one. The "real" Tepoztlán is probably an amalgam of both perspectives.

There is always a selective factor in what an investigator chooses to research and in the various generalizing theories he uses to marshal his data. The selection is based not only upon the critical evaluation of theories he receives in the classroom but also upon personal interests. Theories, like definitions, are not sacrosanct. Basically, generalizing theories in the social sciences are only more or less useful, productive, and illuminating frames of reference. They can't be *proved* though they may be discredited as intellectualizing frames of reference change and the accumulation of new or additional data reveals the limitations of prior "explanations." The so-called "personal equation" is always present, not only in the construction of theories but also in the choice of "significant" areas of research—even in the formulation of problems—and in the methodologies applied to them.

The case of the objectivists, however, often turns on the issue of replicability, on the extent to which those who follow the original investigator can use his methods to either confirm or deny his conclusions. The model is that of the natural and experimental sciences where laboratory conditions can be duplicated and an experimental situation can be repeated again and again. Situations approximating these are possible in the social sciences when methods are specified precisely and the problem is not only pinpointed exactly but is also usually limited to small and, from some points of view, relatively inconsequential matters; but I do not think replication is a possible or even a necessary test of the validity of ethnographies.

I hasten to add that ethnographic facts and the explanatory framework in which they are placed may be disputed. No ethnographer is omniscient. The possibility of errors in judgment cannot be eliminated entirely, even in trying to identify the customs and the rules of any given culture; and the possibility for error increases when the investigator is concerned with beliefs and ideologies, with world view and ethos. Even when the "facts" reported are not questioned, there is always room for differences of opinion on how they should be interpreted, but these differences are inherent in the process of theory building and are themselves subject to future reformulation.

No ethnography gives a complete account of any culture. Probably the most comprehensive ethnography of one culture by one observer is Malinowski's *oeuvre* on the Trobriand Islanders, but even that enormous body of work has lacunae, and his generalizing framework has been largely discredited. But apart from the changing perspectives of theoretical models, replication—as it is understood in the experimental sciences—is virtually impossible in the art of ethnography. The passage of time alone prevents it, for there are extremely few, if any, people in the world whose lives are so secluded or isolated that they represent a stable and immemorial tradition. All ethnographies are "past histories" by the time the investigator has left the field and his work reaches the printed page.

Even though it is still physically there, The Columbia I have described is also past history. The quality of its "order of activities" has changed since I began my work, and there were some perceptible changes during the years when I was most intensively associated with it. At the beginning of the study, for example, police harassment was an almost nightly probability. Often it was no more serious than handing out tickets for jaywalking in an area where there was very little nighttime traffic, but the ticketing officers usually returned ID's with demeaning gestures, presenting their citations with one hand placed on their hips in a simpering fashion and remarks such as "Here you are, honey. Be a good girl in the future."

This kind of harassment gave a subtle flavor to the life of the tavern, accenting its clandestine and disparaged values and reinforcing the "inside" understandings of those who found a relatively safe commonality on passing through its doors.

Such petty harassment is rare now. The state in which Port City is located has repealed its criminal sanctions against private homosexual acts between consenting adults while maintaining, however, legal sanctions against lewd homosexual conduct in public places. As I said earlier, legislation doesn't necessarily effect changes in entrenched attitudes. I do not think that even the most sweeping legislation favoring the civil rights of homosexuals will produce an unevaluated acceptance

of their life-style as an "equally reasonable" alternative to hetero-
sexuality. Something "clandestine"—something "odd"—is likely to be
attributed to the homosexual for the foreseeable future, and, as with so
many other attempts to legislate civil liberties, all that seems to have
been gained may be erased almost overnight.

Some official attitudes toward homosexuality have altered since I
began my study of The Columbia, and these changes have to some extent
altered the quality of visiting it. But its major changes have been
"internal," having nothing to do with the revision of statutes and an
increased wariness and tolerance on the part of police. Anyone who
might look for it now will not see what I have described—some similarities, perhaps, but not the same picture. Moreover, I doubt that any other
independent observer would necessarily have "seen" what I "saw."
Another observer may have fastened upon a different set of questions
and may have been blind or relatively indifferent to those that interested
me. If I had had a co-worker, perhaps these lacunae could have been
resolved, each of us enlightening the other about matters that were not
central to our individual interests.

But although *this* Columbia—*my* Columbia—no longer exists, other
researchers may question, correct, verify, or discount my interpretations
by observations in "ethnographically" related situations across the
country; for although in one sense my ethnography is unique—as all
ethnographies are unique—it is representative of a *style:* a variation of
more generalized patterns of behavior. The analogy that comes most
quickly to mind is the anthropological construct of "culture," or
"ethnographic," areas. In the culture area of Melanesia, for example—
and it is surely the most internally diverse in the number of its localized
variations—there are underlying similarities in world view, goals, and
social institutions. Melanesian specialists may—and do—dispute how
these similarities should not only be delineated but also expressed in
principles. But enough is known to question the veracity of ethnographies that seem to depart radically from the accepted range of
probability.

There are other "Columbias" in the United States—taverns whose
customers share the same multiple disadvantages as those that characterized the members of my population in Port City. They are easily
located, and I believe that there are similarities in their orders of activity
—common elements in structuring of interpersonal relationships, in the
cognitive and perceptual dimensions of world view, in the lores associated with the "inside-outside" quality of stigmatized lives, and in the
"mirror" symbolism of the more ritualized behaviors.

The literary frame of reference I have used for analyzing the symbolism of the ritualized behaviors is outside the methods and theories that are most commonly employed today by anthropologists who are interested in symbolic analysis, but is the one that I have found most useful for illuminating the data and other cognate behaviors that are more widely distributed among male homosexuals. I believe it is *one* valid approach to the material and serves my overall purpose of trying to understand the processes of communication between people who share a particular style and a common range of stigmatized experiences and understandings.

Appendix 1 — Observations on the Current State of Anthropological Research on Homosexual Behavior

I began the first draft of this book in 1973. It is now April 1979 and nothing that has happened in the interim suggests there is much need to modify my position that the American public, in the foreseeable future, is unlikely to give unevaluated acceptance to homosexuality as a "legitimate" alternative sexual life style.

The first successful and most highly publicized blow to the contemporary "Gay Movement" was the Save Our Children campaign, led by the entertainer and former "Miss America" Anita Bryant, aimed at repealing a Dade County (Florida) ordinance protecting homosexuals in housing and employment. The campaign was nothing more than a witch hunt—resembling the communist witch hunts of the McCarthy era—whose spokesmen invoked highly emotional but spurious issues. Yet it is reasonably certain that a large number of those who voted for repeal were not moved to do so by the strident fundamentalist religious arguments. Their support illustrates the deep entrenchment of homophobia in American culture.

The anti-homosexual forces won three subsequent victories in rather quick succession, one in Eugene (Oregon), one in Wichita (Kansas), and one in St. Paul. It was not until November 1978 that the momentum was

halted in Seattle, Washington, with the defeat by a two-to-one margin of
an initiative to rescind an existing city ordinance similar to the one
repealed in Dade County and by the overwhelming defeat of Proposition
6 in California that would have barred homosexuals from teaching in the
public schools.

In Port City, the campaign for Initiative 13 (that is, repeal of the existing anti-discrimination ordinance) was headed by two members of the
Port City Police Department (one of whom subsequently dropped out
following a controversial shooting incident) and was supported by
"Bryant-style" religious fundamentalists. I was asked to speak, as a
"humanist," at a citizens' meeting at which both pro and con views on
the Initiative were presented. I have seldom heard such specious, viru-
lent, and misinformed "arguments" as those presented by the sponsors of
the Initiative; but in fairness I must also note that many of those who
spoke against repeal were professed and believing Christians and Jews.

The successes in Port City and California represent worthy attempts
to resist demogoguery and bigotry, but I do not think there is any long-
lasting comfort in them. Many of those who voted against both measures
were not proclaiming their support for and acceptance of homosexuality
per se. They voted with homosexuals because the wording in each case
threatened to open a Pandora's box of innuendo and possible invasions
of privacy. The homosexual issue was contained in a package of larger
and more threatening dimensions.

I do not think these two victories are a sufficient reason to revise my
prognosis. The issue of homosexuality and homosexual rights does not
have the mass implications of the debate over the Vietnam War, the
draft, the black civil rights movement, or the women's movement. There
was and is a moral issue at the core of all these movements, but the moral
issues are not of the same kind or magnitude in their impact on the daily
lives of the total population. The stark events of the Vietnam adventure
and the prodigal expenditure of lives and treasure—a daily spectacle for
anyone who watched the TV news during those unfortunate years—
eventually generated national disgust and compelled millions of people
to reappraise the ideal image of America and its world significance. The
same kind of difficult questioning was involved in the black civil rights
movement. It is not as palpably present in the gay movement.

Both the gay movement and the women's movement touch far more
deeply entrenched attitudes and values, as I said earlier "striking directly
at the tender heart of cultural definitions of gender and gender roles";
and the difficult progress of the Equal Rights Amendment through the
constitutional process is an ample illustration of the way in which principles of justice can be obscured or buried under spurious moralizing and

doomsday prophecies of what will happen if there is any tampering with such "natural" definitions. Indeed, the probable fate of the ERA—failure to secure the number of state endorsements necessary for ratification—seems to dim the hopes of the homosexual movement; for if the rights of a sexual majority are so difficult to define and secure, those of a "questionable" minority are less likely to receive constitutional recognition and protection.

Finally, because this study of the Columbia tavern is a work in anthropology it may be useful to make a few brief remarks on the status of research on homosexuality within the discipline.

In his Foreword to this book, Lewis L. Langness remarks that "it is safe to say that anthropology has no theory of homosexuality." This is true, and it is also striking that in the thousands of articles and ethnographies published since "modern anthropology" began about the first decade of the twentieth century there is scant reference to the subject and very few "full scale" treatments of homosexual behavior in particular cultures. Thomas K. Fitzgerald (1977, p. 391) summarizes the status of the research for three-quarters of a century by saying that "most anthropologists mentioned the phenomenon, if at all, only in passing or hid such descriptions in the most obscure corners of their ethnographies." A case in point, which Fitzgerald cites, is E. E. Evans-Pritchard's belated (1970) "note" on institutionalized homosexual behavior among the Azande, coming more than thirty years after the publication of his major work on these people. Evans-Pritchard may have decided that the information was not central to his other intellectual concerns, yet its omission raises questions concerning what we "know" about Zande ideology, Zande sexual relationships, and sociopolitical structures.

Homosexual behavior is almost certainly a panhuman phenomenon, even more global than Ford (1960) and Ford and Beech (1951) were able to suggest by using the "world sample of societies" contained in the Human Relations Area Files. Anthropologists have questioned this source for comparative studies of human behavior, and it seems to be an absolutely necessary reservation in using the Files for cross-cultural studies of homosexual behavior. As Margaret Mead (1961) has pointed out, one should be very skeptical of reports that deny the existence of homosexual behavior in a given culture or that dismiss it as limited and insignificant. If the behavior is not conspicuous—institutionalized to some extent—the ethnographer may not have observed it, may have been reluctant to enquire about it, or, if he did, reticent about publishing his data as well as being predisposed to cast the information in the mold of his own culturally negative response and even aversion to it.

My own articles and ethnography on the Gahuku of New Guinea may be "tainted" in several of these ways. When my editor was preparing the final draft of *The High Valley* for publication, I received a rather distressed long-distance telephone call questioning the propriety of including a few sentences dealing with homoerotic exhibitionism in a ritual context, for "we [that is, the publishing house] want this book to be available to high school students as well as adults and professional anthropologists." I replied indignantly that I did not think anything I had written could possibly subvert the morals of teenage Americans at that time, most of whom (it was the mid-sixties) were far more sexually sophisticated than I was. Yet I think now that there are lacunae —possibly important gaps—in my analyses of Gahuku male ideology and institutions. "Homosocial behavior" was highly conspicuous in Gahuku culture, not only in the ideological, ritual, and social separation of the sexes but also in customary familiarities between males. I remember that when the late S. F. Nadel, who was my academic mentor, visited me briefly in the field, he remarked, on observing these "familiarities," that "there must be a good deal of homosexuality here." The words may not be his precisely but the suggestion (the accusation?) was clear and I reacted (protecting "my people"?) with a defensive "no." Now I am by no means so certain. I have described homoerotic exhibitionism in the culminating stage of Gahuku initiation rites (Read, 1965) and I have documented and demonstrated the dominance of male homosocial ideology and values but I cannot ignore what may be missing from my record, gaps that have been suggested by more recently published data on "cognate" New Guinea groups (Kelly, 1976; Scheffelin, 1977) and by a presently unpublished article by Gilbert H. Herdt (1980) on the Sambia, whose ideology of maleness and whose male rituals have much in common with those of the Gahuku.

The gaps in my record of the Gahuku cannot be retrieved now and I advise skepticism in accepting my statement in a footnote to one article (Read, 1955) that homosexual practices did not exist. A pertinent question is why my record may have these lacunae and could even be downright wrong in the only passage that mentions homosexual behavior. The most simple and obvious answer is that I failed to "ask the right questions" or did not follow up on some possible clues, but I think that something more fundamental and more culture bound is involved.

Until quite recently, the overwhelming majority of professional anthropologists have been persons raised in Western cultures and Western intellectual and moral traditions. Homophobia, excluding a few of the classical forebears of Western culture, is closely associated with these traditions and particularly in the nineteenth century, when anthropology was "coming of age," references to homosexuality and descriptions of homosexual practices were often presented in Latin in the body of English-language texts, and a few more clinical studies could be bought only by members of the medical professions. The acceptance and the ascendency of the "doctrine of cultural and ethical relativity" in twentieth-century anthropology had almost no effect on attitudes toward and the evaluation of homosexual behavior cross culturally. As a "legitimate" study, homosexuality remained the "vice without a name" or at least the "virtually invisible vice" in anthropology, and even homosexual members of the profession, who might have been expected to be more aware than their straight colleagues, were prudently deeply closeted and cautious about the possible risk of "exposure by innuendo." Prejudice, moral aversion, and in some cases naivety almost certainly inhibited many from pursuing the matter. The "liberal" anthropologist, wanting to demonstrate the validity and "rationality" of all cultures, tended to shy away from the one practice that his own cultural tradition presented as unequivocally unnatural, against all "reason." It was far easier to look at and to "objectively" justify the practice of infanticide under certain circumstances than to "justify" the practice and acceptance of homosexual behavior. The former, though abhorrent by Western standards, could be "excused" (that is, shown to be "rational") in some demographic situations, but homosexuality, since in a sense it "produced" nothing, was simply "unnatural." If the anthropologist's informants denied the existence of homosexuality or of any homosexual practices, and they often did, the investigator sometimes "thankfully" accepted it at face value, for the denial absolved him of enquiring further into a painful and morally tainted dimension of human behavior, a dimension presented as *the* most fundamental betrayal of "nature."

There is little doubt that many anthropologists have been intellectually, morally, and emotionally uncomfortable in even approaching the phenomenon of homosexuality, and, since the subject has been more or less tabooed, many of them are also naive in their approaches to it. To most heterosexuals, sodomy is the sexual practice that "typifies" the homosexual male; and although there is no way I can prove it, I suspect it may have been the only practice some anthropologists enquired about in "probing" into homosexual behavior. If this is so, the placing of some societies in the "no homosexuality" category may be unwarranted, for the absence of sodomy, even a negative evaluation of it, does not mean the absence and may even suggest the acceptance of other homosexual behaviors. The three New Guinea societies I have referred to (Herdt, 1979; Kelly, 1976; Scheffelin, 1977) have "institutionalized homosexual behavior" in certain ideologically sanctioned and ritualized contexts; but in two of them the positively sanctioned implanting of semen male to male—necessary to "making a man"—is by fellatio only and in the third by sodomy. Fellatio and sodomy may be mutually exclusive, and if one enquires only about the latter one may indeed receive the answer that it does not exist. However, this answer should not be interpreted as evidence for the absence of all homosexual practices or even a negative evaluation of all such behavior. And if male anthropologists—that is, most of the profession—have been inhibited from facing the occurence of homosexual behavior between members of their own sex, they seem to have entirely ignored even the possibility of female homosexuality. This is possibly more excusable, since the male observer has extremely limited access to the female side of life in many cultures; but I wonder how many of them broached the subject to their male informants. I suspect a kind of tacit "chauvinistic conspiracy," not, perhaps, deliberate but nevertheless reflecting male ignorance of female sexuality and male assumptions of the "inevitability" of their superior sexual attraction for members of the opposite sex.

There may be some professional risk in publicly recognizing one's own naivety, but twenty-seven years after my field work with the Gahuku I do not mind admitting it, for others who have used or referred to my work should be aware that I was naive in certain areas of sexual behavior (and I do not think I was the only young anthropologist, male or female, who was naive). Gahuku denied the existence of sodomy among them. They knew very well what I was talking about when I enquired, and their invariable reaction was amusement, *not* moralistic condemnation of the practice. "Oh yes," they said (and I am condensing the import of many conversations) "some of those people over there [other tribal groups] do that," and they also stated that some of their youths had been propositioned to "pus-pus" (pidgin English to "fuck") by American servicemen. They laughed, as though it was a curious request, but they were not morally outraged. In the matter of sodomy, they were thorough-going cultural and ethical relativists.

I do not think that any Gahuku engaged in sodomy with another Gahuku male, though in culling my old notes it appears that I never posed the question directly to a male informant, probably because I thought it would not be any more "proper" to do so than to ask the same question of another male in my own culture. I was reared in what seems an "earlier age" today, taught to consider the expression of sexuality as a peculiarly private domain, and some of these attitudes almost certainly inhibited me from looking at my subjects, who had become my friends, in a solely clinical light. It was only some years after leaving the field that I realized such direct questions probably would not have caused even the raising of an eyebrow, for Gahuku notions of sexuality were not as private or "not to be spoken about" as my own cultural heritage had led me to believe.

But sodomy aside, which was clearly not placed in an anathematized and "unthinkable" category, what of the existence and even, perhaps, the approval of other homosexual practices? I simply do not know, though I suspect, based upon clues in my published work and on some scattered references in my notes, that fellatio may have had a place in the ritual process of "making a man."

It is certainly true that culture-bound attitudes have played a part in the way in which anthropologists have looked at, or have failed to look at, homosexuality. With very few exceptions, the anthropological record, such as it is, is obtuse (cf. Fitzgerald, 1977, p. 390 ff). Carrier (1979), summarizing these attitudes, remarks: "At the turn of the century, such adjectives as disgusting, vile, and detestable were still being used to describe homosexual behavior; and even in the mid-30s some anthropologists continued to view the behavior as unnatural. In discussing sodomy with some of his New Guinea informants, Williams (1936), for example, asked them if they "had ever been *subjected* to an unnatural practice" (italics added). With the acceptance of the view in the mid-30s that the behavior should be classified as a mental illness (or at the least dysfunctional), many anthropologists replaced "unnatural" with the medical model. This model still finds adherents among researchers at present.

I do not think that F. E. Williams actually used the word "unnatural" in questioning his informants. It is simply a "delicate" way of rephrasing the question for "sensitive" Western readers, but in conjunction with the verb "subjected," it is indicative of the culture-bound attitudes and evaluations that have implicitly or explicitly informed anthropological approaches to homosexuality.

There has been immense difficulty and much confusion, for example, in labeling. As Carrier (1979) points out, almost all forms of cross-gender behavior, including cross-dressing, have been included under the rubric of "homosexuality"; and in our own culture today persons whom I have called "transgenderals" tend to be regarded as "homosexuals" even by "sophisticated" social scientists. These culturally bound assumptions have bedevilled the entire anthropological literature on the *berdache* in Native American cultures, and it is because of this that I have followed the lead of Angelino and Shedd when referring to the phenomenon of the *berdache*-transgenderal, for as Fitzgerald (1977) points out: "A *berdache* . . . may be a transvestite, but a transvestite need not be a *berdache*; and neither need be homosexual."

The English dictionary definition of the word "homosexual" is quite precise, but this does not mean that its cultural connotations are either precise or easily transposable to non-Western cultures. For example, there is little doubt that there is no concept of "homosexuality" or of "a homosexual" in many cultures where "homosexual behavior" occurs, particularly in those where it is accepted or institutionalized under certain circumstances. This seems to be the case in a number of New Guinea societies. Among the Sambia described by Herdt (1979) homosexual behavior (fellatio) was positively sanctioned and encouraged for males between the ages, roughly, of six to eighteen. It was necessary for "making a man." But following heterosexual cohabitation it was not fully approved though, apparently, not "outlawed." Sambia not only considered the behavior "natural" and "necessary," given their ideology of male and female biology and physiology, within this range of ages but it is also clear that they had no concept or cultural category of "a homosexual." This is also true of the people whom Williams studied and, it seems, of other New Guinea groups. Indeed, the absence of a word equivalent to our "homosexual" in some languages does not mean the absence of "homosexual behavior"; it may simply imply that such behaviors have some recognized and more or less "legitimate" place in the spectrum of human sexuality.

Since anthropology has given the subject little attention, the study of homosexual behavior has been left to psychiatry, psychology, and sociology, and it is not unfair to say that it has been the study of only a single case: cultures of Western tradition if one stretches it to its broadest limits. The title of the first Kinsey report, *Sexual Behavior in the Human Male* (1948), is misleading. It is a study of such behavior in the United States alone and also of one segment of the population: white and mainly middle-class males. This is also true of the most recent report from the Kinsey Institute (Bell and Weinberg, 1978); only an insignificant few nonwhites were included in the sample on which it is based. Homosexuals are also critical of the fact that most studies of their life-styles have been made by heterosexuals. While this criticism smacks of the charge that "only the native can know the native," many of these "objective" studies are colored by the homophobic bias attributed to their anthropological counterparts. Even where adverse moral evaluation is not obvious, "heterosexual ethnocentricity" informs most descriptions and typologies of homosexual relationships. The model used is a heterosexual model—a "unimodel" as Fitzgerald (1977) calls it—and it is often also an ideal, not to say naive, model of heterosexual relationships. The investigators fail to recognize that the homosexual universe is not simply the obverse of an ideal heterosexual universe, not simply a negative impression of the face side, though the face side has to accept responsibility for many of the impressions the other seems to present.*

*Evelyn Hooker (1965, pp. 25-26) points out that "heterosexual ethnocentricity" has caused confusion in addressing the psychosexual identities of male homosexuals: "The perspective of the two-sexed heterosexual society has dominated all attempts to classify the patterned relationships between sexual performance and psychological gender in male homosexuals."

"Heterosexual ethnocentricity" has led to some puzzling statements when social psychologists, sociologists, and some anthropologists have looked at "homosexual marriages." Marriage as an institution—that is, with all its legally, socially, economically, and morally protected rights and obligations—is simply not an available choice for persons of the same gender in our culture. "Marriages" performed with the blessing of some nondenominational homosexual Christian churches have no force at law or any other kind of recognition except the approval of other members of the congregations. Yet some homosexuals use the term "married" to describe the public, private, and accepted qualities of some same-gender relationships. Is the difficulty merely semantic? Perhaps to some extent it is, but the strain to compare and to contrast homosexual relationships often obscures and falsifies the "other reality." Why, for example, asking the question that Fitzgerald (1977) asks, does anthropologist David Sonenschein (1968) reserve the term "actual homosexual marriage" only for those couples, and they are an extremely small minority, who have gone through a mock heterosexual marriage rite; and *why* (with a justified emphasis) does he include *only* "kept boys" in the category of "permanent homosexual relationships" (Sonenschein, 1968, p. 75; Fitzgerald, 1977, p. 394)? Other investigators attempt to get around the semantic difficulties by referring to some homosexual relationships as "quasi-marriages," or they try to avoid it altogether by using such "neutral" terms as "close-coupled" or "open-coupled." The latter at least recognize that the sociocultural institution of marriage in the United States is not a possibility for persons of the same gender, but none of the terms correspond to the realities of relationships as they are perceived by homosexuals within their own social universe.

Despite criticism, David Sonenschein (1966) was the first anthropologist in recent decades to call upon his colleagues to study homosexuality. His call, as Clark Taylor (1979) has said, brought no immediate "rush to commit professional suicide," but it had some effect. I know of about fourteen young anthropologists who are presently studying and intend to study various aspects of homosexuality. Some of them are students who have not yet completed their higher degrees. It will be a few years before we see the results of their research. A small number of more senior anthropologists (for example, J. M. Carrier, Clark Taylor, David Sonenschein, Thomas K. Fitzgerald) have published data on homosexuality in the United States and Mexico, and a few (such as Gilbert Herdt and others I have mentioned) have made admirable departures from the usually cursory treatment of the subject in more exotic cultures. All told, they amount to a small fraction of professional anthropologists, but perhaps their work will help to "legitimize" homosexuality as an important area for research within the discipline.

Four years after Sonenschein published his "call" to the profession, the American Anthropological Association at its Annual Meeting (Fall 1970) in San Diego passed a series of Resolutions (introduced by Clark Taylor) that gave its scholarly imprimatur to research on homosexuality and supported the rights of openly gay anthropologists in matters concerning professional employment (see Appendix 2). According to Clark Taylor (1979) the resolutions "passed overwhelmingly at the business meeting, *but barely passed* [italics added] on the mail ballot to the general membership." In the following years, a few members of the Association, at considerable personal risk, attempted to found and to develop an organization of members, homosexual or heterosexual, to implement the Resolutions of the Association. Despite a great deal of effort, nothing much happened, but efforts to resurrect the Anthropology Research Group on Homosexuality (ARGOH) began at the Annual Meetings of the American Anthropological Association at Los Angeles in 1978.

Quite by accident, I fell into the elected position of "convenor" of the reconstituted ARGOH. One year in that office has convinced me that research on homosexuality remains a very questionable stepchild in anthropology, notwithstanding the wording of the Resolutions accepted by the Association in 1970 and reconfirmed in 1978. Since 1974—when one hard-fought-for symposium was included—no papers on homosexuality have been presented at the Annual Meetings of the largest professional organization of anthropologists in the United States. All of those offered have been rejected in the "blind" reviews (by three persons) which are ostensibly required before a submitted abstract is accepted for inclusion on the program. Reasons of "quality" and/or "lack of space" are cited for rejection. Both are difficult to respond to without suggesting there is some reluctance to recognize research on homosexual behavior. The subject matter of papers given at the Annual Meetings is highly diverse and their quality is highly variable. Presumably, "blind" reviewers are chosen because they are assumed to have some knowledge of the subject of the paper they are reviewing; and since very few anthropologists have contributed anything to or have any interest in the study of homosexual behavior, they are a very small number. Yet not one person I know who has such an interest has been asked to review a submitted abstract. Whether it is warranted or not, the outcome tends to reenforce the impression that anthropological research on homosexual behavior is not "professionally significant" and should perhaps be avoided in the competition for professional recognition.

Given virtually a century of neglect—if not some degree of proscription—it is not surprising that the state of anthropological research on homosexual behavior trails behind other substantive and theoretical areas in the discipline, and it will be a self-perpetuating situation as long as current lack of interest penalizes, in some sense, those members of the profession who have the temerity to suggest that anthropology *has* something to say about an important though, as far as we know, always a minority panhuman behavioral phenomenon.

Indeed, anthropology has not been greatly interested in the study of "deviance." All members of the profession recognize that behavior varies within permitted and expected limits against an ideal norm in any human group. It is the "norm," however, that has been principally addressed by anthropologists in their cross-cultural studies. Partly for this reason, the entire discipline in recent decades has been branded increasingly as "ultra-conservative" by many educated members of Third World and Fourth World "nations." I do not think the charge is fully justified, though it is not without foundation.

The supreme paradox, however, is that since about the nineteen-thirties the discipline that calls itself "the science of man" has contributed minimally to and hardly influenced any panhuman understandings. There are a few—and, indeed, they are a few—notable works in anthropology that have had a considerable impact outside the profession, and within the profession it is fair to say that they have been given grudging recognition when they have not been regarded as déclassé. Anthropology, as Lewis Langness (1977, p. 5) has said, "deals with the most intrinsically interesting subject matter of all the sciences [but tends to] remain a dull subject." I suspect that "dull" if not "boring" is the adjective most university undergraduates would apply to their first experience of anthropology.

One cannot place all the blame on the individual instructor. Almost all of the introductory textbooks I have read are "boring" and excessively didactic. but aside from this, anthropological science has failed dismally in communication with the general public. Debates within the discipline center on issues that are of interest only to the initiated, that is, to members or would-be members of the profession. Anthropologists speak only to anthropologists (as do most scientists) and in a language that is characteristically obscure if not downright arcane. I can imagine only a few nonprofessionals picking up any of the hundreds of ethnographies of the ways of life of exotic people and reading them with pleasure or, if they persevere, putting them down with much sense of enlightenment and any expanded awareness of the "kinship" of human beings. There are exceptions, of course; but these books tend to be those that receive only grudging recognition within the profession. They are not sufficiently "serious" and do not count for much when they are included in the bibliographies academicians must submit in trying to move from one rung to another on the ladder of promotion.

Until quite recently, anthropologists have also shown little interest in turning the "anthropological point of view" upon their own culture, leaving that to the even drier discipline of sociology. Anthropology is still largely the "comparative study of non-Western cultures," and no one suggests it should abandon its traditional emphasis: it may be its greatest virtue and principal reason for existing. But in over half a lifetime of teaching I have listened to "generations" of bemused students leaving lectures on, for example, Crow, Omaha, and Iroquois kinship terminology and asking: "So what? What is the relevance of this to anything we may need to know to cope with the problems of living?" I do not agree with them entirely, though in the case of many kinship studies I probably do, for "relevance," in some immediately applicable sense, is not a necessary test of the significance of many things that scholars study. Yet it is true that a possible majority of anthropologists cannot or do not know how to integrate their vast body of data in ways that are meaningful, illuminating, and, yes, even fascinating to a public that comes to them with the hope that their curiosity may be whetted.

Anthropology, as a discipline, seems to be as "uncomfortable" with the study of homosexual behavior today as it has been for the past three-quarters of a century. There are numerous reasons for this, including some of those I have mentioned above, but probably one of the principal reasons is that homosexuality is a "controversial" and "sensitive" subject and anthropology has not had a distinguished record in dealing with controversial subjects, though this does not preclude raging "internal controversies" within the discipline. In fairly recent years the profession has indeed been "burned" by the alleged activities of some of its members that resulted in the adoption of a Code of Ethics to which all members of the American Anthropological Association are supposed to subscribe. Moreover, anthropologists are still largely dependent upon their acceptance by governments of Third World nations which in the process of image building have become increasingly sensitive about what should or should not be studied. Homosexuality is sometimes on the "not to be studied" list, but I know of one instance (in 1975) when the Executive Board of the Association resolved "not to endorse anthropological research on homosexuality across National borders," a blanket rejection (later removed I think) that apparently had nothing to do with the attitudes of the host government and that some members of the Association challenged as excessively discriminating and tantamount to placing a taboo on cross-cultural research on homosexuality.

When one attempts to unravel this tangled skein, one thread stands out: namely, that anthropological research on homosexual behavior has been and, to a large extent, still is consigned to the dark recesses of the discipline's closet.

Appendix 2 — American Anthropological Association Resolutions on Anthropological Research on Homosexuality*

HOMOSEXUALITY (Clark Taylor)

Resolution 11

Whereas anthropological studies of homosexuality are important to the advancement of Anthropology as a science and to the well being of society, and

Whereas homosexual men and women are a taboo minority group even within the American Anthropological Association, and

Whereas increasing numbers of homosexual women and men entering anthropological fields wish to undertake research on homosexuality and homoerotophobia, and

Whereas such studies, and the training of students to undertake them, are almost nonexistent,

Be it resolved that the American Anthropological Association recognizes the legitimacy and immediate importance of such research, and training, and urges the active development of both.

*American Anthropological Association Annual Report 1970 (April 1971).

Resolution 12

Whereas homoerotophobia in this culture discriminates overtly and covertly against professionally qualified homosexual individuals,

And whereas anthropological data gathered by non-homosexual Western anthropologists is becoming recognized as woefully ethnocentric,

Be it resolved that the American Anthropological Association opposes such discrimination and urges the protection of homosexual anthropologists and encourages homosexual studies by homosexual anthropologists or others.

Resolution 13

Whereas eroticism is an accepted part of life in many cultures, and the same erotic acts are illegal in most Western countries for both homosexuals and heterosexuals,

Be it resolved that the American Anthropological Association go on record as urging the immediate legalization of all consensual sexual acts.

Appendix 3 — Martin Esslin on Jean Genet's The Maids*

The Maids opens in a Louis XV bedroom in which an elegant lady is being dressed by her maid, whom she calls Claire. The lady is haughty, the maid servile. But the two visibly taunt each other. In the end the maid slaps the lady. Suddenly an alarm clock rings; in a flash the whole scene collapses. The lady is seen to be no lady at all, but one of two maids who have been playing at lady and maid in the absence of the real lady. And in fact the maid who has been called Claire is not Claire at all but Solange, and it was Claire who acted the part of the lady, and treated her sister as the lady treats Claire.

Whenever their lady is out, the two maids enact the fantasy game of servility and final revolt against her, each playing the lady in turn. For they are bound to their lady . . . by a mixture of affection, erotic love, and deep hatred. They have just caused the arrest of Monsieur, the lady's lover, by writing anonymous letters to the police. The telephone rings; Monsieur is out on bail. The maids are terrified. Now their denunciation will be found out. They decide to kill the lady when she returns. They will pour poison into her tea. The lady arrives. They keep the news of Monsieur's release from her, but just as she is about to drink the poisoned tea, she notices that the receiver of the telephone is off, and one of the maids lets the news of Monsieur's release slip out. The lady will no longer drink her tea; she hurries off to meet her lover. The maids are left

*Excerpted from *The Theatre of the Absurd* by Martin Esslin. Copyright © 1961, 1968, 1969 by Martin Esslin. Reprinted by permission of Doubleday & Company, Inc.

195

alone. They resume the game of lady and maid. Claire again plays the lady and demands that she be served the poisoned cup of tea. Solange has once before failed to kill the lady. Now Claire is going to show her courage. She drinks the poison and dies in the role of the lady.

The two maids are linked by the love-hatred of being each other's mirror image. As Claire says, "I'm sick of seeing my image thrown back at me by a mirror, like a bad smell." At the same time, in the role of the lady, Claire sees the whole race of servants as the distorting mirror of the upper class: "Your frightened, guilty faces, your puckered elbows, your outmoded clothes, your wasted bodies, only fit for cast-offs! You're our distorting mirrors, our loathsome vent, our shame, our dregs!" Thus what they hate seeing reflected in each other is the distorted reflection of the world of the secure masters, which they adore, ape, and loathe. . . . But the lady and her lover, the masters of the maids . . . are also an image of respectable society itself, the closed world of *les justes*, from which the orphaned foundling Genet had felt himself excluded as a monstrosity. The revolt of the maids against their masters is not a social gesture, a revolutionary action; it is tinged with nostalgia and longing, like the revolt of the fallen angel Satan against the world of light from which he is forever banished. That is why this revolt finds its expression not in protest but in ritual.

Glossary

absurd By dictionary definition, the word "absurd" means "out of harmony with reason or propriety; incongruous, unreasonable, illogical." In its most commonplace usage it is synonymous with "ridiculous." None of the behaviors described in *Other Voices*, however, are "ridiculous," though most "normal" people may decide it is an appropriate epithet to apply to them. My usage of "absurd" relies heavily on Esslin's glossing of the word (1969, pp. 3–5) in characterizing a contemporary genre of drama—the "theatre of the absurd"—represented by the works of such writers as Adamov, Beckett, Ionesco, Genet, et al. Esslin quotes Ionesco's definition of the term: "Absurd is that which is devoid of purpose. . . . Cut off from his religious, metaphysical and transcendental roots, man is lost; all his actions become senseless, absurd, useless." And, he adds, "this sense of metaphysical anguish at the absurdity of the human condition is, broadly speaking, the theme of the plays" of these writers.

Some qualifications are necessary in applying this meaning of the word to the behaviors observed in The Columbia. In the works of the playwrights of "the absurd," various literary and dramatic devices are *deliberately* used to convey a philosophical and metaphysical view of man's relationships to man and to society. The protagonists on the "stages" of The Columbia are not intellectuals. Unlike the playwrights, they are not "standing aside" and making deliberately, consciously constructed statements on their human condition and on the human condition of "everyman." Also, I doubt that any of them— excepting, perhaps, the few who are far advanced into alcoholic depression and ineptitude—regard life itself as "senseless" and

197

"useless." Yet their basic experience is one of *disjunction* with a supposedly "real world," and this is the intellectual core of works belonging to the genre of the "absurd." For the homosexual, the experience of disjunction stems from the relationship between his or her own subjective persona and cultural definitions of gender and gender roles and the social institutions in which they are embodied—the "real world." This supposedly "real" world and the homosexual's relationship with it are basically "absurd," and reaction to the "absurdity" may be expressed in active efforts to change the values that are responsible for it or in rituals that communicate the basic "absurdity" of their condition to members of the excluded "commonality."

basket Male genitals, particularly their size as suggested by their prominence beneath clothing such as trousers.

butch A "masculine" looking and acting male homosexual. Also applied to lesbians who look and act like "men."

chicken Teenage, or younger, males who are sought by older men as sexual partners.

chicken hawk An adult male who prefers sex with "chicken." A "chicken hawk" is a pedophiliac.

chicken queen The same as "chicken hawk." Both "chicken hawk" and "chicken queen," however, are sometimes used for adult men who seek sexual partners who are much younger than themselves: for example, a man of forty who is sexually interested in males in their early twenties.

coming out The act of recognizing homosexual motivation and participating in homosexual life-styles. Currently, it is also used more narrowly for those homosexuals who have identified themselves publicly as such, as in "coming out of the closet." Being "brought out" often refers to a first experience of sex with a member of the same gender.

dike A lesbian. A "masculine" lesbian may be referred to as a "bull dike."

drag Mainly applied to the costuming of male homosexual transvestites. "Going in drag," for men, means dressing as a woman. Possibly, however, the term might be applied to the costuming of homosexual men, particularly in some public territories, that exaggerates supposedly "masculine" and "butch" styles. Male homosexuals who go in "costume" to the "leather" and "S and M" (see below) bars and taverns might be said to be adopting a form of "drag."

drag queen Principally refers to female impersonators or those men who appear fairly regularly in public in female costume.

fag chitchat A gossipy, biting and "bitchy" (supposedly "female") style of conversation.

fag talk As above.

faggot Derogatory heterosexual term for male homosexuals.

fairy A derogatory heterosexual term for male homosexuals. Among themselves, male homosexuals tend to apply it to those who are "feminine" in appearance and mannerisms. It often has a derogatory connotation when it is used by those who emphasize their "masculine" identification.

femme As used by male homosexuals, it is often synonymous with "fairy," but it may also be used to characterize the style of public territories (bars and taverns) that emphasize conventional decorum and middle- to upper-middle-class dress. Such establishments may also be referred to as "cuff-link" bars. As used by lesbians, "femme" usually refers to the more "conventionally feminine" and "passive" individual.

grass Marijuana.

homoerotic My use of this adjective is somewhat narrower than its dictionary definition. In my usage, it applies principally to the intermittent but recurring "homosexual" activities of men who do not identify themselves as "homosexuals" or as "gay." Such "homoerotic" experiences are far more widely distributed in the total male population than those that are exclusively "homosexual," and some public territories (such as men's rest rooms) are used for sexual gratification almost as frequently by "heterosexual" men as by "homosexuals." "Homoerotic" would also apply to the mutual sexual exhibitionism and experimentation between teenagers of the same gender who do not regard such activities as "homosexual" and in later life do not "become" homosexuals. Any sexual act or stimulus between members of the same gender is "homoerotic," but such acts and stimuli do not necessarily result in the adoption of a "homosexual" life-style and a "homosexual" identity. "Homoeroticism" is very widely distributed among the total male population, far more widely than simply between those who are "homosexual," and "homophobia" (the fear of "homosexuality" and of "homosexuals") reflects the cultural suppression and negative sanctioning of such stimuli.

homosexual Both as a noun and adjective, I have used this term only for individuals who have an exclusive sexual interest in members of their own gender. It is roughly equivalent to the term "gay," and it distinguishes "homosexuals" from "bisexuals" (who, by dictionary definition, engage in "homosexual" acts) *and* from "heterosexuals" who engage in "homoerotic" acts.

hustle In the homosexual context usually refers to sexual activity. A "hustler" is a male prostitute. "Hustling," however, may also mean any obvious or blatant attempt to find a sexual partner. In its nonsexual context, it may simply convey the common experiences and world view of those who lead stigmatized and disadvantaged lives, and almost anyone can be said to be "hustling" something, including his or her profession or job. In its most inclusive sense, it reflects an essentially competitive and cynical view of life and of human relationships and social and material success.

jack off Masturbate.

leather Refers to a style of costume, usually leather jacket, cap, and sometimes trousers and boots rather than shoes. It is often, though not exclusively, associated with the "S and M" fraternity (see below) and is a rather exaggerated replication of a type of costuming that is associated with a highly "masculine" identity. A "leather man" is one who presents this public image, though the image does not necessarily have a one-to-one relationship with his role in sex. To those involved in the "leather scene," it is an erotic form of costuming.

Marlboro Man A homosexual who affects "western" (US) dress as, for example, the male models who appear in advertisements for Marlboro cigarettes.

nelly See *femme.*

pot Marijuana.

queen Derogatory heterosexual term for male homosexuals. Among male homosexuals it is frequently used to refer to those who are "feminine" in appearance and mannerisms.

queer Derogatory heterosexual term for homosexuals.

rice queen A Caucasian male homosexual who prefers sexual partners who are Oriental.

S and M An abbreviation of the psychoanalytic term "sadomasochistic." Its primary discipline reference is appropriate for the sexual relationships of male homosexuals who are "into" the "S and M" scene. An exaggerated style of "leather" costuming (above) *may* signal "S and M" interests, and there are some "leather" bars and taverns in which those who are "into S and M" may expect to find others who share their sexual tastes. The "leather scene" and the "S and M scene," however, are not necessarily synonymous.

score As a noun, it is equivalent to "a trick" (below). "To score" means to achieve a successful result of sexual propositioning.

shrimper A male homosexual who has a foot fetish.

sissy A derogatory heterosexual term for male homosexuals. Male homosexuals often use it to refer to those who are conspicuously "femme" or "fairies" (above). Ethnically and socioeconomically disadvantaged male homosexuals, however, often use it to characterize the styles and the clientele of predominantly white middle- to upper-middle-class bars and taverns.

smack "Hard" drugs (as distinct from "pot" or "grass"), but particularly heroin.

tearoom A colloquialism for men's public rest rooms, particularly for those known to be locales for impersonal homoerotic sexual encounters.

trade Most narrowly the clients of male prostitutes; but "trading" also applies to sexual arrangements in public territories that do not involve prostitution and is often synonymous with the more generalized usages of "trick" and "tricking." "Trade" may also be used in conjunction with qualifying adjectives to designate the "styles" of some public territories. For example, "rough trade" may apply to a lower-class bar or tavern. But "rough trade" may also be synonymous with "S and M" (above).

transgenderal A term that is currently being promoted to replace "transsexual" (below).

transsexual An individual who is psychologically motivated to assume the cultural identity, roles, and status of someone of the opposite gender and who views himself or herself in this way alone. Many transsexuals prefer the term "transgenderal." The gender "change" may be made without the assistance of male and female hormones or cosmetic surgery. Transsexual is not synonymous with "transvestite."

transvestite Someone who cross-dresses, that is, who wears clothing that is culturally associated with the opposite sex. Many men who cross-dress are not necessarily homosexual.

trick   The client of a male prostitute, but also any person who is "picked up" to engage in sex. To "trick" or to "go tricking" means looking for a homosexual partner (usually someone who is a "one-night stand"). A "trick" does not have to be someone who pays for sex, though this is the most common meaning of the term in the context of heterosexual prostitution.

watch queen   A male lookout in tearooms (above). Someone who keeps "watch" and warns of the approach of "suspicious" members of the public including uniformed or plainclothed police.

Bibliography — Selected References

Abrahams, Roger D. 1964 *Deep Down in the Jungle.* Folklore Associates, Hatboro. Also available from Aldine (1970), Chicago.

Angelino, Henry, and Charles L. Shedd. 1955 "A Note on Berdache." *American Anthropologist,* 57: 121–125.

Bateson, Gregory, and Jurgen Ruesch 1951, 1968 *Communication: The Social Matrix of Psychiatry.* W. W. Norton, New York.

Bell, Alan P., and Martin S. Weinberg. 1978 *Homosexualities: A Study of Diversity Among Men and Women.* Simon & Schuster, New York.

Brown, H. "Rap." 1971 "Poem." Reprinted in Jacobs, Paul, and Saul Landau (with Eve Pelly), *To Serve the Devil.* Vantage Books, New York.

Bugliosi, Vincent, and Curt Gentry. 1975 *Helter Skelter.* Bantam Books, New York.

Carrier, J. M. 1979 "Homosexual Behavior in Cross-Cultural Perspective." In press.

Cavan, Sherri. 1966 *Liquor License.* Aldine, Chicago.

Cory, D. W. 1960 *The Homosexual in America.* Castle, New York. Also available from Arno Press (1975), New York.

Esslin, Martin. 1969 *The Theatre of the Absurd.* Doubleday/Anchor, New York.

Evans-Pritchard, E. E. 1970 "Sexual Inversion among the Azande." *American Anthropologist,* 72: 1428–1434.

1976 *Witchcraft, Oracles and Magic among the Azande.* Clarendon Press, Oxford.

Fitzgerald, Thomas K.   1977   "A Critique of Anthropological Research on Homosexuality." *Journal of Homosexuality*, 2:4:385–397.

Ford, C. S.   1960   "Sex Offenses: An Anthropological Perspective." *Law and Contemporary Problems*, 25:225–248.

Ford, C. S., and F. A. Beech.   1951   *Patterns of Sexual Behavior*. Harper & Row, New York.

Freud, Sigmund.   1928   *The Future of an Illusion*. Horace Liveright and The Institute of Psycho-Analysis, New York.

Gagnon, J. H., and W. Simon.   1967   "Femininity in the Lesbian Community." *Social Problems*, 15: 212–221.

Geertz, C.   1973   "Ethos, World View and the Analysis of Sacred Symbols." In C. Geertz, ed., *The Interpretation of Culture*. Basic Books, New York.

Genet, Jean.   1954   *The Maids*. In *The Maids/Deathwatch*. Grove Press, New York.
1964   *Our Lady of the Flowers*. Bantam Books, New York.
1967   *The Thief's Journal*. Penguin Books, New York.
(*Our Lady of the Flowers* (1976) and *The Thief's Journal* (1973) also available from Grove Press, New York.)

Goffman, Erving.   1974   *Frame Analysis*. Harper & Row, New York.
1968   *Stigma: Notes on the Management of Spoiled Identity*. Pelican Books, New York. Also available from Prentice-Hall Spectrum Books (1973), New York.

Herdt, Gilbert H.   1980   "Fetish and Fantasy in Sambia Initiation." In Gilbert H. Herdt and Mervyn J. Meggitt, eds., *Male Initiation in New Guinea*. University of California Press, Berkeley; forthcoming.

Herndon, James.   1969   *The Way It Spozed to Be*. Bantam Books, New York. Also available from Simon & Schuster Touchstone Books (1977), New York.

Hite, Shere.   1976   *The Hite Report*. Macmillan, New York.

Hoffman, M.   1968   *The Gay World*. Basic Books, New York.

Honigman, John J.   1976   "The Personal Approach in Anthropological Research." *Current Anthropology*, 16:2.

Hooker, Evelyn.   1956   "A Preliminary Analysis of Group Behavior of Homosexuals." *Journal of Psychiatry*, 42:217–225.
1957   "The Adjustment of the Overt Male Homosexual." *Journal of Projective Techniques*, 21:18–31
1958   "Male Homosexuality in the Rorschach." *Journal of Projective Techniques*, 22:33–54.
1963   "Male Homosexuality." In N. L. Farberow, ed., *Taboo Topics*. Atherton Press, New York.
1965a   "An Empirical Study of Some Relations Between Sexual Patterns and Gender Identity in Male Homosexuals." In John Money,

Hooker, Evelyn *(con't.)*
ed., *Sex Research: New Developments.* Holt, Rinehart & Winston, New York.
1965b "Male Homosexuals and Their "Worlds." In J. Marmor, ed., *Sexual Inversion.* Basic Books, New York.
1967 "The Homosexual Community." In J. H. Gagnon and W. Simon, eds., *Sexual Deviance.* Harper & Row, New York.

Humphreys, Laud. 1970 *Tearoom Trade: Impersonal Sex in Public Places.* Aldine, Chicago.

Jacobs, Sue-Ellen. 1968 "Berdache: A Brief Review of the Literature." *Colorado Anthropologist,* 1:25–40.

Kelly, R. 1976 "Witchcraft and Social Relations: An Exploration in the Social and Semantic Implications of the Structure of Belief." In P. Brown and G. Buchbinder, eds., *Man and Woman in the New Guinea Highlands.* American Anthropological Association, Washington, D.C.

Kinsey, Alfred C., et al. 1948 *Sexual Behavior in the Human Male.* Saunders, 1948.

Kochman, Thomas. 1969 "Rapping in the Black Ghetto." *Trans-action,* 6:26–34.

Langness, L. L., ed. 1977 *Other Fields, Other Grasshoppers: Readings in Cultural Anthropology.* J. B. Lippincott, Philadelphia.

Larrain, Gilles. n.d. *Idols.* n.p.

Leach, E. R. 1976 *Culture and Communication.* Cambridge University Press, London.

Lewis, Oscar. 1951 *Life in a Mexican Village: Tepoztlán Revisited.* University of Illinois Press, Urbana.

Leznoff, M., and W. A. Westley. 1956. "The Homosexual Community." *Social Problems,* 3:257–263.

Lieber, Michael D., and Mary Agnes Lewis. "Mamas and Motherfuckers: Another Look at the Dozens." n.d. Unpublished paper. Quoted with the permission of the authors.

Lloyd, Robin. 1976 *For Money or Love.* Vanguard Press, New York.

Lurie, Nancy Oestreich. 1953 "Winnebago Berdache." *American Anthropologist,* 55:708–712.

Masters, William H., and Virginia E. Johnson. 1979. *Homosexuality in Perspective.* Little, Brown, New York.

Mead, Margaret. 1961 "Cultural Determinants of Sexual Behavior." In C. W. Young, ed., *Sex and Internal Secretions.* Williams & Wilkins, Baltimore.

Mileski, Maureen, and Donald J. Black. 1972 "The Social Organization of Homosexuality." *Urban Life and Culture.* 1: 187–202.

Millet, Kate. 1971 *Sexual Politics.* Avon Books, New York.

Munn, Nancy D. 1973 "Symbolism in Ritual Context: Aspects of Symbolic Action." In John J. Honigman, ed., *Handbook of Social and Cultural Anthropology*. Rand McNally, Chicago.

Newton, Esther. 1972 *Mother Camp: Female Impersonators in America*. Prentice-Hall, Englewood Cliffs, New Jersey.

Read, K. E. 1955 "Morality and the Concept of the Person Among the Gahuku-Gama, Eastern Highlands, New Guinea." *Oceania*, 25:233–282.

1965 *The High Valley*. Charles Scribner's Sons, New York.

Rechy, John. 1967 *Numbers*. Grove Press, New York.

Redfield, Robert. 1930 *Tepoztlán: A Mexican Village*. University of Chicago Press, Chicago.

Riesman, David. 1952 *Faces in the Crowd*. Yale University Press, New Haven.

Ruesch, Jurgen, and Gregory Bateson (*see* Bateson)

Sartre, Jean-Paul. 1964 *Saint Genet: Actor and Martyr*. Mentor Books, New York.

Scheffelin, E. L. 1977 *The Sorrow of the Lonely and the Burning of the Dancers*. University of Queensland Press, St. Lucia.

Sonenschein, David. 1966 "Homosexuality as a Subject of Anthropological Enquiry." *Anthropological Quarterly*, 39:73–82.

1968 "The Ethnography of Male Homosexual Relationships." *Journal of Sex Research*, 4:69–83.

Sperling. S. J. 1953 "On the Psychodynamics of Teasing." *Journal of the American Psychoanalytic Association*, 1:458–483.

Taylor, Clark. 1979 "Background Information on the Organization of Gay Anthropologists and Researchers on Homosexuality." *Anthropology Research Group on Homosexuality Newsletter*, 1, Appendix 1.

Tripp, C. A. 1975 *The Homosexual Matrix*. McGraw-Hill, New York.

Turner, Victor W. 1967 "Betwixt and Between: The Liminal Period in *Rites de Passage*." In V. W. Turner, ed., *The Forest of Symbols*. Cornell University Press, Ithaca, New York.

Williams, F. E. 1936 *Papuans of the Trans-Fly*. Oxford University Press, London.

Wright, Richard. 1940 *Native Son*. Harper & Brothers, New York.

Index